The Jesus Bag

Books by
William H. Grier
and
Price M. Cobbs

THE JESUS BAG

BLACK RAGE

The Jesus Bag

by
William H. Grier, M.D.
and
Price M. Cobbs, M.D.

McGraw-Hill Book Company

New York St. Louis San Francisco
Düsseldorf London Mexico
Sydney Toronto

Free at last,
Free at last,
Thank God a'mighty
I'm free at last!

Contents

I.

Black Survival

1↗↗↗

Black children from birth are exposed to heavily systematized hostility from the nation and for their own survival must reject the community's code of behavior, containing as it does the injunction that they themselves are to be the object of hatred. The formulation is simple. The community hates blacks and blacks return the favor.

We feel no patriotic fervor, more, perhaps, contempt. We yearn for a home, but in a way that centers on the earth and sky and a remoteness from the man-made institutions which hold us in thralldom. Thus we cannot afford to embrace the rules of law for fear of their being the instruments of our destruction.

How does that affect our developing codes of behavior? If we become so cynical at so early an age, what kind of enrichment is available to our conscience from a broader world? We know how often it has been necessary for us to conceal our true nature.

For example, blacks have for hundreds of years found it often prudent and lifesaving to assume a completely passive posture in the face of overwhelming odds.

Observers have been inclined to misread this passivity as a characterological response to fewer opportunities, to fewer options—or as a massive slowdown of operations which had the subverting of the system as its prime purpose.

No such answers were in any way primary. The passivity developed in response to a deadly threatening social system which gave the black man no option but to yield (passively) or die.

Passivity was thus an adaptive device of lifesaving importance.

A broader means of maintaining balance was found in religion. Religion is a matter of such importance and one which touches on so many aspects of black life that even though only one of many survival techniques, it is the central structure from which we have drawn the title of this book.

The psychological trail is as follows:

1. White Americans act and have acted murderously toward blacks.

2. Blacks, in response, have felt murderous toward whites.

3. The overwhelming power of the hostile white environment demands the inhibition of such impulses.

4. The black tells himself that the reason for the inhibition of such murderous impulses is religion, not the white man.

5. As is the case with other protective psychological devices, the inhibition is excessive and spreads to curb a wide range of aggressive and competitive acts, most of which are healthy.

6. The result is that blacks are bound hand and foot by self-defeating inhibitions.

7. Thus the commands of conscience and the strictures of religion which have haunted blacks from slavery to this day, we call *The Jesus Bag*.

2↟↟↟

What is the effect on the character of our kids when they are rejected and openly threatened by their neighbors and coincidentally burdened with unending poverty?

We suggest that different children bring a different genius to the problem. The intense character-shaping pressure black kids are under has to be seen to be believed. Certain uniquely black experiences have had a profound impact on children.

Let us consider "the dozens," a degrading, humiliating custom of mutual vilification practiced by black boys for as long as anyone can remember. It forms part of the black environment from childhood through late adolescence.

Essentially, the dozens are rhyming obscenities describing the speaker and, most often, the mother of the victim involved in some gross sexual act. The more outrageous the sexual practice, the better.

> I fucked your mother on an electric wire;
> The fire in her pussy made us both jump higher.

And again:

> I fucked your mother on the railroad track;
> Her pussy's so hot even the train backed back.

Then there were stylish variations:

> I hate to talk about your mother,
> She's a good old soul;
> She's got a leather-lined pussy
> And a brass asshole.

There was also the "denial":

> I don't play the dozens 'cause the dozens' too bad,
> But I'll tell you how many children your mammy
>   had;
> She had one, she had two, she had a dirty
>   cocksucker when she had you.

The whole process is ritualized. It is never appropriate to "put someone in the dozens" unless it is known or established that he "plays."

Once "in," both participants play to the everpresent crowd, trying to make each rhyming riposte funnier than the last. The crowd, moved by the wit and innovation of one, will, by responsive laughter and tumult, indicate a favorite. The winner, if capable, will dismiss his opponent with a final thrust of virtuosity, such as:

> And tell your mother to keep her drawers on
>   around my dog;
> I don't want him to catch nothing.

It is a further possibility that the loser may turn on the crowd and, singling out some less skilled players, "score" on him:

> Tell me, how long has your mother been playing
>   fullback for the Chicago Bears?

The laughing crowd is a crucial part of the drama, rewarding the witty and scorning the inept. There is always the potential that any of the observers might be drawn into the game. The loser may broaden the number of potential players to include all who laughed, declaring, "If you grin, you're in."

The dozens are like sin. There are a few who by youth or special circumstance are innocent and spared combat—but once innocence is lost all are fair game.

If an experienced player "loses his cool" and fights over the insults, he is exposed to universal loss of face. It is a more worthy response for him to retire to his muse and come back with more imaginative ammunition.

The one who out of his innocence knows nothing of the game may respond with anger and fisticuffs, and such a response is understandable to all.

"Leave that cat alone; he don't play that stuff."

And there are always surly, ill-tempered lads who fight under any provocation and who demonstrate their thin skin whenever they are scored on.

In the deepest sense, the essence of the dozens lies not in the insults but in the response of the victim. To take umbrage is considered an infantile response. Maturity and sophistication bring the capability to suffer the vile talk with aplomb at least, and, hopefully, with grace and wit. Without doubt, the most mature boys smile at the humor and decline to join in the game.

Whatever its origin, the dozens have been a way traveled by all black boys. It is a trial which obviously cannot be shared with grown-ups. It requires that a boy gulp, swallow, and set aside that special sanctification held for mother. He must suppress the natural inclination to defend her honor and he must move away from her to a world of men where his love for her now is perverted in the medium of wit.

The dozens are thus a dark passage leading to manhood, a puberty ritual, a way of recognizing secret sin and vicariously participating in insulting mother. The boy emerges knowing that he is free of the stifling aspect of the maternal bond; he knows as well that in freeing himself he has betrayed her.

Having participated in the dozens affects a boy's pride and its linkage to things outside himself. It is a means of learning how to react to any insult. A verbal attack need not be a call to arms but conceivably a summons to the competition of wit and self-control. One may wonder if the hostility black men feel for their mothers may in a small way have its origins in a necessary, reactive turning of love to hate which better arms the combatant playing the dozens. And the question also comes, if having mastered the dozens he can ever again bind his selfhood to anyone or anything with that deep, innocent abandonment of earlier years.

Finally, it is possible that the most important effect of the dozens is a pronounced degradation of the spirit. It may be more than chance that the introduction of the black boy to manhood is made via insult and that manhood is proven by an ability to stand by while those whom he holds dearest are vilified.

*   *   *

Ronald had always been a surly, sensitive boy and man, dazzling academically, but having so repellent a personality that few people cared to be around him. Though not effeminate, he was one of the few boys thought to be lacking in some essential maleness.

He looked angry all the time but no one recalled explosions (with one exception). He simply brooded and looked threatening.

In treatment it was discovered that the only time he had a fight was when someone spoke disparagingly of his mother; then he became the raging, threatening dreadnought otherwise only suggested.

*   *   *

In the miracle that is culture, the dozens may be a highly evolved instrument of survival by means of which black boys are introduced to the humiliations which will become so intimate a part of their life.

A variation of the dozens is a word of infinite uses and meanings, "motherfucker." It is an epithet and a challenge to battle. Among younger boys it may be incorporated into the dozens and the challenge turned aside, but as adulthood comes it can be used with impunity only among closest friends. With this word the elaboration and ritual are dismissed. The victim is accused of an act universally condemned. The challenger does not ease the blow with humor but lays on the insult cold and bare.

And, even here, there are men who use the term without the object of their attack feeling annoyance. The settings are fiercely masculine, isolated, and violent. Typical are prisons, military units, and criminal groups. It would suggest that where such abuse is tolerated without reaction men feel themselves banished in ultimate isolation from society.

The exchange of obscenities, or, rather more precisely their tolerance, is akin to the utterance of blasphemies. Either is tolerated only as part of ritual, in special settings, surrounded and protected by one's peers. Otherwise, such words are spoken only by lost men who have no hope of redemption, who live already in hell and who have no further fear of punishment.

Out of all this ugliness comes one of the funniest and most famous legends of black life, the story of the monkey who enjoyed the verbal battle and who, for the sheer bystanding pleasure of it, promoted hostilities between dull-witted characters.

*   *   *

The Signifying Monkey

Said the monkey to the lion one bright and sunny day,
"There's a big burly motherfucker down the way;
And the way he talks about your mother, I know he ain't
    your friend;
When you two meet you're bound to bend.
He talked about your mama and your grandma too,
Say if you show up he'll talk about you.
He talked about your sister and all your cousins
And everybody knows you don't play the dozens.
I'da fought him myself," he said with tears in his eyes,
"But that dirty motherfucker is twice my size."
Off ran the lion in a hell of a rage,
Creating a breeze which shook the trees
And knocked a giraffe to his knees.
He saw the elephant resting under a tree
And said, "You big-eared motherfucker, it's you or me."
He dove at the elephant and made a pass;
The elephant ducked and knocked him flat on his ass.
He picked him up and stomped him all in his face,
He kicked in his ribs and pulled his ass out of place.
They fought all night and they fought all day
And I still don't see how the lion got away.
He dragged back to the jungle more dead than alive
And that's when the monkey started his signifying jive:
"King of the jungle, now ain't you a bitch,
All swelled up like you got the seven-year itch.
When you came by here yesterday the jungle rung,
Now you come back with your asshole hung.
Shut up motherfucker, you better not roar
Or I'll come down there and kick your ass some more!"
The monkey started laughing and he jumped up and
    down,
His foot missed the limb and his ass hit the ground.
Like a bolt of lightning and a streak of heat
The lion was on him with all four feet.

The monkey looked up with tears in his eyes
And said, "Please, Mr. Lion, I apologize."
The lion said, "A signifying motherfucker always will;
You gonna fuck around here and get somebody killed.
So you might as well stop all your hollering and crying,
I'm gonna put an end to all your signifying!!"

*   *   *

One addicted to signifying deserved everything that happened to him and as a disturber of the precarious peace got no sympathy when punished.

The universal military experience dating from World War II has exposed large numbers of white men to the dozens and its derivatives and the whole complex is gradually drifting into more common usage. (It is a pity that the reactions of the young white soldiers when first exposed to the dozens were not recorded, for surely that must have been the purest example of "cultural shock.") While white men first exposed to the insults must either adapt or avoid the encounter, their experience is nowhere as fundamental nor does it have the potential for molding character as does the experience of the black boy who is scored on at ten and who must for the next eight years learn to master this challenge as an integral part of growing up.

We suggest that when black boys leave that era of childhood governed by parents and delimited by home, they enter school where an unfiltered rush of the world engulfs them and where a significant preparation involves sustained degradation. It is a road of ritual cynicism and alienation from love.

To suggest that such a complex tradition is a dysfunctional caprice is to have too little respect for the responses people perpetuate. If this practice has persisted it has done so at the expense of other rituals which have contested for dominance. It has persisted because it meets a group need, accomplishes certain work, and does it all in a universal language. It takes the medium of childhood sexuality and the intense passionate involvements within the family and with this as the vehicle introduces the boy to stoicism as a requirement of manhood. It insists that he understand that humiliation may be the texture of his life, but states also that manhood can transcend such onslaught.

No doubt the most instructive aspect of boys' response to the dozens is the reaction of healthy youngsters, the grace and balance developed under this vicious pressure.

*   *   *

As a boy, Victor was bigger, better-coordinated, and smarter, no doubt, than his peers. He was clearly en route to leadership. The dozens did not trouble him; when scored on he smiled benignly and nothing said about his mother could rouse him to battle.

He had achieved a maturity early in life and, whatever other problems he had, there was a grace to his walking, talking, and intercourse with others that his more troubled peers never managed.

Later, as an adult in treatment, he concluded that a close-knit supportive family, a relatively benign neighborhood, and early academic success provided a fortunate combination of circumstances which gave him a relative immunity to this specific provocation.

*   *   *

By ordinary (or white) standards, the dozens would seem to prepare a man to be a vicious warrior without conscience. Not here, however, since the system makes the warrior posture suicidal. For most black boys it is a complex maturational experience which influences much of their later lives.

The dozens has no doubt developed as a microcosmic reflection of the social system for which boys prepare. And, if one wonders what the life of black men is like in these United States, one could do no better than to look closely at this tradition which prepares them for manhood.

It is a tradition which suggests that life is an obscenity but that grace and a fine variety of manhood can yet be maintained. The grace, poise, and self-contained masculinity which have come to grow out of profane soil are rooted now in the individual's own pride in himself.

The young man has developed a code of behavior out of his concept of the right thing to do, although it has remained an intensely personal code.

He has lived with the dozens and no part of his world has moderated the fury of its assault. No one said it was too harsh; no one said that the world was different. All stood back, cold-eyed, and watched, and when he survived they looked away to something more interesting, something else small, helpless, and trapped. In a bitter way, successful navigation of these waters fosters a vigorous maleness of character, a loneliness and an emotional detachment from women, but strength. It is more often the troubled kids who fail to survive the challenge of the dozens.

3

People say, among other things, that whites are shattered as well as blacks; they say that while housing is poor for blacks, it is inadequate for ninety percent of the nation's families, black or white.

White people add that not only are blacks discriminated against in employment; they say that *all* poor people face degrading mistreatment in the area of employment.

Finally, they say that while there is no doubt that racial prejudice is rampant in America, the primary problem is *class* discrimination. The conflict, they say, is between haves and have-nots and since blacks rarely have anything, then . . .

The logical conclusion to be drawn from this line of reasoning is that we have been mistaken. They would have us believe that there is no difference in the way that black and white fare in America and we simply ought to be more precise in our social criticism.

While such reasoning is obviously garbage, it is quantitatively important because it is indulged in by so many otherwise reasonable people who look for similarities and close their eyes to disparities.

One important difference lies in the inhibitory pressure applied on blacks by the white community and transmitted through parents to children. The children grow up in an environment in which efforts to master the world are actively discouraged. The sharpening of man's essential weapon, the mind, is discouraged and inhibited.

The specific circumstances of the case that follows are mercifully rare, but poverty and illness and cruelty and hatred and the overriding enmity of the white world toward the average black man are not rare at all. The case illustrates the impediments placed before *one* boy and it shows *his* solution.

*   *   *

Albert is a slender, black college sophomore who is effeminate. His movements and speech leave this in no doubt and he makes little attempt to conceal it in his ordinary actions.

He is a brilliant student, majoring in art, with a minor in English literature. He is considered by his instructors to possess exceptional gifts and they have urged him to pursue his art studies in Europe. Pleased with his academic performance, he looks forward to a career in art and is only mildly troubled by what he sees as minor problems related to his homosexuality.

He is currently an active homosexual, finding a string of partners among other students. There have evolved two relatively lengthy relationships with older men. In one of these, a middle-aged college instructor developed a deeply affectionate, paternal attitude, advised Albert on his career, bought him clothing, and generally looked after him for the several months their liaison lasted.

Albert viewed the instructor as a convenience. He was pleased with the man's generosity because he needed the money proffered but was amused by the older man's protestations of love. He was struck by what he saw as the hypocrisy in the man's position: by day providing instruction and leadership for college students, by night begging Albert for sexual gratification. He tormented the instructor with this picture of himself and it was this taunting hostility which led directly to the breakup of the relationship. Albert still finds the whole affair greatly amusing.

There was another involvement with a professional man, with a similar ending. The older man showered him with gifts and seemed devoted. He bought him expensive clothes and rented an apartment for the boy's exclusive use (and for their meetings). Albert regarded the man as foolish and as a sucker who was just *asking* to be "taken." He swindled him out of several thousands of dollars and then broke off the relationship. He is amazed, he says, at the frequency of perversity in high places!

Albert's early life is an instructive study in the "making of a homosexual." He is the oldest of four children. The mother is an astonishing woman. Never married, she lived with his father long enough to bear Albert and his younger sister. Since then she has had a series of lovers, or, perhaps more precisely, paying guests. She apparently does not know which of several men fathered the two youngest children.

She has been supported by welfare, but male friends have consistently contributed to the family's care. She drinks heavily and shows only minimal interest in the health and well-being of the children, frequently abusing them both verbally and physically.

Through his high school years Albert lived with his mother and found partial relief by spending time whenever possible with a cousin, a maternal woman who had no children of her own and who was fond of him. Whenever fights with mother made home unbearable, he could go to his cousin and spend as long as he liked with her and her gentle husband. They provided a haven which made it possible to tolerate his own household. His mother seemed to focus her hostility particularly on him, claiming he resembled his father. She felt wronged and abandoned by that man and directed all the rage she felt for him toward the boy.

She beat him, criticized him, and scoffed at him from his earliest years. She behaved as if his schoolwork were a senseless waste of time and money—she said he should be working and contributing to her financial support. Albert got to college with the help of high school teachers and his cousin. His mother said she would not waste *her* time on such foolishness.

From his earliest years he remembered his mother entertaining one man after another. She ordinarily had sexual relations with her friends on a sofa which converted into a bed. Aside from a television set, this was the sole item of furniture in the living room and, since the front door of the flat opened directly into this room, the boy at times came through the door to face the scene of his mother having intercourse with a strange man. He would walk around the figures on the couch and go back to his room to study. At times she would ridicule him as he went by, saying to her partner, "Don't mind him, its just 'stupid-ass.' "

His most vivid memory is from his sixth year. He came upon his mother and a friend both nude, drunk, and copulating. He must have exclaimed in surprise because they stopped and laughed at him—his mother made him watch them—the man waved his penis at him and made threatening gestures toward the boy as if to "stick him" with it. His mother told him that the man would assault him sexually if he were not a good boy. Albert was petrified; the couple resumed their sexual activity and ignored him. The most painful part of the memory is of his mother taunting him in the presence of the strange man and literally offering him to the man to be punished sexually for general misbehavior.

His relationship with his mother contained an additional complexity. She showered him with infantile, indulgent care whenever she thought he was "legitimately" ill. She became maudlin and weepy, and spoke "baby talk." There was little to explain her attitude save her apparent feeling that somehow sick children were legitimate recipients of a mother's love and well ones were not.

Albert felt a responsibility for the health and well-being of the younger siblings. As a result they turned to him in crisis and he assumed the role of mother-father-older brother. Their relationship with him was intensely ambivalent and they alternated between extreme dependence and vicious hostility.

But in *his* relationship with his younger siblings we see an answer to how he found stabilizing experience in a home dominated by so pathological a mother. He was above all a *mother* to the younger ones. He tried hard to be a *good* mother and, for the most part, succeeded.

He surely succeeded in being a better mother than his own mother was to him. In his determination to improve on her, his reactions were organized in a purposeful manner. His own goodness highlighted and emphasized her misdeeds. She was mean and thoughtless with the children—he was considerate and sensitive to their needs. She was impatient with them—he was patience itself. She attacked him verbally and physically on little provocation—he maintained a neutral, non-critical attitude in the face of extreme provocation. The more cruel and damaging she strove to be, the firmer he felt in taking an opposite position and in warding off and "neutralizing" her cruelty.

It was a rare and ingenious way of relating oneself to a parent: He gained strength from her cruelty. By this means he survived and functioned effectively in his daily affairs. He was nourished by the affection of his cousin and drew encouragement from teachers. He synthesized these positive emotional experiences into his character and balanced these things against the nightmarish times endured with his mother.

In a real sense, Albert showed creativity of the highest order in working with the various elements of his life. Selecting pieces or, rather, shreds of an outrageously discouraging situation, he fitted them together in a manner which allowed him to escape the more flagrantly anti-social character traits, to avoid intellectual inhibition, and, most of all, to free other creative tendencies. That he was not wholly successful is to be expected, and that he paid a heavy price—his heterosexuality—does not surprise us.

In early childhood he tried desperately, painfully to please his mother—to be a good boy. He was alternately beaten and fawned over and periodically exposed to the gross sexual scenes described above. His own sexual feelings were thus stimulated intensely and from his third to his seventh year he engaged in constant sexual play with neighbor children. At seven he was punished severely when he was discovered in sexual contact with a neighbor girl; and he dates the suppression of heterosexual interest to the ferocious beating of that occasion.

Psychological study suggests, however, that during that period his attachment to his mother was at a peak and, no doubt, a series of incidents involving *that* sharply increased interest lay at the bottom of his abandonment of heterosexuality. Whatever the truth, he was sexually inactive for some time. At ten he was lured into mutual masturbation by an older boy and thereafter seduced into fellatio and anal intercourse.

Up to his fifteenth year he was involved in regular homosexual activity with his peers. At first, he took active or passive roles as the situation allowed, but, consorting more often with older boys, became a favorite and was pressed into regularly assuming the receptive role.

His first involvement with an adult came early in his fifteenth year. A man offered to drive him home but insisted on a detour by his hotel room. Asked to go along, Albert went to the room and once there accepted a drink and later submitted to anal intercourse. He recalls the entire episode as one in which he was tricked, duped, and finally raped, but he engaged in similar assignations with increasing frequency. He was often picked up by "cruising" homosexuals, and he made contacts in libraries or at concerts. It was a regular part of his operational style to extract money from partners, to induce them to buy him clothing and to give him gifts.

His hostility toward them was even more direct. To him, they were suckers, perverts, hypocritical old men who deserved to be fleeced. He seemed to be reenacting with his lovers the role his mother took with her lovers.

Albert had seen her as a grasping, bitter woman who returned affection with hurt. In his relationship with men he, too, adopted a castrating role, identifying with a mother who had seemed the stronger one in relationships with men.

With her son, she also faced a weaker male whom she completely dominated and finally psychologically castrated. In his inner self, Albert wanted to be aligned with the strong partner, the winner, and in his sexual life he related himself to men after the manner of his overpowering mother. He lured them by allowing them sexual access and then took their money, played with their affection, and held them in contempt. He was, in fact, a castrating (fe)male.

This remarkable identification with his mother stands in contrast to his complete rejection of her intellectual values and to his movement into new creative worlds. It is as if he "rendered unto Caesar that which is Caesar's" and, having done so, became able to function with freedom in areas of artistic importance.

*   *   *

One final note: Albert took a grotesque life situation and made it a medium for the expression of his talent.

It is a task that has burdened black men for a very long time.

4 ↙↙↙

The two harrowing passages, homosexuality and the dozens, fall among the many obstacles black kids face. (A thoughtful psychologist once said that *The Labors of Hercules* might be retitled *A Day in the Life of the Average "Blood."*)

For blacks, one of these trials, the dozens, is common, ubiquitous, and perceived as part of life simply because all other black boys either have dealt with it or will deal with it. It becomes a shared suffering and contributes to brotherly emotions.

Being ubiquitous only in the black community and confined to blacks, and being an activity of which one is ashamed, it can and does reinforce feelings of worthlessness. It plays a most important part in feeding attitudes of self-deprecation. If for no other reason, it needs to become public knowledge, to be co-opted by the white community and used openly. This is desirable not because white usage will purify the practice but because its wider adoption will speak to every black child whenever a shriveling of the spirit seeks reinforcement in the dozens. Instead of uniquely black shame, the child will find rather a body of lore and a shared obscenity common to all Americans.

Up against the wall, motherfucker!
We're all in this obscenity together.

The dozens and homosexuality are extremities of experience in another way. One of them (at least up to this point) is an experience confined to blacks, while the other could in no way be seen as exclusively or especially black.

The black experience is as deeply rooted in daily American life as the contempt of a headwaiter or the shotgun in a southern sheriff's car. The important factor is the expression of the white man's hatred for blacks—and *that* is the essence of the shared experience.

Albert's cruel childhood was exceedingly dangerous and solitary and certain to twist his personality. He will no doubt suffer from grave emotional ailments all his life. He may be fortunate and never cease functioning, but he will bear scars and he will know it.

Those men who seek a homosexual solution to their personal miseries often turn to artistic and intellectual pursuits as Albert did. But white America is hostile to homosexuals, to intellectuals, and to blacks. When these three categories are joined in one man he has *one* hell of a hard way to go.

Black boys grow up in a culture onto which certain characteristics are impressed from without. The white community in innumerable ways encourages an equating of anti-intellectualism with virility.

In centers of power—political, commercial, or otherwise —blacks are systematically excluded and, in fact, any such directed ambitions they might have are squashed. It is still assumed in America that blacks are not smart enough to hold positions of power. They are permitted to express their male vigor only in areas remote from centers of importance.

Even now maleness is tightly linked to physical strength and the capacity for violence in the mind of the dominant white community. Blacks are seen as heavily endowed sexually, not intellectually. Many black scholars feel driven to compulsive hypersexuality as if to erase the notion of the effeminate scholar.

America has created a climate in which black anti-intellectualism is seen as virile and where scholarship becomes an effeminate pursuit. Intellectual activities are thus actively discouraged and the few rewards generally available to scholars are withheld. The vigor with which America wages war on the intellectual development of blacks is patently evident from the frenzy with which our white fellow citizens have fought to *keep* education for blacks inferior.

What few rewards there were, awaited boys who turned away from intellectual callings. Little save a marginal academic experience lay before the potential black intellectual. Only aberrant types, "sissies," and "queers" were said to find pleasure in studies; it was assumed that there was little to attract ambitious, competitive, masculine boys.

And, although black parents could not help absorbing some of the attitudes of the white community, they often engaged in a vigorous counteractivity, stimulating boys to learn, to obtain maximum educational experience, and to persist in scholarship in spite of the few palpable rewards. But they struggled against a strong, persistent, contrary tide.

There are no studies which suggest an increased frequency of homosexuality among black men, but there is to be found everywhere evidence of a determined attack on black masculine strivings.

Our own psychiatric studies suggest that one factor accounts for more male vigor than might be expected. It is that blacks at crucial points often do not take the white world seriously when it devalues them. No thoughtful black man assumes that Senator Edward Brooke is the first black since Reconstruction to be capable and qualified to serve in the United States Senate. Would white people really expect us to believe that there are so few of us in places of political distinction because we are *incompetent?*

And consider those key positions in business which have never been filled by blacks. Are we further to believe that such a phenomenon is also due to our intellectual incapacity?

The case is just as bad in sports. Are we really to believe that for all those years nowhere could a black football player be found *smart enough* to be a quarterback?

Perhaps if blacks had truly believed all the things these discriminatory acts implied, they would have been unmanned by doubts about themselves. Fortunately, black men and women saw clearly that they were unrewarded because of the hatred of white men and not because of their own deficiency.

Other factors are of serious import to a black boy in conflict about his future. His white peer has many options and may delay vocational decisions knowing that *some* kind of job will be available *somewhere.* The black boy has no such certainty. Indeed, he has only the certainty that whatever course he takes will be harder because he is black. He must therefore make his simple survival a matter of highest priority. He must take his ultimate vocation into account as early as possible and he can under no circumstances count on opportunities appearing in the future at the right time.

The common observation that homosexuals are often interested in more delicate, more "refined," more intellectual pursuits takes on greater significance when the boy facing such a crisis of identification is black.

To announce "I am a homosexual" is to take a stance before one finds out how the enemy is deployed.

And some boys like Albert find life too threatening, largely because of personal experience but augmented exponentially by the fact of being black. They move into homosexuality propelled by a pattern of motives often different from those of whites. If they have "given up their balls for a brain" then that brain is of vital importance. Their existence, constantly under threat, will rest on the maximal use of intellect.

The worlds of blacks and whites are different and blacks need special armor to wage their wars.

II.

On Being Violent and Being Black

1*

Slaves had to survive incredibly hard work which lasted an eternity; if they obeyed their overseers, it was a killing schedule resulting in certain death within a few years. (Banking houses financed the purchase of slaves with the assumption that a prime field hand had a working life of seven years.) Black survival required that this murderous level of work be avoided at all costs. There are frequently recorded instances of slaves smashing farm equipment, injuring themselves, and using all the techniques at hand to avoid the lethal work pace.

Between the slaveowner's need to see blacks as subhuman and the blacks' need to avoid man-killing work there are several points of contact. The blacks might pretend to fit themselves to some image in the slaveowner's mind and add an elaboration of their own, namely, "If we are a separate breed, you can hardly expect us to be moved as you are, by the promise of reward."

The slaveowner, preoccupied with the "laziness" of his

23

slaves, found this situation both amusing and exasperating and, saddled by conflict, allowed the slave some occasional relief.

The whole concept of the "lazy nigger" was useful to whites who preferred to view blacks as bizarre, primitive, and infantile and who might have felt that an unwillingness to work arose from any or all these categories. It was also useful to blacks who, struggling under a life-and-death burden, were quite happy to be considered "lazy" if that made them less desirable for murderous field work.

The development over the years of a posture of black passivity grew thus out of the interweaving of the economic demands of the planters and the psychological needs of blacks. Added subtleties appeared with time.

The worker, for example, who promises to complete a certain job but never quite gets to it or never quite completes it, or who stretches fifteen minutes' work into two days, is, as any supervisor will tell, doing violence to the emotional well-being of the boss, and we may be sure that though the aggression inherent in the "laziness" of the worker may be obscure to us, it is evident to the supervisor.

The passive posture, in other words, was an adaptive choice of behavior which allowed the black both to contain his aggression against the white owner and, importantly, to minimize the likelihood of retaliation.

If the black worker openly defied his white master, he placed his safety, if not his life, in jeopardy. In fact, open rebellion brought the whole economic system under fire and repression was necessarily swift. The solitary slave, however, might adopt a foot-shuffling, head-scratching, slow-moving mode which the white had come to expect, and so minimize his labor without labeling himself a dangerous rebel.

*   *   *

A black laborer, newly hired, was assigned a hazardous, man-killing job avoided by all workers.

Within a few days he sensed how the white foreman expected black laborers to act. And so he grinned and shuffled and did only a fraction of the work. The foreman, exasperated but amused, reassigned him to sweeping the floor.

In his more comfortable situation he reminded himself that if sweeping ever got hard he would grin and shuffle himself into another easier job.

*   *   *

But the overriding purpose of this shuffle and drawl was to save his life. Secondarily, by denying the economy his labor, he struck at the heart of the system.

Sambo may well have been our first black militant.

2

It is tempting to speculate about recorded history. It recounts wars following upon wars, distorts the facts of the past, and records incidents such as the overthrow of kings and the collapse of nations. To understand our state of affairs, past and present, we cannot ignore the citizens who have been the instruments and the fodder of war.

The frequency of wars which laid waste the people and land in other countries has had only scant disrupting effect in America. This nation was isolated by the oceans and, secure in such isolation, experimented with social systems which had long since proved unwieldy and maladaptive elsewhere.

Slavery was such an experiment. White Americans created a

commendable ethical system which banned violence, but suspended it when the victim had darker skin. Violence against
blacks was sanctioned and is yet sanctioned.

The roots of violence in America are deep and have come
to be associated with heroes of myth and legend. The legends
of fame of Daniel Boone and Kit Carson rest on the slaughter
of dark-skinned aborigines. The fact that the white men
brought far superior weapons to that struggle is concealed by
emphasizing their fewer numbers.

The enemy at the Alamo has been contracted to a symbol
alone and is hardly visualized in human terms. Gold was discovered in California and the tens of thousands of Indians
who occupied the land were murdered without a sound and
without a trace.

It is unfair and untrue to suggest that the settlement of the
United States was any more brutal than the settlement of
lands in other parts of the world. The exploitation of every advantage is surely more a general characteristic of man than a
narrowly defined American trait.

But massive violence *is* part of this country's way of life
and this nation has developed highly refined techniques for
making ugly facts into palatable half-truths. Morality can be
suspended if the victims of violence are not white. America
has worked its deceptive magic on its past and has made it
into a harmless fantasy of Disneyland, or, more precisely,
Frontierland.

If our children take unto themselves this violent quality of
America, they are more likely to act in dominating, exploita-
tive, thoughtless, and cruel ways which produce other men's
deaths as readily as knocking over toys.

If the reader feels that the above is too strong a statement
of America's heritage of violence, he has only to consider the
experience of American soldiers in the course of war.

In World War II, the Korean and the Vietnamese wars, it has been unfeasible to *fully* inform the public about the callousness of our soldiers in their treatment of civilians. Their treatment of captured enemy troops has been more than brutal. There has been, however, one exception in the ordinary chronicle of American soldiers and their treatment of the captured enemy. In World War II, German prisoners were treated with more respect and dignity and handled in a way as free of mindless brutality as any prisoners since the Civil War. Few observers have commented on the phenomenon, and even fewer have speculated on its explanation.

It does not require deep social-psychological analysis to determine that the long-standing American admiration for the Germans played a large part. The allusion to the Civil War is not idle since much of the relationship between the United States and Germany resembled the fratricidal war between the States, even to the deification of the defeated generals, Lee and Rommel.

Moreover, a thread of fascism, Nazi-style, still runs through this nation. The American Nazi Party is the most obvious example, and periodically police uncover a nest of wretched, close-eyed young men who maintain a basement stocked with firearms, swastikas, and photographs of Hitler. Even though they wither when exposed to light—like creatures of the damp —their regular appearance suggests a deep and pervasive infection.

Or, perhaps more accurately, it speaks for an alternative style of life, which in America remains a live alternative, never eradicated, only driven underground to sprout from time to time in white sheets or white hats.

*   *   *

A ninety-three-year-old woman still shivered with fear when she spoke of "the patty rollers." These slave patrols were vicious state-sponsored gangs assigned to gather runaway slaves.

These patrols were disbanded in 1865, but their savagery made them a symbol of terror—a symbol still alive.

*   *   *

There is much to suggest that the ethos of the frontier, immortalizing the two-gun hero facing wild murderous outlaws, remains a played-down but still important part of America's character. If a black American expects to reach maturity in possession of a sound body and mind, he must contain his rage, else risk the concerted attack of such "two-gun heroes."

So it is no great mystery that many black men *appear* passive. Their mothers and a hostile white community have impressed upon them that being a "bad nigger" increases one's chances of being a "dead nigger."

Black mothers are forced to devise ways to crush aggression in their sons. Their efforts, joined with white hostility, rob the black child of positive, self-assertive feelings which could lead to violence against whites.

As a result of such inhibition, black children direct their violence against the white establishment and the result is called delinquency.

There are special qualities of black delinquency. A white child may initiate an anti-social pattern with a break away from the authority of parents, while a black child's anti-social activity may begin when he first ignores the attitude of the surrounding community.

Often the toughest boys and the ones first arrested are those who have most bitterly abandoned hope for the esteem of black people.

They may be dutiful at home, kind to mother, but they have learned how insignificant the white world considers their parents to be. The mother does what she can to prepare her son for a hostile world; she curbs his ambition and urges caution.

The central issue to this is the relationship between family, child, and community. The black parent, acting to transmit important truths about society to the child, feels obligated to inhibit his growth toward mastery of that society.

The predominantly white environment in which the parents live is hostile toward black life and the child sees through his parents' eyes a dangerous world outside.

The mother controls him by the admonition: "If you misbehave I will be angry." Implicit is the further message, "The community won't like you, either." And ultimately, *"White folks won't like you."*

Early he perceives himself subject to anonymous white people who have great influence over his parents.

Sooner or later he will see himself as the victim of those whites, finding common cause with the Indians and the Mexicans and with them taking arms against the Carsons and the Crocketts and the Boones.

3↗↗↗

Some years ago a magazine photograph showed the body of a black woman whose head had been severed and thrown by the murderer into a trash can. The headless body lay on the sidewalk with blood pouring into the gutter. It was a hideous and gory sight and, occurring as it did in the black community on a Saturday night, it was a reminder of the wide range of depredations black people visit upon each other. These things raise the question of why we are so violent one with the other. And why murder is so common a thing in the ghetto.

It is certain that there are uncritical apologists for the black circumstance who would say that murder and violence are no more common in the black community than they are in other areas. And while the authors are not mesmerized by statistics gathered by untrained, unskilled, and often biased observers, still, all observations indicate that the incidence of personal mayhem is more common in the impoverished black ghetto than in comparable white communities.

Some important details must be added concerning this higher level of violence. Explosive rage seems more frequently directed against those closest to the murderer. Men generally, black or white, are more likely to murder friends than strangers, more likely to murder a wife than an unknown.

Thus, in the black community few murders are perpetrated against white people. This is familiar to all students of human misbehavior. The victim is rarely other than an intimate because only someone close can inflict a wound of such pain as to open up the potential of homicide. It is the dear friend or the co-worker who has been needling, making life miserable, who at the moment of extreme stress is turned upon and slain. It is the mistress or the wife who the murderer feels has been unfaithful, who has made life a living hell, whom in a moment of extremity he kills.

Most experts think that the majority of such murders are committed under circumstances of temporary mental derangement. They take place when the man has expended his psychological controls and is whipped into fury so violent that orderly mental operations—judgment and reality-testing—are suspended. Voices may be heard, visions seen; by any measure he would be deemed grossly unbalanced. It is in such a state as this that most murders—white or black—take place. This being so, we are dealing then with a crime of one who is emotionally ill, or has within him the potentiality for emotional illness. Since this is the case, we need to look to the frequency of emotional illness in the population at large.

It is our contention that life in America places stress on the development, growth, and maturation of black Americans of such a kind as to make the incidence of paranoid illness much higher than among white citizens. We suggest that the natural suspiciousness, the natural wariness that black men develop in order to survive make a fertile bed for the potential development under stress of a frank, florid paranoid illness. With the relatively larger number of emotionally disturbed blacks, we would expect to see more of the unhappy consequences of such sickness and among them a higher incidence of murder.

In addition to the more widespread emotional disturbance, another factor contributes to the greater frequency of crimes against the person which take place in the black community. Blacks as well as whites have grown up in a culture which conveys clearly and eloquently the low estimation it places upon blacks and emphasizes the ease with which one may take out hostility on them. Such a message is communicated as readily to a black as to a white and both, if they feel driven by inner needs to a homicidal attack, feel less in the way of restraint and greater permission if the victim is black. Such circumstances make for a higher number of serious assaults and, indeed, murderous assaults on blacks no matter what the race of the criminal himself.

This message is not lost on the police. In many communities they are, literally, killers of black youth.

*　　*　　*

A young, black community worker was murdered by a white off-duty policeman who by all accounts had been drinking across the street from the police station for five hours.

The investigation included an examination of the dead man's blood for alcohol. No blood studies were made on the killer. As might be expected, the speedy conclusion was "justifiable homicide."

*   *   *

America claims that it follows the commandment, "Thou shalt not kill." But it adds, If, however, you must kill, we look with less disfavor on a murder where the victim is black." And, if the person receiving such a message is himself black, it is understandable how the whole ethical system, of which the admonition, "Thou shalt not kill" is only a part, comes under critical review.

4⟋⟋⟋

Whatever the nature of violence in America, there is no doubt that blacks constitute special targets and have themselves adopted this typical Americanism.

The brutality of master to slave was to terrify the slave and thus force him to maximum effort. If he disobeyed or ran away, he was punished with special cruelty to discourage repetition of the act and to frighten other slaves. The acts of violence and cruelty had a savagery which has always characterized whites' mistreatment of blacks.

This is spelled out in the case of the Klansmen in Birmingham, Alabama, who, in 1957, set upon an innocent black man and who, apparently for their own perverse reasons, amputated his penis with a razor blade.

The same quality of violence was shown in the murder of the child Emmett Till in Mississippi in August of 1955.

These and countless similar acts reflect a special way of

feeling about black people which is distinct. It speaks eloquently to the fact that blacks are regarded as subhuman, beyond the circle of kinship established by the brotherhood of
man. The perception of blacks as alien became a factor which
not only made their enslavement an economically profitable
matter, but allowed white Americans to shun any sentiment of
fraternity. Such sentiment might have made the atrocities of
slavery impossible.

As if this victimization were not enough, it further caused
blacks themselves to feel beyond the pale, beyond the circle of
common humanity. They have found that when they feel toward each other as the white man does toward all of them,
they are capable of turning fierce and conscienceless against
other black men.

At times, this matter of rage augments the dynamic hostile
relationship between two people.

*   *   *

Charles was a jealous black man married to a fair
Negro woman. He grew up on an island off the coast of
Georgia. While his family was deeply religious, on reaching adulthood he cast religion aside. He was coal-black,
had a lilting speech, and developed a reputation of being
mean and violent.

His wife described him as a good provider who
worked hard, loved his children, and was unbelievably
cruel to her.

Each day after work, he put her through an inquisi-
tion in which she was to account for every minute of her
day. Charles would seize upon some aspect of her activities which struck him as false and focus his questioning
around that point.

Rarely could she satisfy him and, after a beating or
slapping, she was allowed to retire for the night. He
would then awaken her after a few hours to resume his
questioning, often till dawn.

While there never came to light any objective evidence to support his jealousy, at times he became uncontrollable. And, finally, on one such occasion, Charles shot his wife seven times, killing her on the spot.

Subsequent examination showed him to be a surly, self-righteous man whose jealousy could obviously attain pathological levels, but who was surprisingly intact in other areas to have been so unreasonably jealous for so long.

*   *   *

The classic explanation of jealousy associates it with the projected wish to misbehave. According to this formulation, Charles might have wanted to be unfaithful himself, but projected such a wish onto his luckless wife. On the other hand, he may unconsciously have wished that she betray him with another man to relieve his own guilt or to contribute to his own sexual excitement.

Moreover, when such a man marries, he is likely to select a mate who has a wandering eye or one who, by her beauty, attracts others. The selection of mates is an endless thread twisted upon itself and related in a thousand ways to man's secret mind.

Charles chose an attractive woman and the formulation holds thus far. It is, however, his blackness, her fairness, and their joint negritude which elevate the matter to tragedy.

He thought his wife beautiful. He knew of the striking appearance she presented in public and watched other men's eyes to see their envy. He was pleased when they admired his wife and doubly pleased if he detected puzzlement as to why she had chosen a dark-skinned man. He had himself never dated a dark girl and was convinced that all humans' desirability was a direct function of their fairness of skin.

Charles was therefore firmly convinced that his wife found him, black as he was, repellent. He was further certain that he had to prove himself a better husband than any other man he knew in order to retain her loyalty. And, finally, he deeply believed that, all his virtues notwithstanding, she would one day choose another, lighter-skinned man. It was this certainty that drove him to kill her.

He had added to the commonplace elements of the jealous husband's emotions the incendiary characteristics of America's racial disease. By selecting a woman who appeared to be white, he set the entire social structure in opposition to his marriage and, like an avenging angel, was then determined to avoid cuckoldry and to punish the wife who he was sure would give him horns.

At each step of the way he used the racial sets of the country to establish the framework and heighten the drama of his personal hell. The result was an inter-digitating of racial prejudice and a uniquely black American paranoid jealousy.

*   *   *

Jim was the classic image of a "bad nigger." Squat, muscular, he sported a shaven head and a small gold ring in one ear. He had spent most of his adult life in prison. Now a weather-beaten forty years, he had a quick, apparently ungovernable temper and there was no reason to disbelieve his statement that he had killed nine men and was "looking for number ten."

He was secretive about his early life and only gradually spelled out a story of being orphaned and left in the care of a grandmother. He "went everywhere with her" and there seemed to have been great love between the old woman and the boy.

As they walked along a country road, a speeding car struck her down and she died before his eyes. He remembered the car—an A-Model Ford filled with white men which never slowed down.

Later, as an adult, Jim became a boxer and developed the fine art of inflicting deadly punishment without actually knocking out his opponent. His hostility was turned against all his adversaries, but he conveyed a special quality of hatred for white men, and in the ring, they were the ones he tried to hold up for fifteen rounds while delivering peppery little blows to the head. He was trying deliberately to damage their brains.

Of late, he had become a thief and a mugger—a deadly little black man who specialized in assaulting white men.

*   *   *

If we touch Jim with magic to make him white and leave him with essentially the same past, we might have an adult just as angry, just as cut off from love and compassion as this unfortunate man; but, as a white, Jim might have assembled the fragments of his life differently, and the tragic death of the grandmother would never have fitted into the pattern of murderous hostility framed by a dominant group against him and all his kind.

For this black boy, it remained simply the most deeply penetrating of countless wounds he had suffered from the same antagonist.

Jim is by all criteria psychopathic and anti-social and a menace to society; but, given his cards to play, it is hard to imagine many of us doing better.

III.

Poor Niggers and Hard Times

1↗↗↗

"The dog's next move is the extermination of black people!"

"When honkies sneak into the black community, cut their tires, beat the shit out of them, waste the motherfuckers."

"White pussy is sapping our strength."

"Police are an army of occupation."

"The cities belong to us."

"The honkie is an impotent pervert."

"Cut the pigs down to the hocks."

"The Germans didn't make enough lampshades."

"Birth control is genocide."

"Get your shit together, the man is going to move on you."

"Toms go first."

37

"They are running dogs of the imperialists."

"Off the pigs."

"Black men get their revenge between a white woman's legs."

"Burn the motherfucker down."

"We demand 100 million dollars reparations."

"I have quit talking to white folks."

"How come black men keep running after the stringy-haired beast?"

"They're trying to starve black folks to death."

"When the revolution comes you got to get ten beasts."

"Urban renewal equals black removal."

"The beast is fucking with the minds of black children!"

"We want five states for our own black nation."

*   *   *

The reader may consider the above statements extreme and irrational. If so, we propose to spell out even more irrational and obscene social strictures within which blacks live and which are considered to be "the natural order of things" by their white fellow-citizens.

The rigors of poverty make the above comments by comparison conventional, even tame. At worst, they are epithetical and in no way approach truthful description of the horrors meted out daily to the poor and helpless in health, educational, and welfare facilities all over this country.

2*

Is impoverishment defined as $2500 per year for a family of four? If so, can the resources of a family receiving $3100 per year be adequate? And what meaning do such debates hold if economists find that more than $9000 per year is required to decently support a family in major cities?

For our purposes, we will accept the figure of 40 million impoverished Americans, aware that their condition is defined by dollars and not by what those dollars will buy. A more functional definition of poverty might be: that level of reduced income which requires that adequate clothing be sacrificed in order to procure adequate food, or that the diet be inadequate so that housing may be obtained. It does not seem to ask too much of economists and demographers that poverty be clarified as "too little money to provide the necessities of life."

Poverty also implies poor health, since good health bears a price tag and must usually be sacrificed to allow for more immediate necessities. One of the most sensitive barometers of the inclination and ability of citizens to spend money is the amount they spend for dental care. Thriving dentists connote a confident community willing to spend money and with money to spend.

When things are tough, dental care is sacrificed first, so the poor generally have bad teeth. This in turn leads to digestive and gastrointestinal ills.

The ordinary health aids are also soon given up by poor people. Eyeglasses are only sometimes available and, if broken, require a long time for replacement. Hearing aids, properly fitted shoes, clothing appropriate to the weather—any or all may become luxuries to be relinquished.

A varied and nutritious diet is an expensive item and something few people of even borderline incomes can afford, much less the frankly impoverished.

The health problems, indeed all the problems of the poor, are of great importance to blacks. The most modest estimate would make 10 million of that 40 million poor Americans black—one in four, while our distribution in the general population is one in ten.

To put it another way, almost half of us are poverty-stricken. And everyone knows how close the rest of us are to the line.

We are poor because we are sick and sick because we are poor. Many simpletons want to believe that healthy black people remain on welfare by choice. They resist the truth of the matter, which is that by far the majority of welfare recipients are unable to work because of age or illness.

One cannot help wondering about the farmers who have actively resisted programs to give away food to the poor. We assume that they thereby hope to keep the demand for their products high. What would it take to remind them that the subsidy given them by the government is no different from the subsidy given the poor?

Favorable postage rates represent in effect a subsidy for every business using the mails. Every form of commerce receives direct or indirect subsidy by favorable tax laws and yet the beneficiaries of these and other such subsidies are generally the most determined opponents of public assistance for the poor.

Since relatively more blacks than whites are poor, poverty is a matter of great concern to us. The whole cycle of poverty and sickness has become an intimate of ours. Since blacks are so often reviled and mistreated and denied outlets for their talents they turn frequently to manifestly destructive actions—alcohol and drug addiction—direct and indirect suicide. There is also more sickness because of the discriminatory practices of health professionals.

And there is a further clear-cut but less known consequence of being black, and perpetually angry, and unable to express it or do anything about it. High blood pressure is more widespread, more serious, and responsible for more complications with a proportionately greater number of deaths among blacks.

The most common psychological cause of high blood pressure is the active repression of hostile feelings. Current research supports this as the primary reason for its greater frequency in blacks.[1]

It lends quantitative support to the proposition that blacks are angry and that they hold their rage in check by monumental self-control, in the exercise of which their blood pressure soars.

[1] The greater incidence of high blood pressure and hypertension among blacks is a matter of medical fact. It is also well-known that the disease is more difficult to control in blacks and causes more deaths.

In Appendix A we include a selected list of *recent* articles related to *some* aspects of this problem.

The length of the list is instructive in several ways. It suggests the massive amount of published material which must nowadays be studied and evaluated before one can make knowledgeable commentary in a field. The vast majority of these articles show that one or more of the factors under study can *not* account for the greater incidence of high blood pressure in blacks. Only a handful note that, with other possible explanations excluded, the only remaining explanation is a psychological one.

Some people are inherently disinclined to believe whatever a black man says. For them, the appendix of references by predominantly white authors may prove convincing. But then, sadly, we must admit that in the case of others the autoerotic embrace of their own preconceptions is too gratifying to allow the interference of a new idea.

For them, nothing helps.

3*

A black minister—young, empathic, short on formal training but long on love for humankind—was telephoned by a blind woman whose apartment had been robbed. The minister was working with a team in a poverty area. The woman was panicky because the burglar had disturbed her possessions, the location of which she had by necessity carefully memorized. More frightening, however, was the prospect that the burglar might have left a door or window unlocked which would allow his re-entry into the apartment at any time.

The minister raced over, picked up the woman, took her to his own home, and arranged for appropriate housing the next day. Criticism from colleagues poured in. He answered with contempt, saying he responded to the cry of a human in need and found it hard to hear a critic who in turn could not hear such a cry. He was a dominating, officious man at his worst, but he had the spiritual resource his parishioner needed.

A caseworker who was aging, childless, and depressed was also fearful that her husband was losing interest in her. She encountered a poor unmarried black mother as a client. This young woman was overwhelmed by the real life problems presented by four children and the task of balancing a budget on minimal public assistance. The caseworker threw herself into the problem with a passion. She aroused officials to increase the woman's allowance, arranged for new and better housing, secured comprehensive medical care for the family, and enrolled the mother in a training program leading toward skilled employment.

She was praised all around for her heroic work with

this family and only her *own* therapist knew how vitally important it was for her to "save" this young mother. And when she succeeded, only her therapist knew how grieved she was that her own life remained unimproved.

She had started with the feeling that in saving the client she could perhaps save herself. After her task was done she became depressed again, realizing that she was still personally miserable and unable to change those events which made her life a burden.

*   *   *

The black woman who saw the above caseworker was fortunate. She found herself with an energetic, imaginative, capable helper who was determined to effect worthwhile changes in her life.

The fact that the caseworker was driven by her own neurosis is of interest to a study of her work, but of greater importance is the character of the service she offered her client. It was of superior quality and there was nothing in her actions to suggest her having anything but a favorable influence on the young mother's life.

4↗↗

Poverty strikes particularly close to black family life, and, indeed, often defines it. Millions of blacks have an income too low for the least semblance of comfort and all blacks share a history of poverty, knowing that it is infinitely easier for a black man to lose what little he gets than for a white man.

Poverty stands in relation to black America much as it does to the people of India. It is a sea surrounding islands of affluence. The poor must rely for sheer survival on the generosity of charitable agencies and public assistance. For many, welfare or public assistance has necessarily come to constitute a way of life and the white community has linked poverty to immorality.

Nowadays, welfare programs have multiplied in number, if not in sensitivity. They all employ legions of "workers" whose task it is to provide real aid and to bring whatever skills they have to benefit the recipient. The purpose of these workers presumably is to inject a personal touch—to provide a compassionate response to emergencies and to invest the bureaucracy with human flexibility. It is a pity they are so often forced by local governments to abandon a sympathetic role which might ideally reflect the conscience of the community —it is as if no community dare admit its love for fellow men.

As we have said, the country generally holds a strong bias *against* the poor. It is a bias which springs directly from the social climate of America. It harks back to the nation's Puritan origins and it maintains that to be unemployed or to be on the dole is sinful, that, in fact, to be poor is sinful. Some caseworkers are able to resolve these feelings, but few can keep such sentiments from affecting their relationship with clients.

It is difficult to discuss helping agencies and related governmental organizations without appearing unduly harsh and critical. These agencies seem to beg for criticism. But we hold no unrelenting animus toward them; rather do we have respect and abiding sympathy for officials who are required to formulate rules and administrators who must observe them.

In an ideal world there would arise no conflict between the primary interests of the foregoing and those of the client. In the world as we know it, however, as we think the reader will agree, such conflict does develop more often than not. It should be obvious that we side with the client.

5*↑↑↑*

It now seems well-authenticated that a higher incidence of mental illness is to be found among the poor than among people of higher income. Let us, then, accordingly speculate on the implications of this fact for the poor and for those associated with them.

Our society considers mental illness a "bad" thing which affects the wealthy more often than it does the poor. The poor are thereby seen as suffering not so much in the way of mental illness but from realistic problems of simple survival which take precedence over neurosis. They are thought to be somehow more deserving because they need only the absolute material necessities of life, not some complicated psychotherapy which is inexact and poorly understood at best.

On the other hand, and in another sense, and simultaneously, our society sees the poor as suffering from *more* psychopathology than are their affluent neighbors. They are imagined to be sicker and more deviant in every sense when placed alongside middle-class folk. Their illnesses are therefore not considered ailments peculiar to the individual and his unique circumstances; rather they are seen as disorders common to all persons at this income level.

Such extreme attitudes may be modified or mixed in any proportion.

*   *   *

A caseworker who had dealt effectively and compassionately with poor clients for a long time found herself involved with "better-off" families. She said she was immediately struck by the "complexities" of neurotic defenses in her wealthier clients. Her second reaction was to observe the higher value she placed on the "more complex" defenses, and the almost unnoticed pleasure she found in working with "more complex" problems. It was suggested to her that, although she would not have guessed it herself, she viewed her poor clients as "simple people," good but plain, who offered her less professional gratification than did the rich.

*   *   *

Certain advantages may attach to the situation of her poor clients being considered "good" and "plain," but they would no doubt feel short-changed if they ever sensed a differential in the worker's feelings between the poor and the rich.

Poor people develop more mental illness because they have more crises, more stress. There is less room for a "minor" problem: All problems are major, and, in fact, for a problem to receive any serious attention it must *become* major. One may find it difficult to justify taking an hour out of a day to talk about a child's sleep disturbance if the family has inadequate living quarters and if every waking moment would properly be spent searching for better housing.

Under such circumstances it is psychologically necessary that "minor" problems be ignored. Conscience, if nothing else, demands that "major" problems take priority.

This attitude has great significance for the American society. In this highly mobile social system, many influential people, now no longer poor, grew up in poverty where minor problems—and as we said they defined all but the most severe emotional problems as minor—were ignored and where "stout folk" paid attention only to truly serious matters.

If policy-makers grew to manhood with such attitudes, then we can be sure they will turn a hostile face to any program which strikes them as pampering weaklings, or calling upon the stout, self-reliant "good people" to support the weak, dependent "bad people."

It is widely believed that emotional concerns are a luxury poor people cannot afford; and it is a mischievous belief, whenever it appears.

Poor people develop more mental illness because the built-in "tension relievers" of our social system are less available to them. We are speaking in part of recreation, but primarily of the *leisure time* to consider recreation or unplanned activities undertaken solely for pleasure.

Rare is the working man or woman who has not had to take a "sick day" off when a crisis was brewing. When a man feels mounting anxiety and is free to go bowling, buy a new tie, or take off a week, he engages in mental hygiene in its purest form. He prevents a worsening of a bad condition, often pulls out of it, and gives his psychic structure time to heal.

When a breather is not available because other matters are "more important," the resultant situation sets up the same requirement for repression that is seen in childhood. Powerful outside forces make the expression of inner concerns impossible and minor pressures must either abandon the quest for direct expression or find an outlet by some disguised means.

Repression of strong drives builds up a store of ever-enlarging future troubles. Thus, the poor develop more mental illness because the concentration exclusively on major crises means they feel themselves required to deal with problems actually incapable of human mastery.

People with ample financial resources don't have to deal with such a flood of major crises. Critical circumstances arise from time to time, but there are fewer of them. And when they do appear, lawyers, physicians, and other experts are at hand who respond as agents of the victim to strengthen him and make it possible to master these crises.

This issue is of central importance because mastery of problems is vitally important for the psychological apparatus of all people. When confronted by crisis, the adult needs leisure in which to "play with" the problem—to turn it over, look at it in every way, reduce it to manageable dimensions, and, in his own good time, develop techniques for mastering all or part of it. Moreover, should he consult a lawyer, whom he hires out of his own resources, he is simply summoning aid *out of his own substance.* In fact, all the experts he uses are *his* experts, extensions of himself. If, with their assistance, he surmounts the crisis, *he* has done it and the ascendancy is his, giving him new energy for future encounters.

Consider then the poor citizen who has no respite from difficulties, whose life becomes an exercise in brinksmanship and who finds scant opportunity to use his talents in the leisurely process of problem manipulation. Poverty robs him of the time for contemplative intellectual handling of problems. Thinking a problem through can take time and time is what he has least of all.

There is little opportunity to turn to outside resources to strengthen his hand and because he cannot purchase such aid, he feels diminished. Lacking support, he finds more and more problems overwhelming.

The cruelest blow comes, however, when charitable agencies offer inadequate aid (legal, medical, or other). It may help the victim over the immediate crisis but he gains thereby no feeling of mastery. It was not *his* strengthened hand which dealt with the crisis, it was another's. He acquires no newer feeling of greater capability, only a brief respite before the dragon of circumstance must again be faced by a protagonist no stronger, no wiser, no subtler, than before. He has been denied the chance for personal growth and he is the lesser for it.

This is no pamphleteering against helping the helpless. Far from it. Rather it is an assessment of just what help can and cannot do. Even a little help may provide relief from repetitive overwhelming trauma and such relief may be lifesaving. But if there is sufficient time between crises, the victim can gather his resources and develop his own techniques for mastery.

We say that outside help *should* provide breathing room for the poor, allowing them time for their own capabilities to catch up with the demands made on them. If this outside help is to provide such an opportunity, it must be *major* help, readily available, and sustained over a long enough period for the individual to gather together scattered psychological resources and develop his own capability for meeting stress. The latter is illustrated in the following case history.

*   *   *

Mrs. Lewis is a chunky, dark woman, breathless, overweight, and chronically depressed. Her worsening hypertension and diabetes were impossible to control because of chronic eating binges. Every few days she gorged herself on bread and sweets. In between times, she moved about brooding, restless, trying frantically to control her appetite.

Her physician despaired of curbing her overeating and referred her for counseling, convinced that her voracious appetite was related to emotional problems.

Although she had once been married, both her children were illegitimate. The fifteen-year-old boy had a severe behavior problem and was receiving psychiatric treatment. Her eight-year-old daughter was extremely close to her and, while the child presented no behavior problem, the mother was troubled about her excessive dependence.

The family was supported by public assistance grants and this had been true for many years. Mrs. Lewis did occasional domestic work to augment her income, but concealed this from her caseworker. She was genuinely worried about her health and feared for her children should she become completely disabled.

She spoke of her past with detachment. She had been orphaned in the South early in her life and reared by an older couple, distant relatives. From her tenth year onward, she attracted the attention of her foster father who forced her to submit sexually. This continued through her menarche and, shortly after, she became pregnant. She bore the foster father's child at thirteen. The wife's scorn and suspicion made the girl keep silent about the paternity of the infant and, taking over the child, the foster mother spoke of the baby girl as her own. She refused to let the young mother care for her and raised the baby as her own daughter.

Mrs. Lewis quit school at her foster mother's insistence and obtained domestic work. She was sent to live with relatives in another town—and there, a lonely adolescent, she came under the influence of a lesbian with whom she developed a lengthy intimacy. Years later, having borne two more children and been involved in one brief disastrous marriage, ill health forced her onto welfare and gradually into the situation first described.

Her therapist made every effort to obtain better housing for her, more complete medical care, a higher monetary allowance, and took a keen interest in the children's welfare. Mrs. Lewis responded favorably to these efforts and her depression lifted sufficiently for real communication to begin.

She revealed among other things impressive intellectual gifts. She was a subtle critic of the social system and felt a deep, inexhaustible maternal concern for her children. Moreover, she was able to view herself with clear-eyed detachment.

"I am fat, aging, and unattractive," she said. "What

man would want me? I am sick and helpless with no one
to turn to. I am eating myself to death. I know it, but I
feel so desperate for love sometimes that only by gorging
myself with food can I fill up the emptiness inside me.

"If I didn't go on eating binges I would go crazy and
kill myself.

"I understand all this and am depressed but I don't see
how you or anyone else can help me.

"I don't understand why the doctor sent me to you.
You should be talking to someone you could help."

The circumstances of her life, being in fact so dismal,
gave little reason for optimism. Her self-appraisal was
cruel and crystal-clear and there was a compelling quality to her statement which drew the therapist momentar-
ily into agreement and the two sat silently pondering this
truth.

In subsequent sessions, the therapist turned to the two
aspects of the pattern which had been most telling—
Mrs. Lewis' intelligence and her helplessness. The
worker concurred gently that Mrs. Lewis' life might be
shortened by illness, but added that all of us live under a
sentence of death. In any event, it seemed a pity that she
allowed herself to continue in such a self-destructive state
when she had such intelligence and capability for changing it.

The therapist recognized that Mrs. Lewis probably felt
the most acute and constant psychic pain as a result of
her helplessness in the face of mountainous odds. Anything which could support a feeling of mastery would relieve pain. And it was toward this end that a therapeutic
campaign was planned.

*   *   *

We say that the community betrays its conscience or lack of
it in dealing with the poor and helpless. It uses programs and
people to carry out its will and makes certain that its agents
have a precise understanding of its wishes.

All citizens must rely to a frightening degree on supportive services provided by the community of their neighbors. A man develops a portion of his own self-esteem in terms of how his neighbors regard him.

When a town treats its poor and its blacks as expendable filth, the town will earn their unrelenting hostility and the victims will feel toward themselves as the town feels toward them.

But possibly the greatest loss is the tendency such treatment has to grind out love, hope, and idealism in its victims. The first casualties of the spirit of the poor are those sustaining fantasies that promise a better day, and, with this disappearance of hope, the town can be absolutely certain that it will reap the bitterness it sows.

IV.

No Blacks Have It Made

1*⚹⚹*

The events followed each other in an orderly causal train.
Martin Luther King, Jr.—civil rights demonstrations—politics as usual—*disenchantment*. Malcolm X—black rage—
Watts, Newark, Detroit—rebellion—hasty placation and
cover-up—then more politics as usual, effecting more bitterness. And now we stand even more bitter and puzzled than
before.

Some institutions, their eye caught by the racial violence,
suddenly brought blacks in in greater numbers than ever in
their history. Prestigious universities were quick to recruit
black students and black faculty. The results were sometimes
strange.

            *   *   *

Women's colleges, old and famous, admitted scores of
black girls. Scholarships were made plentiful and most of
the schools genuinely wanted the blacks to do well. The
new recruits were smart, no doubt about it; and the situ-

ation seemed ideal—the faculties outdid themselves spotting and tutoring students whose inadequate preparation made problems.

But these smart, favored, looked-after black girls suffered. They came to hate their surroundings. Many transferred to black schools after the freshmen year; others, unable to find another college with so favorable a financial climate stayed on and remained miserable.

Their parents considered college a dream fulfilled, and, out of pride, sent more money than they could afford.

The colleges themselves had some less-than-noble reasons for suddenly wanting blacks, but, on the whole, it was a good thing, and a necessary thing. The effort and money expended on the new students could not be cynically dismissed. The colleges could not understand why the girls were so unhappy.

Everything had happened so quickly, no one thought to look ahead. If someone had, it might have been noticed that over the years the colleges had shaped themselves after the interests and needs of the rich families whose daughters they served.

No one remembered that although many of the students were of modest means these schools were shaped for *very* rich girls. The social life was typical of rich families and the interests were "rich white folks" interests.

The black girls, gathered up and thrust into this place, saw quickly that it had nothing to offer them. Alongside the daughters of the world's wealthiest families, all the black girls whatever their financial status felt dirt-poor and, however pretty, felt clumsy and ugly.

In large measure the schools were designed to bring rich white girls into contact with rich white boys. Black girls, being neither rich nor white, were in no way served by this function of the school.

It was easy for them to imagine that the fault lay in them, that they were crude, unsophisticated, homely, stupid. And to assume that all this was due to something intrinsic in the self was "too much."

Maybe, if the schools had tried to match, in deeds, the idealism of the girls . . .

Or if the administrations had talked frankly with the girls about the college and what black girls might expect . . .

Or maybe it couldn't be helped, the country being the way it is and people hating the way they do. Maybe many of the black girls were doomed to suffer, and maybe all the school could do was to try everything and keep offering its insufficient best. In time, the girls might themselves teach the college how to serve them with the greatest success and the least pain.

2✓✓✓ The Silent Blight—The Secret Mind

The overwhelming majority of black children never get a chance at college. Intellectually, they are wiped out early. They become of necessity so occupied with the demands of surviving as blacks that their capacity to learn suffers.

The statistics are shocking. Many blacks, angry, deny them outright, accusing racist investigators of perpetrating some massive lie against blacks. Others indict the instruments of measurement, the language, the family income—indeed everything under the sun.

The facts *are* alarming enough. In standardized tests of verbal and non-verbal skill, reading comprehension, arithmetic skill, and general information, black first-graders score below 85 percent of white first-graders.

This relative disparity continues and increases throughout

elementary and secondary school. A six-year-old who scores below 85 percent of his classmates is one year behind while a sixteen-year-old is more than two years behind.

The facts speak plainly: The minds of black children are early blighted and damaged in the ability to learn.

We all know that tests do not measure the social skill and cunning black youngsters develop in the challenge of city life. We know for example that within the context of survival a black child in South Philadelphia may be a genius. Still, we need scientists, professionals, intellectuals, and our children now have small hope of reaching that mark.

All children, black and white, have learning problems, but very few white children fail altogether to respond to the learning demands of school, home, and community. These elements combine to push a white child steadily through the sequences of ordinary educational establishments.

While most white children do emerge from the other end of the education process intellectually stifled, they experience no economic penalty. Not so with black children. Tests record a steady deflection away from academic interests and competition. By the sixth grade, most city kids who are black are so far behind that, unless removed from the situation, they will never catch up.

The genesis of this decline is the hostility of the *white society* to the child's learning. It is so pervasive, so powerful, that it can be likened to a shower of deadly radioactive dust. Exposed to such a shower long enough these children wither and die intellectually.

We submit that the high intensity of white hatred for black and the boundless opportunity for its expression produce an environment in which black children are terrified, but go through the motions of schooling nevertheless. To a great extent, our children are prevented from developing confidence in the environment. A specific inhibitory effect is acquired as children explore with adults the world outside their homes. The alert child sees white people in control and notes their attitudes.

Such events have a deep effect because the child's maturation depends on his ability to read the hidden meaning in adults. He *must* know how mother *really* feels and he learns how to search the face and listen to the voice and arrive at the most important judgments: Does she love me? Will she protect me? Does she dislike me? Will she harm me? May I love her?

These are the only questions of importance for the helpless child who must position himself within the family in such a way as to be loved and protected. And it is the keen, highly developed penetration into the inner life of adults which informs the child as to the nature of the adult's fundamental convictions.

Children get hostility and contempt from whites. From black adults they get the idea that some whites hold even more deadly feelings against black people *and* black children. And, no doubt, the most important truth they find behind the eyes of those adults they love is the hopeless helplessness to protect the child against those who hate him. (And this is his most precious defender.)

The driving, developmental forces innate in children thrust them out toward the world with eyes, mouth, hands, feet, and mind—all those sensory and motor instruments with which the child is armed for the mastery of his environment.

We would propose that it is here—where the inborn driving life-force of a man-child for triumph collides with every element outside him—that here it is he learns that all the machinery of that limitless world out there is geared to block his gain of ultimate dominance. He learns that he is blocked because he is black.

Once the truth of his situation sinks in, it would be most natural that he take less interest in matters of the mind. It is, after all, with mental instruments that man brings his world under control and if that objective is from the outset denied him he is likely to neglect an instrument now made purposeless.

Who would develop a sword arm if combat is denied?

The societal climate disarms and unmans. Through its unceasing war on black men and women the society affects the child. Parents have no choice but to convey to the child the truest nature of their world. Through the eyes and lips and mind of his most beloved, the child is told early of the nature of his world.

And under the silent, subtle, steady, unrelenting, drifting, malignant fallout of hate, the child loses heart and seals tight the undiscovered temples of his mind.

3*

"Look at Ralph Bunche, or Jackie Robinson, or Joe Louis. If *they* can make it, you can too."

"They should serve as an example to your people."

*   *   *

Ralph Bunche said once that his most annoying and senseless burden was being made an "example" of what black men can accomplish in spite of everything. He added that if his achievements were to be explained in terms of the influence of only one person, it might be that his grandmother should be memorialized rather than he.

When she discovered her grandson's assignment to a high school course which did not prepare him for college, single-handedly she fought the Los Angeles Board of Education and succeeded in having the boy switched to college-preparatory courses. Her hopes for Ralph were rooted in his education and she fought for it.

Dr. Bunche has mentioned other bright children among his friends who had no such advocate and who dropped out or were put out of school. Some settled for a precarious living, others went to prison.

*   *   *

For millions of black youngsters, it often seems that no matter how clever one is or how hard one tries, at a crucial point one must rely on a parent or someone standing in a parent's place. If society has cut down the older person before one needs him or has so harassed him that he is unable to respond to the child's need or has so crushed his spirit that he does not sense the need, then the child is lost.

Since America is engaged in the business of killing blacks, in spirit if not in body, we might do well to look at blacks who have "made it." We might take a special interest in the family and parents who stand shadowed in the background but who have more often than not made success possible for the generation following.

Our inquiry must move beyond frivolous concepts to real understanding of these families. There are far too many mediocre and dull-witted whites in high places for the standard explanations of black inferiority to hold up.

Ralph Bunche's grandmother may not have been unusual in her ambition for her grandson. Who knows exactly how she helped him? His fate may have depended on her tireless testing of the system and her determination to find a way for the boy.

One might ask just how black families made it possible for their children to prosper? Our experience tells us that exceptionality cannot be separated from its setting. The most barren land produces an occasional flower of beauty. We must draw a lesson from these families, not to exculpate white America but to give hope to black America.

The very existence of 22 million blacks hangs in the balance.

4 ⁄⁄⁄

Disaster struck the Jenkinses in 1936. The father lost his job in the South and took the family north just in time to encounter the depression of the late thirties.

They barely subsisted living in one room, surviving on welfare payments and surplus commodities. The mother worked as a domestic; the father did whatever common or uncommon labor he could find. The sons and daughter went to school, worked at odd jobs, and watched the parents struggle.

As the years passed, there was no noticeable improvement in their economic condition—they simply all grew older. The situation was particularly bleak as they looked ahead to the children reaching college age. There seemed to be no way to obtain money for higher education.

Within the younger son's last year in high school, the whole picture changed. In the fall following his graduation, Sam was enrolled in college and, aided by his parents, was able to complete undergraduate and graduate school. His older brother had been drafted and later was unable to organize himself to use the veterans' educational benefits. His sister, two years older, worked as a clerk, was married at 18, and had two children by 20.

The crucial factors were that Sam was ready to go to college in 1941 and that the Jenkinses lived in Pittsburgh. 1941 was the year when the industry of war exploded upon the city, and men and women, black and white, suddenly found plentiful, well-paid work.

From 1941 through 1946, both parents worked in the mills and, with the additional good fortune of not being drafted, Sam was well-launched into graduate school by the time the boom faded.

Had he been ready for college in 1940 or earlier he could not have attended. He is now a trained professional because he graduated from high school in the right town and in the right year.

*   *   *

The barrier opened to let one child through.

Thus, the pattern is that an ordinary family, even modest in aspirations, moves from one generation to the next with its members achieving or failing—within the limits—no higher than this and rarely lower than that—all quite evenly and predictably until the unusual one, the mutant, appears.

It may be that a family which can offer the oldest child scholarly opportunities can offer those who follow no such luxury. If such a situation includes a gifted child then we have a setting for potential grandeur.

No matter the size of the sibship a family in the struggle of its ordinary affairs for a brief period may encounter favorable winds and a buoyant sea. The child at hand to benefit from such a respite may forever after stand apart from the others in exploitation of talents and in serenity.

Such phenomena have intriguing implications. The family maintains steady unrelenting pressure on the children but their ambitions are blocked by *external circumstances*. Once an opening appears, the child is pushed through. If the opening is shut quickly, then his achievement appears due solely to exceptional gifts. The conclusion is drawn that he arises born of elements with no intellectual antecedents or ambitious parents.

For some, among them occasional scholars and "experts" who ought to know better, the pattern described above suggests that most blacks are genetically sub-par and rarely gifted. This is despicable, but some people need such notions of intellectual inferiority to reinforce their prejudices.

In recent years an old line of reasoning which comforts desperate minds has gained new adherents. It suggests a chance lurch of fate which operates to elevate one man and reduce another—but, no matter what the nature of the misery, the lowered wretch brought it on himself!

With this logic the blame falls on the less fortunate themselves and the assumption is made that all had had equal opportunities.

Nothing could be further from the truth. We suggest, rather, that the mutant is different *not because* he was brighter than the others but because his brightness met an opportunity for flowering. Otherwise, he, too, surely would have been stifled, his bright potential shriveled, and he would have slogged through a pedestrian life along with his brothers and sisters.

The mutant is, then, no mutant at all—only the beneficiary of watchful parents who seize even the smallest opportunity to save a child.

5′′′

Blacks have produced a small but important group of families in which parents who have only modest attainments manage to inspire each of a host of children to a high level of distinction.

When black families accomplish this, we must ask what about them was significant to the success of their children.

Sometimes the parents had education or respect for learning. Those with educational experience felt they had glimpsed a sliver of freedom and power available to an educated black man.

These families had to have the means for educating their children. While the amounts of money available were pitifully small, for such a pittance to represent advantage simply tells us how stark was the poverty of other black families.

Special skills often meant special opportunities. For example, one mother was expert in the making of fancy pastries. What made the difference was the advantage of this skill coupled with an intense ambition for her children and the father's steady, though modest, employment. Five of her six children became college graduates.

In other cases, the fathers were incredibly resourceful farmers who made poor land support a family and educate the children. But most blacks were without land.

There were in addition many barriers firmly opposed to blacks improving their lot so that for a whole family to stream through, some extraordinary circumstance had to open a crevice.

*   *   *

The Bullocks exemplify one way in which black families lifted the next generation en masse onto a high level of accomplishment.

There were seven children and all lived lives of distinction. The two oldest sisters married ministers and presided over important households. George, the first son, became a high school teacher; Ben took degrees in rural education and was a college instructor. Joseph was a successful dentist. Lula was a teacher of English and Latin. Jessie, the youngest, had a master's degree in home economics and was a college teacher.

This distinguished group was fathered by a farmer, George Bullock, who married Martha Johnson in 1879. His parents had been slaves and he himself had been born into slavery. The mother of the clan was the daughter of Ben Johnson, a man who bought his freedom, and Rebecca Norris, a freeborn woman.

The father, with his growing family, moved from one sharecropping situation in North Carolina to another, all unsatisfactory.

A young black educator, Thomas S. Inborden, was hired as the principal of a newly founded school. Excited about his new assignment, he drove over all the neighboring counties talking to black parents, urging them to enroll children in his new school.

In Martha Bullock he found his most enthusiastic convert. She thundered through the community exhorting every parent to seize upon the great educational opportunity. She registered all her children who were of age and, in addition, recruited a small army of neighbors.

When George Bullock came to a final disagreement with his most recent landowner, he was persuaded by Inborden to move onto the school grounds. The parents farmed and worked in various capacities around the institution. The children worked, attended classes, and, out of this special setting, moved on to higher education and distinction.

*   *   *

This impressive story covered a period from the 1880's to the present. The parents were poorly educated and could contribute little formally to their children's education.

They could, however, seize each opportunity and widen every door and shout so loud as to deafen them with the statement that education would free them—mind and heart and soul.

Such chance happenings as the foundation of Inborden's school were seized by some black families. An influential white person on occasion helped obtain learning for the children. Stories are plentiful of ambitious parents who, employed as maid and butler for rich white families, maneuvered the financial aid and personal intercession of whites and obtained educational advantages for their children.

In their roles as protector and interpreter of the environment for the benefit of their children, some black families have engaged in mental acrobatics.

Some parents fired up their children to function as examples of black intellectual excellence, which was to demonstrate to whites that blacks were capable of high-level functioning. It was supposed that white people, seeing such scholarship, would relax their opposition to the advancement of blacks.

This reasoning was, of course, naive. The students did well, displayed their accomplishments to whites, and the whites ignored them. No change occurred in the system, save a tightening of the meshwork to make certain no black slipped through simply because he happened to be bright.

The black scholar, disappointed, resigned himself to work in that narrow corner allowed him by a segregated world. If he had an abundance of spirit and drive, he might set out on another program designed to further prove that blacks could be outstanding scholars. There were more than a few blacks whose whole lives were a series of vigorous efforts to produce some accomplishment which could be shown to whites in hopes that *this* would let them through.

The repetitive efforts and the repetitive rejections are intriguing in another way. These are blacks who accepted the idea that there was a legitimate question about their inferiority, and they embarked on what seemed to them a sensible method of refuting this premise.

They assumed that the hostility toward the advancement of

blacks was due solely to ignorance. They thought that whites simply did not know they were capable of the same level of intellectual functioning. It must have seemed that whites had only to be shown.

We contend that these parents saw things this way deliberately because it allowed them to convince the children that by their school performance they could shake, if not break, the system of racial oppression. This gave a great push to the scholarly drive, and allowed the children to persevere in academic efforts despite terrible odds.

The parents need not have made so conscious a choice. They may have simply avoided thinking the matter through to its logical conclusion, or they may have wanted so desperately to believe it themselves that they *were* convinced. They had sufficient belief to convince the children, but they were hardheaded realists and in their hearts they no doubt knew it made no difference what their children accomplished. The structure of bigotry and the hatred of blacks remained.

The lie simply drove them harder.

There was another lie parents told their children, and whether they believed it or not is less important than that again they had to *seem* to believe it.

They seemed to believe, and in large measure induced their children to believe, that if one were prudent, diligent, and so on down the list of Puritan virtues, if one were all these things, then one was likely to rise to a position of prominence: Success awaited—wealth and position was theirs.

Now one would have to be a very special kind of ninny to look around at the universal disenfranchisement of blacks, to see the abuse of blacks of every condition, at every turn—one would have had to have a serious intellectual impairment to see all this and yet believe that opportunities were unlimited for the deserving black man.

Education, preparation, and all the rest made a difference if one were white, but they had absolutely nothing to do with the heights to which a black man could rise. This was determined by the caste system that is still operative in this country.

The best black student became a physician, dentist, lawyer, or educator. The ceiling was low: He could only rise to the top of his field in a small community. If that community were Atlanta or Washington, D.C., the field might be large and a certain local distinction might be achieved. In no way could he hope to gain fame beyond a white-defined limit.

Dr. Matthew Walker's great surgical skills are probably unknown outside the small circle of Meharry alumni. Benjamin Mays' renown as an educator, however wide, is fractioned by his being viewed by whites as limited to the black academic world.

The world in which black men of learning have worked has made few opportunities available. What sense could it make to study cultural anthropology if only a demeaning post was available to reward the most prodigious scholarship?

Our few architects, engineers, astronomers, mathematicians, writers, and poets all at some point had to consider the difficulties facing them and their possible impoverishment if such a calling were pursued. It is, we think, understandable that there was a wide diversity of talents among those who survived and all this diversity was filtered through a few professions.

*   *   *

In the 1940's a black student embarked on a course in journalism. For most blacks it seemed patently ridiculous to waste four years of college on a discipline with such limited opportunities.

A brief survey by his fellow students revealed that there were no black journalists employed by white publishers and black publishers offered woefully underfinanced and understaffed weekly newspapers. On none of them was a job likely to develop that would justify the years of training. It required a combination of courage and a selective inattention to the facts of life for the young man to complete his training.

*   *   *

At best a family has a hell of a job. At worst it is a nightmare.

6*

Consider for a moment the matter of the perennial conflict between mother and daughter. Theirs is a war which flares openly at times but is always a smoldering bitterness.

At some point in pre-adolescence, the mother feels that the child should assume the responsibility for cleaning up her room. A battle is begun which will last until the daughter ultimately moves out on her own.

It is one of the wonders of nature that all the psychological tendings which push mother and daughter into such intense and prolonged conflict should so regularly center on the "cleaning of the room" as the battleground.

We speak of the wide diversity of American families, white and black, and find that it becomes a regular phenomenon—a thing to be expected if one has a daughter—the battling between mother and daughter over the room. The room is never clean enough for mother and it always satisfies daughter.

Depending on how much pressure the mother brings to bear and how much it is diluted by her love, she will force the child to yield, and in so doing there will be the implicit agreement that the girl was dirty before she yielded—that she was willing to live in filth until her mother forced her to clean up.

Perhaps the issue of cleaning a room is a minor thing, but the matter of being filthy and dirty might be more of a problem for a black girl who lives in an environment which treats her like filth and considers black synonymous with dirt.

A black family would want to neutralize this kind of thing, but how? In its attempt to reinforce seemingly uncomplicated habits of cleanliness, it finds instead that it is reinforcing in the child community-generated attitudes of self-depreciation.

Or take the business of sleeping late. We know that there are day people and night people and that any or all may do well. But generations of parents of all colors have pegged kids as lazy simply because they were not on the same biological clock as older members of the family.

Similarly, some human organisms are equipped to handle a greater quantity of food without piling up fat—others gain weight if they get too close to the refrigerator. It all seems related to the functioning of regulating hormones. There is nothing innately slothful about a fat boy and all thin children are not necessarily starved.

These are hormonal truths which few parents have known themselves and which even fewer have shared with their children. As a result, children of all ages have been led to the conviction that they were in the essence of their selves piggish, and had reason to be ashamed—or that they were thin and therefore sickly in spirit as well as body—or that they were too large and ox-like or too small and therefore worthless.

We might try to list all the miseries of childhood, but we would fail. We might succeed in reminding the reader, however, that childhood is a period of shame and mortification relieved by dazzling moments of joy.

Fortunately, we remember mostly the latter, but it is the

mastery of those long, dark periods between that makes us men. And it must lie within the power of parents to kiss a hurt and make it well—to gaze on a lumpy nose with affection and make it beautiful.

Black children have been simply too vulnerable to the ordinary misery of learning about themselves and the world. The child who eats too much is in danger of developing a doubly enforced feeling of self-depreciation: fat (black), ugly (black), grotesque (black).

Or he may be lazy (black) for sleeping too late.

Negative descriptions have been so often made synonymous for black people that one critical world does double duty, carrying as it does another unspoken epithet.

The lines can get so twisted one simply doesn't know.

*   *   *

A six-year-old girl had tolerated her mother's regular working absences quite well for most of her life. The mother explained that after her divorce she had to work and the child seemed to understand. Much of their talk had centered around race and the mother's attempt to explain that she was white, the absent father black, and the child by her own description "brown."

There had been much matching of skin color and speculation on the child's part about what color *her* children would be if she married a white man or a black man. She wanted her mother to remarry and acted the busy matchmaker whenever a man visited.

All went well until a series of misadventures disrupted the regular schedule. The mother faced additional heavy work responsibilities. Her comings and goings became irregular, and on several occasions the child was left at school not knowing how she would get home. Once she became hysterical and another time she wet herself and continued to wet each day for weeks.

During the same period she started "worrying" about being "brown." The girl said she was darker than another child and that no one would play with her because she was so dark. She said the teachers picked on her because she was brown. Finally, she said she would pray to turn white and searched the palms of her hands where she said she was beginning to "turn."

Her mother was heartbroken at this turn of events. When she regained her composure, the mother remembered that she had checked carefully and found that none of the child's complaints about ostracism were true. The child was popular with other children and the teachers.

When seen in consultation the child was a charming, well-mannered little lady, verbal and quite at ease. She was much more poised than her mother, who felt that all the years of careful work preparing the child for the puzzlement of racial conflict had suddenly and mysteriously gone down the drain.

Aside from being slightly sad, the child seemed otherwise normal, and it was only when we looked past the child at the harried mother that the truth emerged.

The little girl was simply punishing her mother for being away so much and for frightening her. She had chosen to attack by exaggerating a "worry" long ago spotted as the woman's Achilles' heel. The mother was distraught over the idea of her daughter being so miserable about her color that she would pray to be white. No doubt the daughter's worries were exaggerations of some nucleus that lay buried, but now she was simply punishing her mother.

Proof came when the mother told the child how the "worries" had come about and changed her schedule, adding that she wanted to please the child and had not known how miserable the previous schedule had made her.

When this was done the wetting stopped, the unhappy

look evaporated, and all those heartrending stories about the misery of "brownness" ceased.

*　　　*　　　*

The story is more than a little instructive, illustrating as it does the excessive sensitivity of an adult and a clever child's exploitation of it. It is even more sobering to realize that it is precisely a defenselessness on the part of parents against racial attack that renders their children equally defenseless. The older generation has no strength to lend the young.

We add one further description.

*　　　*　　　*

Mr. Camp was a laborer, regularly employed at menial work. He lived with his wife and five children in a run-down house in the black ghetto of the central city. His three oldest were sons seventeen, nineteen, and twenty-one. All the children were well-behaved and obeyed their father.

He had organized a home auto repair business, and each of the boys had learned a different skill. After school they all worked together under the oldest brother's leadership. When the father came home, the leadership was turned over to him, and so it continued as father and sons worked together each evening putting aside what money they could for a shop of their own.

Such a family relationship was uncommon in that area of the city or indeed in any part of the city. Black boys particularly seemed to rebel against father and society as if they were one, and rarely could one find sons willing to seek the realization of their own ambitions through a vocational vehicle provided by their father.

Finally, they seemed at peace and found pleasure in the company of brothers, father, and sons.

The other singular thing about this family was that they were Black Muslims and had been for the full life-span of the oldest boy.

*　　　*　　　*

Theological considerations aside, we feel that it was the peculiarly intense involvement of the family in the Muslim religion which allowed them to develop a social framework which, augmented by the mosque and fellow parishioners, was sufficiently engrossing to neutralize the effect of the surrounding environment.

Lastly, it must be noted that the American black family has been unable to perform the essential familial function of conserving the gains of earlier generations. It is well known that families which acquired land and wealth lost that substance when they became the object of predatory white men. Laws which in other circumstances guarded a patrimony were here interpreted by thieves, and, helpless in an atmosphere of pillage, the blacks were quickly robbed.

In like manner, one generation's gain of position and learning is difficult for the black family to conserve.

In confusion, some blacks are willing to assume that, if they are suffering, then they must somehow deserve it. The explanations stretch from the quixotic Biblical event of Noah's cursing the son of Ham and condemning him ever after to be slave to his brothers, to the rhyming existential fatalism of Bert Williams' philosophy:

> A man born of a dark woman
> Is bound to see dark days.

*   *   *

A group of black scholars, convened to help the poor youth of the community, discovered in the course of their discussion that many of their own children were delinquents and school dropouts.

Astonished that so many had been unable to aid their own children, they regrouped and took the rehabilitation of their sons and daughters as their initial task.

*   *   *

The atmosphere of hostility in which blacks are required to exist makes it exceedingly difficult for a parent who has succeeded intellectually to know what formulas to use to protect his children's minds from the unceasing rain of hatred.

The sum and substance of all we are saying is that these are no ordinary families. They were ferociously determined that their children get the very best. When this kind of fierce determination meets the barest fragment of opportunity we see a string of black kids streaming through to distinction.

V.

The White Expert

1✓✓✓

Only with the recent riots in the cities have the discontents of black people been taken seriously. But even in the midst of the rioting, whites seemed to feel that blacks had no *real* reason for rage. The various governments and all their instrumentalities are held blameless . . . decent white folks trying to do a job . . . occasional mistakes . . . "they" sometimes over-react. Given the blamelessness of everyone else, blacks are left themselves to be blamed for the riots—and when they burn the property nearest them they are asked in wide-eyed innocence:

> *"Why do you burn your own homes?"*
> "They are not homes, they are not ours, and they are so filthy they ought to be burned,"

is the answer.

> *"But where will you live?"*
> "Somewhere else."

"Will you make that new place as filthy as the old one?"

"We don't create the filth, lady, the owners simply don't maintain the buildings."

"Seems to me if you live in a place you ought to keep it clean."

"The whole city forces us to live here and pay high rent."

"I thought you people wanted to live together."

"The privilege is getting too expensive."

The racial wars in America have offered an opportunity for some white people to talk with a few blacks, walk about the ghetto on a Sunday afternoon, and emerge as experts on black life. Moreover, such activity sometimes pays well, and an ambitious man can make great political use of this expertise. It has become, in a way, America's newest cottage industry, requiring little experience and no training.

Meanwhile, the White Expert caroms about the dangerous black world playing it by ear, out-shouting the Mau-Maus and out-praying the preachers.

He has something to say on everything!!

Consider the following dialogue.

2↗↗↗

When Minnie married Joe he was a soldier hurrying the Second World War to a close. He had complicated plans to train in business and management and complicated justifications for why such a thing made sense for a black man.

"Good Plan! Blacks need to get well trained so they can get a piece of the good life. There is less prejudice than you think when a man has needed skills."

Black men entered the service in the early 1940's never having been part of anything in American society. But now they had made the break and became participants in the nation's biggest business, the winning of the war. Blacks wanted so desperately to believe the wartime rhetoric of "saving the world for democracy." They were convinced that a changed world held the hope of full participation in the nation's affairs; that the war was being fought to bring democracy to the world; and that the war was changing the United States so that they, like their white colleagues, need only work hard, exercise prudence, and prosperity would follow.

Upon resuming civilian life, Joe spent five years in college and worked as a laborer forty hours a week for every week of those five years. Minnie worked as a dietician and their combined income allowed for a few comforts.

Joe had always been occupied with the importance of hard work. He could not tolerate unemployment even as a student. For some ambitious black men, hard work is a badge of honor which takes on a religious and patriotic quality.

After college, Joe took two jobs, one in management, a low-echelon trainee position, and the other, hard physical work with good pay. He worked long hours and advancement came regularly. He rose steadily until his promotion to executive rank in a large company with a salary of over $20,000 per year. When he accepted the new job, Minnie quit working and within the year unexpected financial problems developed.

"Urban life places great strains on the Negro family. The historic matriarchy is poorly suited for survival in the modern city."

But the greatest trouble came when Joe's interest turned to a pretty young girl. Minnie, who had just turned forty, was furious and raged at him day and night. Her anger made hell of the household. For the first time in their marriage there were fist-fights: attacks by Minnie—defense by Joe. Both parties started and stopped divorce actions. Minnie finally developed flagrantly paranoid outbursts, and for the first time Joe was frightened.

Minnie was born in the Deep South and was lost in the large family her tenant-farmer parents tried to raise. Her mother was ambitious and never let any of the children forget that education was the most important thing in life. While both parents worked hard to give them more and more schooling, first the mother and later the children came to hold the uneducated father in contempt. The mother said openly that the father was cursed and doomed because of his lack of education.

"Education is the key to an improved life for blacks."

Minnie was determined that she would never marry a man who worked at manual labor and tolerated Joe's labor only because it was linked to schooling. She said she could never respect an uneducated man. She herself had grown into a woman who saw only the orderly, perfumed world she wanted to see. In her view, all parents knew best, all men were brave, and all husbands faithful. She fell in love with Joe, and for her their love developed a concrete permanence. Their life was perfect—she even looked forward to aging as a new adventure.

Joe held a more pragmatic view. He knew that evil existed and that justice was a sometime thing. He conceded that Minnie's view of life was good if one could manage it. He was convinced that hard work and diligence paid off, and, as opportunities opened up for black men and he moved forward, each promotion became an affirmation of the principle that hard work is in fact rewarded.

Minnie and Joe were well on their way to realizing their personal view of the ideal life. Joe was involved in hard work and "success," and Minnie enjoyed what she saw as the perfect marriage.

But with Joe's last promotion several new factors appeared. He was for the first time the boss over half a hundred men and women and was answerable only to the president of the company. His salary had reached a figure which he later realized had special meaning for him. On the way up he dreamed of an income of five, ten, or even fifteen thousand, and he envisioned the opportunities and restraints imposed by each figure. He was vague about the limits imposed by $20,000, but felt that somewhere north of this figure the kind of restrictions with which he was familiar disappeared and one could be said to be rich. Now, surely a $20,000 salary is not riches, but it signals that the recipient has a headstart in the right direction. For Joe it meant the achievement of part of the American Dream. Finally, he had known few black men who earned money of these proportions and it was a simple fact of life that most bosses were white.

"He may have risen too fast."

Joe worked hard. He put in twelve, fourteen hours every day, worked on weekends, and attended endless meetings. He was, in fact, an excellent administrator, so that in addition to the title and money, he regularly received praise from highly placed men.

It is not clear what was his frame of mind when he first made a serious move toward another woman. We can speculate, but all we know is that this was the first woman other than Minnie with whom he had become involved. And we know that it came at the height of his powers. Joe said that he felt like a man for the first time —a big man—free. No doubt it was in this mood that he reached out for another woman and chose a beauty. There were problems with Minnie, but he had lived through those problems before, and now the only new variable was his high rank.

"It will no doubt require many successful generations before the black family develops the internal strength of white families."

As Joe moved up Minnie had become more restive. After she quit her job they bought a new house. Joe was able to carry the load financially, but he resented being led to count on Minnie's salary only to have her quit at the crucial moment.

Where in the past she had urged him to take every promotion, she now questioned even obviously favorable moves. Joe had always valued her support and enthusiasm. Lately he avoided talking things over with her; she became a persistent source of discouragement.

When she discovered his new romantic interest she exploded as if she had expected it. She collapsed in a series of fainting spells. She physically attacked him and left the house, ignoring all responsibility.

While it was a shocking, disorganizing thing for her to hear, there was an element about her reaction which suggested that she had expected and feared it. She later explained this as more than the usual dread any wife has that she may be supplanted.

In the course of treatment, it was found that among the unreal things she chose to see was herself as a beautiful girl who had her choice of men. Although she had no grossly irregular features, she simply was not pretty. But perhaps more to the point, she was dark-skinned and *she* equated blackness with undesirability.

As her feelings of being personally unattractive came to the surface, she opened up an entirely new view of her marital adjustment. Minnie learned that in a way she had seen herself as ugly, but she also had seen Joe as an ordinary black man who was not likely to go far. In light of his status and his prospects, *she,* homely face and all, was as much as he could expect in a wife.

"Joe's irresponsibility is to blame, not her narcissistic preoccupations with her appearance."

Her apparent ambitions and her seeming pleasure in *his* ambitions served neatly to counterbalance a deeper contrary trend which in her mind organized the marriage. The whole relationship was further stabilized by Joe's "enfeeblement" and his necessarily having to be satisfied with an "inferior being" such as she. All this set the stage for her coming apart when he hit the jackpot.

"This is a perfectly ordinary marital conflict which in an ordinary and predictable way comes apart with a change in status of one of the partners."

We see a set of most extraordinary forces at work with this couple.

For this black woman from the rural South denying her mud-caked origins and turning away from the debasement and humiliation she saw there was a major task. From such origins, the devalued identity of Minnie was so overpowering that to organize her life around superficial niceties and dilettantism was to place a great strain on her psychologically.

Many women see themselves as ordinary and feel that their unpromising mates deserve no more, and would be dismayed if the spouse began any movement toward success.

But any test of the health or pathology of a marital adjustment rests ultimately on how realistic is the couple's view of their world. Obviously a poor man who based his marriage on the acquisition of riches would be a poor choice. Likewise, the woman who marries a man for his youthful good looks has some disquieting years ahead when the husband ages.

But Minnie was sounder and wiser than either of these examples. She founded her marriage on one of the most certain verities of this nation.

She took the position that a poorly educated black man is not likely to prosper in the United States.

"Not so! There is plenty of opportunity for well-trained, hard-working, ambitious blacks."

She assumed that prosperity was not likely to come in the form of high salary, directorships and community esteem. Frankly, she could not have made a sounder wager. Few black men out of the millions who have breathed this air have reached Joe's level of achievement.

We cannot fault Minnie for a poor reading of the environmental signs. She saw all she needed to see and understood it well.

She was subtle enough to anticipate the interaction between the nation eroding away his self-esteem, *its* view of her as homely, and Joe's attachment to her.

And hidden deep in all of this was evidence of her love for her father. In a way, she paid lip service to ambitions her mother wanted for her. She felt contempt for the father as her mother wanted her to feel—still, she chose a man who she thought would be a common man —one who loved her and who labored in the expression of that love.

It was a neat fit bringing together elements of her life to support a marriage with solid underpinnings of fact, and what seemed to be a clearly perceived future.

Her reason would have demanded looking into if she had banked on a future in which Joe's hard work brought him money and position.

So, while forty is an unsettling age under the best of auspices and makes women look at husbands with a more analytical eye, Minnie had reason to sense approaching catastrophe. Joe was, in fact, moving up, and with that *unlikely* event she had to consider the possibilities that he might no longer be satisfied with her. Her expectation of his infidelity may well have come from her own certainty that with success he was sure to turn to another woman.

We are suggesting that Minnie and Joe illustrate only one way the racial environment affects the marriage experience among blacks.

"The problem is not confined to blacks. Whites have marital problems, too."

*   *   *

Blacks have had to establish a marriage on the certainties of their lives. When social scientists attack the black family as a social organ with little internal glue, they would do well to examine the lack of certainties in the lives of black people.

Indeed if any one thing characterizes black life in America, it would be its uncertainty. The task of establishing a family in such a dangerous world is great.

Minnie and Joe present us, though, with the final irony. After launching a fairly good marriage, "the man," with a capricious change of heart, allows Joe to succeed, and the marriage, so imaginatively braced, is down the drain.

But it is common knowledge that when black men are denied jobs, their family relationships are imperiled. It is grim testimony of how precarious our life has been that many of our most intimate institutions have been based on the one certainty of black life—failure—and the readjustment to a measure of success may be more than a little painful.

"Sounds like you're saying black people can't stand success!!"

3↑↑↑

Katie's figure was close to perfection. Her face was attractive—not beautiful, not particularly mature, but startlingly feminine and definitely spoiled.

What went through the mind of the personnel man when she was hired is anyone's guess. But his appraisal of her must have given little weight to past experience. She had graduated from a commercial high school near the bottom of her class and had done no work for six months. When she presented herself for work, she was a poor typist and had mastered few clerical skills. It must have been obvious that she was disinclined to work hard, but she worked, after a fashion, for eight months, and quit at that point to marry the fellow she had been dating for a year and a half.

Jack was, at twenty-four, a busboy in a restaurant. He was studying auto mechanics in night school, but after two years in military service the only job he could get was as a busboy. He was going through the motions at school, but had little drive and Katie complained about that. On the other hand, he was deeply in love with her. He was handsome, made good tips, and both enjoyed each other immensely.

When they married, Katie was nineteen. She had never assumed full responsibility for even herself let alone a household, so her management of the apartment was wretched. Jack developed a temper, she became pregnant, and the restaurant laid him off.

She went to her parents and he to his. What began as a separation of convenience soon took more formal tones. He was uninterested in the new baby. Katie filed for divorce and began dating again. The divorce took several years, and before it was final she had another child by her new friend.

As Katie's troubles multiplied, her parents were aging and arriving at an uneasy time of life for working people. They had achieved a toe-hold economically by working long and hard. But their security rested on the father's uninterrupted work and he became ill. They exhausted their savings, but he recovered his health before the home was lost.

The father was sick more and more often and his earning power was dropping. After her second baby Katie could not work because of the demands of the two children. Neither Jack nor the father of her second child contributed to their support. Her parents could offer only shelter, and she finally had to seek public assistance.

*　　　*　　　*

The Katies of the country exist in such numbers, and, along with their children, live such lives of wasted potential that it is a matter of national concern for us to ask how she gets into such a fix and why.

Let us deal first with the question of race.

Critics say that their story is unremarkable, and that such tragedies are experienced by young women of all colors and all circumstances. Indeed, they show statistics indicating that, above certain levels, the higher the income the higher the incidence of marital breakdown.

Even if this were the case, and it would be difficult to prove, it would still not answer the depth of the tragedy facing Katie and those close to her.

White Americans of average income and above do not fall into the system of public assistance as a regular concomitant of marital difficulties. It is a *frequent* thing for black Americans. It has moreover, a degrading, debilitating, self-perpetuating quality which makes it more than a temporary source of financial aid in emergencies. To become immersed in such a system is to risk a major alteration of one's life, and an alteration in most instances for the worse.

Critics will add that our couple is not the most industrious pair of young Americans, and will say that what happened to them might have been avoided with more hustle on their part. They will say that America never guaranteed prosperity to every citizen, only a chance at it.

We will agree and go further.

Katie and Jack might be called lazy and might be held primarily accountable for their misfortunes. We would only raise the question, how it comes to be that Katie and thousands like her, no more or less gifted, no more or less perceptive, fail to respond to the *apparent* opportunities offered by our society?

We can conclude only that the opportunities offered them

are illusory, and that they are reacting to a set of realities much different from what seems to be.

Their lives suggest that *they* perceive a more hostile environment—one offering them little opportunity and one which rather turns a hostile and belligerent face to their efforts to partake of its bounty.

It is conceivable, in fact, that they perceive an environment which is set *against* their independence and participation—a society which does *not* want them to be "successful," but, rather, is determined that they be reduced to dependency.

If such is the case, then we have witnessed an event far different from its surface appearance. We have observed the exuberance and idealism of youth spending itself against unyielding barriers, and, spent, falling back into the space meant for its containment.

It is a matter of great significance how one's world is viewed.

Others may argue that Katie's morality, or perhaps her lack of it, needs to bear part of the blame. They will say that the proliferation of bastards is a matter of community concern, and that among other things the social order encourages childbearing within marriage as a practice which places the responsibility on two people who have the children's interest most at heart. Moral codes rising mainly from religious teachings support and maintain such a social order. It would be easy, therefore, to accuse Katie of being an asocial, amoral, animal-like subhuman moved more by the impulse of the moment than by rational long-range goals and a perception of her own best interests.

Such an accusation requires a response, but it is difficult to make the answer as short and as pointed as the accusation. We can, however, answer in a way we think complete and final. It so happens that in doing so we will learn as much about the critic as we will about Katie.

The answer is to be found in all of this book. We should like here to summarize the matters bearing on this issue.

1. Katie was chaste before her engagement. She was a great flirt and tease but yielded to Jack only after marriage. She was proud to offer herself as a virgin to her bridegroom.

Throughout their marriage up to the time she filed for a divorce, she had never known another man.

Her parents were religious people and Katie had been exposed to greater religious teaching than most young women her age. She was, in fact, burdened with a keen awareness of the teachings of her church.

If we add to the above that like many narcissistic women she was not highly responsive to sexual stimulation, we see the beginning puzzlement.

Why does a chaste young woman with a strong religious background who finds only moderate pleasure in the sexual act produce an illegitimate child?

2. She is clearly a girl who prefers a life of ease. She stopped working the minute she was married. She likes money and the feeling of independence that money brings.

To have children so early in life when life is made more hazardous thereby is against her own best interests.

Caring for two small children is back-breaking work, and as the sources of outside assistance narrow down to public welfare, Katie faces not only a life of harder work but one of degradation as well.

Few men are inclined to marry women with small children and no money, even women as attractive as Katie—and Katie's figure grows less stunning with each child.

So we are left with the question—in view of so many apparently injurious moves, how does Katie see her self-interest?

3. Katie had strong religious training, and was brought up in an intact family. She had sufficient awareness to perceive that with hard work, perseverance, and the dollar-morality of her parents, she could maintain financial independence and provide the same environment for *her* children.

With so many accusations hurled at the black family as a social organ which is falling apart and which lies at the root of asocial behavior—if such an indictment is true, how does it happen that Katie pursues so devastating a course in her own life? How important really is her stable background? What other more powerful influences have acted on her and have canceled out the benign influences of her family?

What happened and is happening to Katie is that she lives in a world far different from the world of her critics. She is dealing with the demands, the options, and the opportunities of that world in the very best way she can.

Others look only at her, and, for reasons dating back hundreds of years, blind themselves to her circumstances.

If we see a soldier on the battlefield in isolation, removed from his environment, then clearly his running, hiding, shooting, digging holes and so on would seem strange, since we see no enemy.

Katie's manuevers to live out her potential must seem equally strange to those who cannot see the hostile sea in which she and her kind are immersed.

4*

Most urban black folk of the generation of Katie's parents came to the city from the South as young adults. They had left the harsh rural land with the blessings of family and friends. They had set out for the city of the North with the same hopes and aspirations of European immigrants generations earlier. They were not learned people, but they were accustomed to hard work.

They had heard that the city offered the opportunity of America—a job for every man and the chance to rise as far as hard work and diligence would allow. The city was a place of unlimited opportunity beginning with the first step—a good job. Jobs were plentiful, people said, and the immigrants came from the country by the tens of thousands.

The great migration from the South to the city began during World War I. It continued throughout the twenties and thirties and reached its peak during World War II.

When blacks arrived they found the city dying. The city, which had earlier embraced and nurtured the European, now had no need for manpower save in the emergency of war.

In time of peace there were few jobs and they paid poorly.

The immigrants found that the first step on the ladder was missing. Good jobs were not available to blacks, and there was a ceiling on how far one could climb in a city with thousands of unemployed, able-bodied men.

The explosion in waterways, railroads, and highways which initially concentrated wealth in the cities now became the instruments of the cities' death. With better transportation, goods could be manufactured at a considerable distance from the centers of populations. As more people crowded into the city, the land rose in value, and companies saw fit to convert city property to other more profitable use and move their manufacturing to other sites.

The political and administrative machinery of the city had been designed in earlier times when problems were simpler and America was booming. They had such graft built into them and allowed such corruption to develop, that over the years they became unable to respond to the now rapidly changing demands of an increasing population.

The cities, where people tended to concentrate more rapidly than wealth, were hardest hit by cyclical depressions, and with archaic governments were less able to exploit boom times. As a result, they sank lower and lower into poverty, and came to represent merely immense collections of impoverished people who had no means to help themselves.

Had the black immigrant come to the city fifty or seventy-five years earlier, it is problematical what his reception might have been. That was a period of industrial expansion and of great need for unskilled workmen. But it was also a time when the North, eager to get about its commercial business, was determined to ignore black people and bore them a peculiar resentment, as if the ex-slaves had caused the war and were themselves directly responsible for the carnage.

Coming when they did, to dying cities when there was no need for unskilled labor, when the governments had grown ineffective, and when the sources of wealth were moving elsewhere—coming at such a time, there was no chance of participating in the bounteous America of which they dreamed.

Added to the foregoing, the omnipresent hostility white Americans have felt for black Americans for centuries, and the oppression they have imposed, makes the way of the newly arrived black urbanite difficult indeed.

They found themselves reduced to the same marginal grubbing economic struggle they had left in the South. Scrubbing floors, digging ditches, or being unemployed and scrimping on welfare payments was the rule, and when times were good they labored frantically in the stockyards and manufacturing plants.

In the fierce competition for jobs, they were further burdened by the bigotry of the powerful. There was discrimination and exclusion in work situations. Black men were assigned the most menial jobs. They were forced to live in the least desirable housing where city services were poorest, and they were required to pay the highest rent. No serious attempt at maintenance was made by the owners because there was no other place blacks were allowed to live. They were excluded from restaurants, intimidated in places of recreation, overcharged by businessmen, and denied protection of the law by corrupt courts.

As if enough had not been accomplished to make their lives unbearable, the community then instructed its policemen to be especially vigilant in seeking out black wrong-doers. In fact, it became the task of the police department to keep the black population in a state of fear and dread by widespread harrassment.

Huddled in the ghetto, excluded from the life of the community, denied economic opportunity, hounded by police, Katie's parents and tens of thousands like them settled down and established homes and families.

That they remained in the city under the circumstances tells us what the South was like. Without exception, the city dwellers chose to remain in the city because it was better than the land from which they came.

They took whatever jobs they could get, worked as hard and as long as they were allowed. They tried to save their money. Periodic depressions consumed their savings and they struggled on the brink of poverty.

Many of them gave up and drifted about the city, adding to a growing population of the disenchanted, asocial, semi-delinquent dropouts from what had been an all but impossible struggle.

They had risen from agrarian origins and the universal objective when they did accumulate money was the purchase of the urban equivalent of land—a house. It was the objective of one's labor and the evidence that one had labored not in vain.

It did not matter that the expenditure of capital for a house, its debt service, and the high cost of maintenance might make the move economically ridiculous. What was involved was the need of a group of harried, insecure people to establish an ownership which *represented* security. It was and is a pathetic, illusory seeking in bricks and mortar those feelings of worth, importance, and permanence—feelings denied them by their white neighbors.

As black people poured into a city, they were crowded into the containment of the ghetto. They doubled up in apartments. Those fortunate enough to have spare rooms took in roomers. There was no other place to live, and it made the payment of high rent possible.

When the ghetto could contain no more, adjoining neighborhoods were made available to home buyers a block at a time. The houses were overpriced, but the blacks had no alternative. They were sold of necessity for a low cash payment and a financing of the balance at brutal, usurious rates of interest.

They bore their children at home or on the segregated wards of hospitals, receiving poor medical care for the highest fees, and were treated as filth in the clinics and waiting rooms of the hospitals.

There were few black physicians and most white physicians discouraged black patients.

There was minimal insurance coverage, so that an illness was treated at public hospitals and the quality of that care was low.

The schools greeted the newly arrived children with dismay

—judged them as stupid—and demoted them, saying that their poor education placed them several grades behind their white counterparts.

Perhaps the white teachers and school administrators most of all reflected the community's contempt for the new immigrants and its determination to withhold assistance from them.

Black children must toe the mark or else; they were to receive no special assistance; they would have to make it "just like everyone else." Administrators had apparently forgotten the countless special programs designed for earlier *white* immigrants.

Immersed in this hostile sea, Katie's parents had hunkered down and worked harder, saved their money and had bought their house. Their preoccupation with staying alive and gathering a few precious acquisitions had been witnessed by Katie. Through them and their struggle she had first experienced the world.

Although she saw their tireless struggle and enjoyed each small achievement of material comfort, she could not see what *they* saw as the alternative to their labor. The old life in the South, with life itself in constant jeopardy, was a reality of which she knew nothing. They, on the other hand, fled to work each day as if thereby they put another mile between themselves and the South.

The difference between their motivation and Katie's was to have great importance. They were involved with an experience as they had known it twenty years before, while she was involved with the city now.

For a knowledgeable nation to vilify Katie as amoral, and to punish her and her children while offering no word of criticism of the sparse and bleak options it made for her, is to abandon all pretense of justice.

For that nation to feel enhanced in grace, whatever minor

charities it offers her parents when they are too old and sick, is little short of obscene, seeing that they are in truth misguided refugees who thought they had escaped the Southern horrors and who were therefore willing to work themselves into an early grave in appreciation.

The white experts don't see it but Katie knows that there had been no escape—that the old folks simply worked just as hard, for little more, in a new place, and thanked the Lord for their good fortune.

VI.

The Killers

1*✓✓✓*

When the pent-up rage of blacks explodes there are always whites who gather immediately to poke in the smoldering aftermath. They were not sufficiently interested in the dilemma earlier to have sensed that a terrible wrong was being done, nor did they guess that such would surely call for a dramatic righting. Rather, these political scavengers of misery recognize the problem only after the event, and rush to the scene hoping for morsels to feed their own immediate self-interest.

After the urban rebellions of 1967 and 1968, the nation missed a magnificent opportunity to step in with needed changes in housing, education, and commerce. Such changes would have benefited the gentle folk who had migrated from the South and who had labored so hard in the cities.

Even more desperate was the need for a series of government fiats forbidding absolutely the abuse of black people by the white majority. Who knows how much might have been accomplished with dedicated leadership and the weight of federal law behind a clear prohibition against the active expression of feelings of bigotry.

Whatever *might* have been done, the fact is that nothing *was* done, and in the vacuum the white scavengers moved in to leech onto blacks and onto their determination for social reform.

Make no mistake, we speak of white pseudo-liberals who mouth a ferocious political ideology but who live in comfort, nay, opulence, while urging blacks on to more and more irrational non-goal-directed attacks on "the system."

Blacks have a cause for hostility against America which runs as deep as the river of life—we need no neurotic children now grown up in body only to urge us to fight their childish battles for them.

These agitators are not Communists. They are as deeply rooted in capitalism as their stockbrokers are. They are often wealthy, educated people, sometimes with powerful connections, but always white, encysted in the American style of life —and off on a lark. They are quite willing for blacks to provide the cannon fodder for their own patricidal struggles.

White radicals have urged blacks on in an ever more rabid attack against an establishment which in turn has grown more and more dangerous. And since there are always a few whites who act as if they are frightened, some blacks have been assured that this fearfulness means that the balance of power favors them and that they should become more audacious.

The most troubling thing about all this is that it devolves into another variety of white leadership and black followship where whites get the benefit and blacks get clobbered.

The same thrusts for social change might have been made by blacks acting independently of whites, but we suggest that it would have had a different quality. We suggest that while life would no doubt have been risked and perhaps lost, there would have been no senseless, purposeless squandering of black youth as has occurred under white radical leadership.

We would not have thrust young boys into the maw of a murderous police establishment. We would not have romanticized suicide-squads of boys who ought to be in school.

Had these matters grown out of black life, we suggest that the old men would have placed themselves in the front rank. We have a reverence for life and a determination to protect women and those whose life is yet to be lived. We would have fought tenaciously as we have done since 1620. We would have conserved our strength and we would have waged war, unrelenting war, that would have lasted, if need be, forever.

As it is, blacks are accused as killers, thieves, and murderers, and brave young men know not where to go. It is suggested that we have now a fearsome army which has initiated a new phase of open warfare on whites.

We have always known that the full power of the United States was, and is, available to crush us. It is a tragedy of our times that white radicals push blacks prematurely into battle, supply them with too few guns, no ammunition, and no plans —and say that in their pushing, they have themselves been a part of the black revolution.

When the dust clears, the bodies are all black.

Although the whole "law and order" scheme has been erected to protect against "murderous killer blacks," we know who the killers are. Both the ones who pulled the trigger and the ones who pushed the boys into the street. They are *white*. The killers are *white*. It is the *victims* who are black.

2*

For white people, the American system works. There are objectives, goals, achievements which are deeply gratifying— so gratifying that the anticipation of them can motivate a child from his earliest contact with the educational system.

Social position and economics and power are all decipherable for white people. There are privileges associated with having a million dollars—if you are white. They surely will be different and fewer for the rare black millionaire.

Employment, or unemployment for that matter, has set meanings if the subject is white. For whites America is in a deep way logical and predictable.

It is illogical and unpredictable for blacks. As a result, they are reluctant to rely on a "sometimey" future. There is no social cause and effect shared by blacks with the white majority. Whites simply don't know that the rules that work for them may not work at all for black men.

In America, success bears its own moral suasion. A man who works and earns "more" money—(more than whom need not be explained)—is a success and the proof is in his bank book.

If he fails at a business or loses a job, there will then be some question regarding his general effectiveness and his adherence to good business practices. His goodness and worth as a person are judged in large measure by his profit and loss statement.

If the successful American is so personally poisonous that his sizable fortune does not outweigh a loathsomeness of character, one only has to wait. In one or two generations his money, if large enough, will cleanse his name, and he will be remembered as a crusty old philanthropist whose great heart and compassion were revealed only after his death.

Self-worth is made much of in psychological circles. If it is important, then the acquisition of money or its equivalent represents the significant *building up* of the esteem one has for oneself. And the loss of money or the failure to acquire it represents a serious *loss* of self-worth.

History suggests that it has never been easy to feel a constant growing delight with oneself—but *some* Americans can chart their pleasure with themselves by the fluctuation in their net worth. When such a one flourishes for a long time, he has come close to getting the whole thing. On every side he is seen as worthy, and he feels a pleasant distension of the belly which echoes a gastrointestinal "yes!" to the accolade from outside.

The matrix of money, power, competition, and all the rest of the social fabric are working for him.

The ability a white man gains to analyze his environment and to predict events within it; to set a course and anticipate the reaction of his fellows should they encounter him at any point; to be able to let go the wheel and know that society has built-in supporting and stabilizing forces to keep him moving on his course; and to arrive at his destination knowing that society damn-near guarantees him rewards; to know all this is to see a logic in the system which is tied to one's comfort and one's effectiveness.

*   *   *

A physician of mediocre talents through a careful attention to opportunism rose to high rank in a medical school. By deliberately associating himself with powerful people and arranging to outlive the competition, his career was one of rising plateaus.

He has always made the arrogant assumption that he is brighter than blacks, more diligent and harder-working. All this in spite of benignly tolerant feelings toward them.

He is not the only "scholar" with such convictions.

*   *   *

It is as if the system might be tested by the promptness of its response to one's own felt needs. Since there is generally a built-in response to the needs of white Americans, they can recognize the sense and order and logic in the system. For blacks, however, the system is seen from an angle which shows none of its orderliness nor any of its predictableness.

It does not work for them.

The environment is unpredictable save for the certainty that it will make a black man's way unnecessarily hard. Blacks can rarely anticipate either the reactions of fellows or the rewards should the goal be reached, save that trouble will no doubt appear at any point of contact with the system.

Moreover, blacks observe that the system works for whites and it seems to work in their behalf whether they have earned it by innate virtue or not (legends to the contrary not withstanding).

Finally, we are all hammered-at from birth to death, morning to night, that the system rewards the diligent, prudent, and hard-working, regardless of color.

So if a black man believes this (and until recent years he had no real alternative to such belief), it makes the whole social and economic system illogical and unpredictable.

He is unable to put together cause and effect, and the whole antecedent world of causality gapes empty before the social fact. It is not surprising that he has often filled it in with projected notions from his own mind.

It was easy to assume that white folks became rich because

they were smart, or that the acquiring of great learning necessarily made white men more humane, or that the difference in speech pattern between whites and blacks was due in the case of the former to higher intelligence and in the latter to stupidity.

Blacks have often assumed a conscious conspiracy on the part of whites to mistreat and do them harm when there was no *conscious* intent, simply the case of motivated white men moving in accordance with an harmonious social system which is *incidentally* designed to crush blacks. The white man need not direct the instrument at all. It was programmed decades ago to exalt the white and demean the black. It is therefore a mistake to assume that the white passenger devotes conscious thought and psychic energy to crushing the black—not necessarily—he may never have given it a thought.

*   *   *

Lars Onsager, a Nobel prize winner, and a gifted Norwegian physicist, arrived in America in 1935, and immediately embarked on the lonely road of genius—occupied with his own thoughts—communicating with only that small group of his fellows who understood him —and in the kindest meaning of the words, remained removed, aloof from the world around him.

There is much unclarity on the nature of genius, but most agree that these gifted few have the capacity to bring great powers of concentration to bear on a problem for an extended period of time, and in a man of imagination and intelligence this concentration is essential.

It was possible for Onsager to concentrate in America. He had only a fragmentary knowledge of the language. He did not know the customs. He did not know the system, and in fact arrived at Yale to occupy the chair of theoretical chemistry without having taken the time to get a Ph.D.

America held out its hands to guide him into the environment he sought, and to protect him against chance misfortune. The social organization held him no malice, indeed even welcomed him and allowed him to continue his all-consuming, all-important thought while he was figuratively guided around lampposts and reminded to step up or down.

The vital requirement Onsager possessed. He was white. It would have been impossible for a black man to have paid so little attention to his environment and survived in America. Even had he known all the social conventions, he would have had to maintain a sharp outlook for the cues signaling danger. He could never have relied on the social system to provide him with early warnings, and he would have had to fight for a place on the faculty even with a dozen Ph.D.s.

*   *   *

The implications are not subtle. The black genius who, like Onsager, required a setting in which the bulk of his energy could be turned to the solitary creative art, would never have emerged in this country, and had he arisen would never have survived.

Blacks have rarely had the opportunity for the long intensive training required to bring native gifts to fruition save perhaps as musical performers. They have never had an environment responsive to and protective of their genius.

Since the numbers of blacks of great talent and accomplishment have been understandably small, that paucity has been seized upon by haters as evidence of black intellectual inferiority. (It might rather be evidence of a sturdy strain which thrusts to the surface no matter what.)

3↑↑↑

What follows is a series of vignettes—black men and women caught in the act of living—doing whatever is necessary to live—but living—at any cost.

*   *   *

Dr. Johnson has "too many" virtues. It is difficult to make him take shape as the warm, friendly man he is. In his relationship with his son, he is too stern, too critical, argues with him over the purchase of a car or auto insurance. He feels he is too extravagant.

Most people would think his son is a fine young man. He has done well in college and is now entering a profession. The father complains about his Afro and beard. If anything, he has curbed his spirit too much. The young man is too compliant, too respectful of authority.

On balance one cannot say he is harsh or insensitive with the rest of his family. He is on good terms with his wife, is the head of a large family of sisters and brothers. He is the responsible member, the big brother. He has more money and is ready to help if anyone is pinched financially.

He is a country doctor in the oldest, finest sense. The community admires him, and he considers the common good as the important governing force in his life.

In sum, one can say only that he is a good man. But the point we want to make about Dr. Johnson is his financial planning. His father died when he was young and the great struggle had left him determined that *his* family was not to have similar problems. In a broader sense, it turned his interest toward planning for the future.

After beginning practice and having met his immediate needs, he looked for a place to put his few excess dollars. The prospects were limited, advice uncertain, and he settled on real estate, more specifically, on a kind of small single-family dwelling common in the black community of which he was a part. They weren't slums. Some buildings were new. The occupants were poor, but then most blacks were poor. It was simply where people lived, and the doctor thought that the return was adequate for the modest investment required.

Over the years he bought these buildings, and computed from time to time that twenty or thirty years of such a program would allow him to retire and would be the cushion his family ought to have after his death.

In his early sixties now, he is troubled. His houses have many vacancies, and while expenses everywhere are rising, he can't raise his rents because the rest of his tenants might move.

Recently Dr. Johnson read that a large, low-cost housing program was planned for the community, and he realized that his entire real estate retirement program was essentially lost.

Earlier in the year, a newspaper article described him as a slumlord who grew fat exploiting his own people. The paper retracted the statement, but it was a painful time for him.

He has placed all of the houses up for sale and is selling to his tenants at a fraction of their cost. He estimates that after years of planning and investment he will get only a fraction of the amount he paid in. He cannot retire. He plans to put the money in the bank and continue practicing medicine.

The doctor does not need our pity. He will live out his days in comfort, and in spite of the newspaper reports, we would be any of us blessed were we loved and respected by one-tenth as many neighbors as he. No, Dr. Johnson is not the object of our concern in these ways. He rather illustrates the consequences of the advice white people give their black friends.

Here is a man who was admired by most of the town,

who could get no decent financial advice at any point in a long and honored career. He was not steered by his banker or lawyer (both prominent white business men and very rich) toward the kind of investments his white physician counterparts were making. Nor did his knowledgeable white friends warn him of the danger of increasing his ownership of property which was becoming less desirable. Finally, the editor of the newspaper allowed the damaging story to reach print even though the doctor had tended members of the editor's own family. A retraction was printed, but such stories never appeared even accidentally about prominent white men in the community.

*   *   *

We think the doctor's story is important; it helps explain the unquenchable, all-consuming rage of blacks. The doctor is typical of blacks who function in the manner of white folks. They follow the rules, work diligently, keep quiet, and are rewarded with gross mistreatment.

Their ambitions, their self-interest, are not considered seriously, and as a final stroke their reputation may be ruined in an oversight. None of this need be done by evil people, simply by white people who look at blacks through detached, dispassionate, apparently ethical eyes.

They didn't do the doctor that much harm, they just killed off his dream.

*   *   *

Steven is an accountant who became "black" shortly after he was certified. From all that can be determined, he was a capable professional up to that time and his present employers had every reason to believe that they had come across a well-qualified, ambitious young "Negro" who could grow with their company.

He, however, had always seen himself as a poor student—one who struggled to keep up and who was passed out of some teacher's generosity. Steven's feelings of inferiority caused increasing stress as he rose through professional ranks. His certification was followed by a significant promotion, and this in turn was followed by his growing an Afro and a beard.

He adopted a belligerent attitude of self-righteousness and interrupted his work to deliver lectures on the hidden and revealed racism in the company. His superiors, for many reasons no doubt, tolerated non-production and disruptive activities for a remarkably long time. Steven demanded to see the head of the firm, and denounced him as a racist.

When friends sought to shield him from the consequences of his acts, he refused their help and continued in an apparently relentless pursuit of self-destruction.

When he was finally fired, he was even more enraged and went to his professional society to preach on their racial sins (which were, in fact, many). They finally acted and suspended his licensure, saying that his behavior violated codes of ethics and propriety, and demanding that he apologize. Only with such an apology would they allow him to practice his profession.

At this point Steve seemed relieved. He spent weeks wandering about his house, leaving it to his wife to work out the sometimes serious consequences of his sudden unemployment.

No official either of his company or of his professional organization suggested that he might be mentally ill. And these large organizations have often been called upon to make such judgments.

*   *   *

Mary turned black a few years ago. She had been the bright daughter of an ordinary family. Both parents worked hard, and Mary benefited by having the time and money to complete her professional training. She became a teacher of the deaf—highly skilled, well-paid, and a busy, young professional.

She has unpleasant character traits. Her parents divorced when she was twelve, and although both remarried, she maintained an intense hatred for her father. Most perceptive friends agree that her present hatred of men has the same passion originally reserved for him.

Beyond the world of men, however, Mary is simply a chronically angry woman, bestowing her bitterness on all who come her way. She has become less committed to her profession since turning black, and now seeks to show that the deafness of black children (to whom she has restricted her work) is due primarily to mean, vicious acts of white people. Her effort toward the prevention of deafness has become a war waged against the white man.

Mary's unpleasantness was not without some ordinary causes. In spite of a distinguished academic record, she had difficulty finding a job when she finished school. And even now, considering the great need for her skills, she is capable of more than her job demands and is in fact under-employed.

Whether due to her plain looks or her temperament, few men have taken an interest in her.

All of this made it more understandable that when a wave of blackness came along she embraced it eagerly. Her voice became more strident. She challenged and confronted a wider range of people. She fomented protest from one end of town to the other, and finally, having made trouble for all concerned, was fired from her job on a shallow pretext.

*   *   *

From a clinical point of view, Mary has neurotic and character problems which no doubt cause her anguish, but which she turns onto those around her to make them share her misery. The black shift provided an ideological screen behind which she remained a bitter, aggravating woman . . . now with a cause.

The black movement gives her a direction for expressing her anger. To the neurotic component it adds the contemporary (healthy) black rage with a real live enemy (the white man), and it gives her a reason based in reality for rejecting authority and intellectualism. She now attacks blacks for not being black enough and whites as racists.

The new black scene offers a complete sociological and political framework within which her personal stresses may find expression.

When, for example, she complained loudly that children's health needs were not only ignored but that actually the agency which fired her was deliberately making children deaf —this her friends recognized as symptomatic of her inner problems.

She found herself passionately pursuing a course much less determined by the external state of affairs than by the dark moods within.

The emotional kinks shared by Steve and Mary are troublesome and familiar. They have inner demons, and they would prefer outer ones. By an effort of will they make it so, and choose to see all their ills as social miseries shared by millions and caused by whites. Given a choice, one might prefer a different kind of hell, but they have no choice.

It is the treatment they receive from their white fellow professionals and administrators that troubles the *logical* mind. These are people who have heard too-zealous advocates of Republicanism, birth control, fluoridation, and Zionism, and they can mark the point when such advocates overstep limits of custom and become fit subjects of clinical examination.

The question of emotional disorder is among the first asked, in part because of the humane concern for a fellow, but also because such a determination removes the responsibility of answering the indictment. Superiors are generally de-

lighted to sidestep the thorny issue of controlling a troublesome S.O.B.—much easier to neutralize the whole thing and
say he is (or was) emotionally ill.

When our two blacks are raising so much hell and causing
such pain to the body of the social system, if the boss forgoes
this easy and appropriate solution to the problem, the question "why" looms large.

Some might suggest that the political situation is so explosive a white man dare not suggest that a militant black is
unbalanced—and that clinical inquiry is withheld because of
this sensitivity by the white man.

It is hard to give this reason much weight when administrators are so grossly insensitive to racial and human subtleties in
every other situation. Even in a confrontation with black militants, such a boss may reach out to rub a black man's head in
an awkward effort to smooth things over. No, we would err if
we attribute too much subtlety and sensitivity to such men.

There are other reasons related to hostility toward blacks
which would probably be important determinants when the
employer overlooks the obvious derangement of our two militants. They might best be introduced with the following vi-
gnette.

*   *   *

Vincent, a young black draftee, became greatly excited as he approached the time and place for his
embarkation to the combat zone. He refused sleep, wrote
endless letters denouncing the racist society, and bom-
barded officers and enlisted men with accusations of racism.

He became frenzied one evening and left the military
base. When he was captured, the authorities set a severe
punitive mechanism in motion which might have sent
him to prison for many years—all in spite of documents
from his parents showing numerous similar emotional

crises in the past, and reports from civilian psychiatrists describing the man's mental illness. Forced by community pressure to treat him as sick, the authorities said they were sorry for the delay of medical care. They had first responded to his "black power statements!!"

They would have preferred to ignore the psychiatric problem and to punish the man for "talking black power."

*   *   *

It is in this vein that we suspect authorities would have preferred to see Steve and Mary as sound of mind and therefore fit subjects for punishment for their beliefs. The fact that in their sickness these two did things hurtful to themselves was judged further evidence of their contrariness and of the perversity of their beliefs.

A less obvious implication of the employer's action lies in the fact that he considers such behavior (by blacks) as normal. He would not judge this action by whites to be rational. Would it be too cynical to suspect that in this way the boss says that he cannot tell the difference between a sound and a deranged black man—that he thinks they are all deranged? Or that maybe he doesn't listen, save to his own prerecorded prejudgments about the man behind a black face.

To give loose, disorganized expressions of a failing mind the same weight as carefully thought out statements of political position is to equate the two and to strike a blow at the cause.

Finally, it is chilling to consider that these two young people were allowed to do grave damage to their careers simply because the ideas they expressed were troublesome to their employers. This illustrates the dangers awaiting black ambition.

Their careers were hard won, but to keep them, they had to

take care in choosing *how* they got ill and what symptoms
they selected.

*   *   *

Calvin's parents died when he was a boy and his early
life was spent in a series of foster homes. The experience
of being a foster child, less important than the natural
children, no doubt played a part in his developing a profound sense of inferiority—this and his own lack of family.

His education was poor; or, more precisely, Calvin
learned little of what was taught in schools. Someone
must have thought he had more than the usual amount
of talent, however, because they arranged for him to
train as a carpenter. After the several years of training
required, he left the Southern school and moved north to
practice his trade. In spite of his unfortunate beginnings,
he had developed an ambitious way about him.

"I'm going to work hard and save my money—and if
I can just get a little break . . . "

or,

"If I can buy an old run-down house and fix it up and
sell it . . . and keep on doing that . . ."

or,

"Maybe if I could get together with somebody who
owned some land I could build some houses and really
get myself together."

He had a blue-sky optimism which seemed to unfold
whenever he talked.

He was trained in a craft that offered great opportunity and he was obliged to assure the listener that he was
busy pursuing bigger and better things.

These lofty words sound thin when one realizes that
Calvin works exceedingly well and exceedingly hard for
a white man, but cannot work in his own behalf, nor can
he work seriously for *any* black man.

*   *   *

A close look at his work will help us understand him.
None of the craft unions allow blacks to enter apprentice-

ship programs in any numbers. The men restrict the numbers in their trade and severely restrict black entry into journeyman status and union membership. If Calvin and those like him could have gained status as craftsmen and union members, they would still have been subject to the whims of foremen regarding job assignments. They would have depended on bitter, hostile men for promotion and job security.

If he sought to start his own business independently, he would be forced to rely on men who regarded him as a subhuman interloper and who could be counted on to block whatever opportunities might come his way.

All of the industry and the workmen would bear some relationship to the banks to which Calvin would have to go for money. The banker could not but be influenced by the mood of the majority of his customers.

Calvin would, moreover, find it most difficult to assemble a crew which would work for and be loyal to a black man. He would lose bid after bid on jobs. He would not know to whom he should pay graft and when found, the "ethical" white man might refuse to accept it from black hands. Other firms might well engage in collusion to block supplies and men and jobs in order to bring him to his knees.

And when he failed he would be told he was imprudent, not honest enough, not diligent, a lazy man who had not worked hard enough.

It is our contention that these impediments cast their shadow before the child. He senses early that he has been born into a hateful place which wishes him ill. He covers his head and goes to make his mark.

We further submit that should the hatred of blacks be removed for one generation, then all the deadly consequences of bigotry would vanish, and Calvin's children could walk proudly and confidently with all their strength in hand and all their cunning in mind.

*   *   *

If ever a lad grew up in the Jesus Bag it was Ben. He never cheated, never lied, never stole. . . . He stayed in school. His family was pious, respectful of authority, and harsh in corrective measures.

"Mother and father leavened physical punishment with love." He purses his lips and e-nun-ci-ates each syllable.

He rarely talks about his early life now—his pompous ways are too transparent when talking about his humble beginning.

Ben went to big universities on scholarships and dishwashing in fraternity houses. He was awarded graduate degrees and settled down to the life pre-war black scholars led—an occasional grant, a research project, a teaching fellowship—anything to say that one was paid for working at his profession.

During this period there were so few blacks in his field that he was never tested intellectually against his equals. He never learned whether he was gifted or not and had no knowledge of how he ranked with white students. He was "special." He was the "only Negro" and like the singing dog was such an unusual act that no one asked *how well* he sang.

As a result it was necessary for him to develop the art of winning friends among powerful white people. Once he was associated with the development of a classic work and his employability increased. He now had only to mention that he was associated with that work.

He obtained better positions and still no one asked about his competence. He became more widely known, headed research projects, and made frequent trips to Washington.

It is not clear at what point he realized that his job was based not on knowledge or competence, but on his exceptionality. Sometime in this period of the rising of his star he must have thought,

"If they *hire* me for no good reason, they can *fire* me for no good reason."

Certainly some such thought must have weakened his reserve because the black movement of the 1960's sounded the beginning of his professional end. When his previously respectful adherents turned to more activist leadership, he sank into an emotional depression—and that depression hurried his exit from the stage.

His is the tragedy of the "only Negro."

He had for so long been the nearest Negro and therefore a policy maker. (The nearest Negro is the first one bumped into by a white administrator who has just rushed out of his office to find out what Negroes think. His influence may be very great, since the white man's public opinion canvass often stops with him.)

Ben gathered followers of lesser and lesser intellectual stature and now stands surrounded by mediocrity.

Finally, he no longer holds the group of white admirers who have so meanly used him and they, also, abandon him.

He is left, a victim of his times, angry with the blacks who have displaced him and trying desperately to woo back the white folks.

He may have been a gifted man. We'll never know. His time asked of him only that he cozy up to white folks and make them like him. For a time he was very, very good at that.

*   *   *

The cost for Ben of staying alive was his manhood. The cost for all the Bens has been more than they should have had to pay. White people, occupied more with the proprieties, have not even recognized them as casualties.

VII.

Black Psychology

1✓✓✓

Blackness has had an exciting effect on Black America. It has stirred groups and individuals to move heaven and earth for the common good. It has stimulated a reversal of feelings about self, and where one had felt a shrunken half-shell, with black awareness the body fills out and a man feels genuinely proud of himself. Attitudes shift from self-denigration to expansive superiority; men and women shed an old identity and with it the wretchedness previously associated with color.

Almost all blacks who embrace blackness for the first time feel a lifting of the spirit—as if they have been freed of a burden. There is an accompanying higher valuation of one's gifts and capacities. Men will embark on astonishingly ambitious careers. For some, the experience of having lived comes to be equated with expert knowledge and learning itself is considered vital only for children.

No doubt the most striking effect is the realization that unknowingly blacks had been accepting, functioning, organizing their lives around the restrictions white people imposed on them.

The realization comes that there are so many dangerous consequences of being black in America that most blacks concern themselves quite consciously with only a few of the highest priority. They simply build their lives around the multitude of carefully ignored lesser cruelties. They do so for reasons of psychological economy. There is simply not enough energy to fight a battle on all the fronts by which a black man is assaulted by his country.

Thus a style of life develops in which much of society's hostility is not recognized—it is explained in other ways and kept from open view.

This is the kind of nest that is upended by blackness. All the hurts are felt as if they were new. No disguises work. The full range of white hatred for blacks is felt every day and seen now by those whose spines have been stiffened and who are of a mind to retaliate.

Black men, feeling wronged, may give white authority a tongue-lashing and threaten physical violence. They may incite group action, strikes, confrontations, any and all, at a moment's notice.

The white man who once was feared can now be called a son-of-a-bitch, and all because of changes *inside* the black man. As experienced black psychiatrists we notice, however, that as some black men discard "white rule" there is the shadow of another internal revolution threatening the overthrow of reason.

Blackness sometimes has unwanted side effects, as do most miracle drugs. By far the most troubling is that under its powerful influence some men go mad.

How often does this happen? What can be done about it?

What does it portend for the future and how can an influence so healing and revivifying have on occasion so disabling an effect?

2 ↟↟↟

Roger, by his mid-twenties, had tried and failed at a number of things. Schools, jobs—neither plentiful nor particularly welcoming—had been tried. Things had always gone wrong, and he was coasting between trying something new and simply relaxing into sloth, when he was struck by blackness.

As the oldest of three children, he was the favored one, the child on whom the family magically centered its yearnings for fame. Roger's background was that cluster of circumstances so familiar to most blacks. The father worked long, backbreaking hours as a longshoreman and spent his time at home in solitary pursuits, sleeping, reading the paper, watching television. He spent little time with the children but it was not willful neglect; he was just tired all the time.

Roger's mother was deeply religious and ambitious for her first child. Early in his life she urged him to read books and "make something of himself." She drove him more than the others and at the age of nine he took piano *and* trumpet lessons.

His mother's urgings never took hold and he was not much of a success at anything. He entered college, and after two undistinguished semesters dropped out and drifted through several jobs.

His friends said he was close-mouthed and secretive, but these descriptions were without conviction. He had been considered an economic and vocational failure, and it was along this dimension that he judged himself and was judged by others.

Even with women he seemed content to accept left-overs. Most people would have called him earnest, willing, always ready to try again, but not gifted with whatever men have who succeed. He was not even bitter.

Blackness changed all that.

His sometimes open, ingratiating good nature disappeared and he developed a permanent scowl. He looked angry all the time.

He wore sandals, daishikis, and as the ultimate affirmation, the symbolically significant Banneker glasses. He read the *Autobiography of Malcolm X,* Frantz Fanon, and soaked up massive amounts of black history.

He spoke knowingly about black culture and developed a way of challenging anyone, black or white. All whites were summarily accused as racists, and most blacks as "Toms." His words took on a life of their own. There emerged a ranting, liturgical quality in his indictments. The genocidal conspiracy of whites, "the killer white man," became a close, immediate threat and dominated his thinking. He was thus able to justify carrying a gun for self-protection, and he exhorted others to join him in the organization of an armed cadre for the defense of the black community against the soldiers who were sure to come. When the blacks declined to join, Roger assumed that they were all in the pay of the enemy. He retreated further and further into an armed, crab-like defense, secret and alone.

In his isolated misery he devoured more books and after a rereading of Fanon, determined that perhaps a black doctor could provide some of the relief he sought. Like so many of those seeking help, he did not think of himself as sick, he only knew he wanted someone to understand.

He came upon a skillful black therapist who over a painful several months drew him back into the community of men and urged that he make a reassessment of his life and times.

Roger's appraisal involved a close look at this country and where he fitted in. He burst into laughter while talking about his mother's insistence on his playing *two* instruments. "Roger, the super-spade," he called himself. The corner was turned. He now spent time wondering what to do with his newly released anger.

Genocide, suggested the therapist, may indeed be right around the corner, but even if we all agree on that (and we don't), there may be more creative responses than holing up in the attic with five hundred rounds of ammunition. We *can* agree that the future of Black America needs all our concern whether it is threatened by guns or by a more subtly enforced Aryanized view of the world. Roger conceded that even the *blackest* militants might slip over the brink and that he had at least come close.

He wondered what help he had been to others in all his activities. Even granting the imminence of attack, had he actually positioned himself protectively between the community and the enemy?

He worked more thoughtfully, and with the help of his therapist, aimed for a more effective future.

Now the place for him was in the street and he became an agitator, organizing rent strikes, welfare strikes, and challenging the police at every turn. He became measurably more militant and active, but with a difference.

He was not more effective—he got more done. He found within himself more love for blacks and saved his vilification for whites. We can speculate and hope that when some whites behave in a way to *justify* his love, *that too* may be forthcoming.

*   *   *

Blackness *does* have an explosive power for creative change. It bursts into the ongoing life of a man and shatters what had seemed fixed components. Roger had grown up in a world in which whites hated blacks and blacks were afraid of whites—a complex system of oppression from which there was no appeal. American hostility to black life has had this consequence, that men have ordered their lives so as to never feel called upon to challenge the authority. They developed a view of the world which said that white oppression of blacks was the most reliable aspect of an otherwise chaotic and completely unpredictable life.

We have seen it happen that a black man has been so burdened by the personally experienced tyranny of the white world that when he throws *this* over, he also abandons the world of reality. White people and their rules, however destructive and senseless, will have become so deeply intertwined with reality that the discard of whites places reality in jeopardy.

In addition to its powerful force for creative change, blackness is sometimes accompanied by a deeply held, mystical view of the profound folk-wisdom of "grass-roots" blacks. There arises sometimes the notion that one need only be black, unlettered, and poor, and by these credentials be identified as men and women of great wisdom.

A poor black man might be tempted to accept such a role but it is sinister for sophisticated whites to anoint some uneducated but ambitious man as a veritable "Renaissance Root." The infusion of blackness may make a man feel sublimely gifted, but there is a cynicism in white collaborators who hope to gain cheap favor by pressing such an ill-prepared man for an opinion, and acting on it as "the will of the community." Responsible white Americans must take the blame for such hypocritical manipulation of this "grass-root" community advice.

To call a white man of some authority a "racist dog" and to threaten to "burn down the institution" are understandably

of great importance to men who have all their lives felt helpless and impotent.

A new leader may strengthen his hand by identifying himself with the black masses. If his idealistic efforts are blocked,
he may invoke the threat of the peoples' revenge:

> "In opposing these demands you oppose the legitimate
> aspirations of the black community!"

As for himself, he says that he has no personal ambition,
but seeks only to serve the people, and he partly sustains an
exaggerated view of his capabilities by forging this union between himself and "the people."

What could be more thoroughly gratifying than to experience the sensual pleasure of such acts and find that one can at
the same time bring about worthwhile social change!

The psychological realities of black life took shape under
the pressure of white hatred. Black men were moved by the
passions that move all men and faced life with the mixtures of
courage and cowardice that all men have mustered—except
with the difference that the complete range of life was lived
under the press of American bigotry.

Blackness has the effect of penetrating and shattering the
pressure bearing down on and distorting black lives. It allows
blacks to cleanse themselves of fear, and, in one act, remove
not only the intimidation of immediate hostility, but also all
ceilings, permitting freedom to move as far and fast as one's
wits will allow.

Freedom from fear is strong wine!

We suggest that it is the *sudden* removal of this pressure
which brings complications. The burden had been so constant
that it had come to be considered a part of one's most intimate world, a part even of one's anatomy. The situation might

be likened to that of a mollusk which feels its body grow, taking on the conformation of the shell which encloses it. Structures deep inside and far away from the surface come into existence *because* the animal is forever encased in that shell.

Some blacks have been injured so deeply in the course of their development that the possibility of a major break with reality lies close to the surface. They may not show outward signs of serious illness, but long-continued observation shows that they move in and out of an estrangement from reality. Under stress they may act most odd, only to pull themselves together once the stress is removed and resume what now becomes an essentially normal life. These people dwell at the borderline between stability and derangement and are gravely affected by blackness.

They will have been the ones who relied most heavily on the externally imposed rules of life and they may live as if they were governed by accurate perceptions of the world. In actuality, they take their cues from people around them. They work when others work, for reasons they have heard others give. They play in the way others play, and fight when they are expected to fight. They are distinguished by the absence of inner conviction and motivation.

Since most of the external structure of black life is imposed as a function of white hatred, blackness, by removing a man's fear of whites, makes this organized hatred ineffective. He now sees as well as fights the enemy. But the structure of the old oppression is gone for some of the newly black, and the troubled borderliners described above have had something akin to an amputation of the white culture which they had grafted onto themselves.

There are new rules, new guides, and these victims float off more and more excited, more and more irrational, finally incapacitated by the freedom they wanted and needed more than anything else. These are people in whom the soil had been prepared for trouble from their earliest years, but who might have made it through life with only occasional excursions into the unreal.

In the South, black men learned to avoid isolated situations with white women; this became a part of their psychic structure, requiring no conscious thought. A driver who has been in traffic long enough soon touches his brake without thinking of it when a red light flashes.

Similarly, black men, North and South, made a wide berth around carousing young white men—and hardly gave it a second thought. The avoidance of danger was automatic and this particular danger was automatically identified.

Opportunities for special pleasure took white hatred into account. People played where no white eyes could see. Happiness was confined to the black community not because the scenes there were so inspiring, but because the hateful whites were absent.

Success, if it meant money, had to be moderated, since too public a show of prosperity attracted thieving men who then used the social advantage of their whiteness to rob the black of his money.

Thus, in so many ways, persistent structures in the personality of black Americans had white hostility as their origin.

When a man has spent a lifetime enchained, he must straighten his limbs with care when the bonds are removed, his body having come to expect the limitations of chains. He might in his new freedom sprain a muscle or break a bone. He must readjust with care. Out of the care and pain and striving there emerges a "Super-Black" whose superiorities are the counterbalancing complement of a previously held feeling of inferiority.

He finds his feeling supported by the intense pleasure and

emotional relief which are part of the rhetorical style and the posture of militancy. Simply to *appear* constantly angry shatters a lifelong feeling of submission. It suggests that one is free to displease the white man and, in fact, to go further. A scowl can be a continuing source of satisfaction and a vehicle for important emotional discharge.

For the newly black, the rhetoric and the militant stance are a welcome outlet for new feelings. The sudden freedom from the oppressive fear of the white man vaults him into a new, unstructured relationship with his world. He is no longer fettered with the limitation of paralyzing fear and there comes welcome relief in his new ability to punish those who harm him.

In view of the reality whereby with each turn of his head the black man sees new outrages committed against his people, his vision and freedom move him to a sustained attack on white America.

The emotional release is deeper because blacks had for so long been told that they were blocking their own progress; that they were their own worst enemy; that their laziness, improvidence, and preoccupation with the superficial—all were the cause of their wretched state.

Black people always knew better, but, threatened by all the structures of the nation, blinded by feelings of inferiority, and weakened by fear, they could not lay hands on the villain. Now they can, and a debt is overdue.

When those who are sound emotionally are taken by blackness they find it removes feelings of inferiority, the fear of whites, self-hatred, and other hurtful things about themselves. It is therefore valued as a healing, pain-relieving anodyne.

No other concept covers so much psychological ground for black people. So long as this powerful new draught is available, sound people will value it and use it.

Blackness, by cutting the ties with the old adaptation to oppression, and by demanding that individuals find more of their own determinants and guides, by these demands has shown us how long and brave a stride men make when set in the direction of freedom. That some men fail may be unrelated to the challenge, having more to do with the questing, sometime over-reaching nature of imperfect man, drawn as he is by the vision of perfection.

3*

Roger is not unusual in seeking out a black therapist. Research in psychotherapy is in a sorry state, and it is difficult to say precisely how many people are helped by black, white, yellow, or red therapists. But patients such as Roger often feel they can be helped only by black therapists.

If we assume the black therapist to be sufficiently knowledgeable, and agree that he is often best for Roger, we may then answer questions about the patient by examining his chosen instrument of cure, the black therapist. Whatever is unique in this situation must surely be of importance and we will profit from knowing of it.

Black therapists find themselves in an anomalous position. Many of them, like their white counterparts, entered the field hoping for a solution to their own problems. When, as often happened, a white analyst encouraged them to think that life would be fulfilled by emulating him, he encouraged their wish to be white, and their genuine neurotic problems which treatment *might* have helped he pushed aside.

They were encouraged to enter an extended and complex

training period and emerged from the other end walking, talking, and acting as if they were part of a white scholarly elite
whose skills were highly valued.

The black therapist was expected to ignore the fact that a
policeman might kill his child simply because the child was
black. He was expected to join organizations of colleagues
which never pushed for social reforms in matters affecting
blacks. And while all the community's services to his people
were dangerously inferior, he was expected to act as if he
could not recognize it.

One might find something admirable in the ability of those
few who carried it off for so long, but it was certain that a rebellion was in the wind. When blackness hit this group, they
embraced the idea with a passion and a unanimity. They grew
beards and Afros and spoke of "the legitimate aspirations of
the black community."

Some have been so deeply moved that they have ceased
functioning as professionals and have adopted the roles of pol-
iticians and provocateurs. Like certain of their white counterparts, many black therapists seem willing to take time out
from the serious, demanding matters of mental health to tack-
le equally serious political issues (but for which they are *completely* unprepared).

Mental illness in the small group of black behavioral scientists is often dramatic and may appear to be relatively common. Whatever the real incidence, as therapists we know it is
too high and is a function of the excessive pressure placed on
all blacks in this country.

For these professionals, turning black has had some frightening consequences. They have become fiercely, uncritically
passionate and exhort their colleagues to join in the new drive.
But as they reorganize their lives around challenging whites,
they seem to be terrified and to rush blindly into ever more

senseless confrontations. The blacker they become the more frightened they seem, or the more frightened they feel the blacker they become.

They adopt a chauvinistic posture which suggests that blacks must serve only blacks, and they abandon the system of knowledge of which they are a part.

Social workers dismiss techniques for working with individuals, groups, and families, and determine to work against the power structure, as if their previously learned skills were no longer needed by black people.

Psychiatrists abandon experience, theory, and the specific needs of troubled people to identify themselves with the movement. They shrink, frightened, from the white world, thrusting all "white learning" away, lest they become corrupted and their warlike resolution weakened.

The result is stranger still. Having abandoned their discipline, psychoanalysts who no longer believe in psychoanalysis, psychologists who no longer believe in psychology, and social workers who no longer believe in social work, all turn to activism only to find that their long specialized training has dulled their senses to the special touch needed for political action.

*   *   *

A black professional who had a history of emotional instability became exercised over what he felt was the exclusion of blacks from positions of influence in a program serving the health needs of a black community. More and more incensed, he argued and provoked a fight. Finally he brought a gun to work and, muttering about "the conspiracy," succeeded in terrorizing the staff to such a point that the police were called to take him away.

*   *   *

A young woman with a brilliant academic background had gained an enviable reputation. She had a wide range of capabilities and assumed many responsibilities in her position as a mental health professional.

With the advent of blackness she became shrill and querulous, a veritable Madame DeFarge as she indicted all whites around her as "imperialist dogs," who, she said, were actively engaged in oppressive racist social action.

Her brilliance turned to tendentious reasoning in which she sought to prove that the very identification of a black man as a recipient of psychological services was a prejudicial act and that institutions sought thereby to ignore his legitimate complaints against society.

She was determined to prove that no black person was emotionally ill and that the whole discipline of mental health was used to silence black dissent.

All this, she said, she did on behalf of the black masses.

*   *   *

We suggest that the above and others like them are disappointed idealists. They are unusual, at least by white America's standards, in the extent to which they had previously embraced the ambition of professionalism. They and their families had been unusual in a willingness to sacrifice for the honor and the security of professional status.

They were idealistic "good boys." They went to school, studied, waited, accepted the ambitions defined by white instructors as appropriate, and they sacrificed, sacrificed, sacrificed.

When one studies the lives of this troubled few of the "talented tenth" of Black America, one is astonished that critics of black life accuse us of an inability to postpone gratification.

It was late in the day when they found that the logical, reasonable, indeed the only goal which could justify such great sacrifice was the goal of being a *white* professional. When they found themselves to be exquisitely trained, polished, experi-

enced, gifted professionals who occupied only modest positions and received even more modest rewards, they became
the anomalous aging "good guys" who had given up everything only to find that they had been deceived. They discovered that their determination to do the right thing had blinded
them to the *wrong* thing "the man" was doing, as he suggested
to them how important it was to be a good "Negro" teacher
or a very fine "Negro" social worker or psychologist or psychiatrist.

They were so honest that they failed to see the true meaning of the adjective "Negro," and that its placement as a mod-
ifier put a low ceiling on the power or prestige to be gained.

They finally rebelled and abandoned everything to embrace
blackness. They turned away from what they now see as the
aristocratic overtones of their previous status and now ally
themselves with the mistreated masses. They have tried it
"Charlie's way" and found that he never intended a payoff,
and now they have come home. They turn their scorn on
scholarship and make of themselves anti-intellectual knights
leading the black majority.

They assume an intensely moral posture as they are determined to come to the black community with clean hands
bearing no vestige of their previous separate state as a scholarly elite.

4*

We celebrate, however, a new and more perfect servant of the
people: a servant who is at heart a black healer—a black man

who has developed the highest skills and acquired so profound a black identity that it is this blood membership which is basic, not the fraternity of the fellows of his craft.

With such an unswerving certainty of who he is, and who his people are, his calling becomes an extension of himself. He has the courage to search the world over for every skill and craft to place in the hands of his brother.

His unity with his own allows him to take all the knowledge white men have come upon, incorporate it, refine it, and turn it to his own use, secure in the knowledge that his motives need never be impugned so long as he can reach out to touch a brother.

The seasoned black therapist has the courage to challenge white America wherever he sees his patients' welfare compromised. In fact, he functions as their advocate. He is not detached and remote, but shares with them a deep, unifying bond. His task is not to urge his patients to accommodate to the viciousness in America. He never asks that they contain their outrage in order to "get along." He never, therefore, assumes that the social order of the nation is a finished piece, shining with perfection, to which reasonable men should accommodate themselves. He is convinced, rather, that those changes which truly have blacks as immediate beneficiaries will in the long run benefit the nation generally.

He thus tests the severity of the ailment by the measure to which it interferes with the patient's effective engagement in the active social change necessary for the improvement of his life.

In his advocacy for improvement in the life circumstances of those who come to him, he frames his therapeutic structure around social betterment. He may use any technique of influence from psychoanalysis to simple instruction and feel no special allegiance to any one of them so long as it works. He is equally opposed to the secularization of treatment along disciplinary lines—such as qualifying only psychologists or social workers or teachers or psychiatrists to perform specific helping tasks.

He measures his worth by the extent to which he frees his patients from personal conflict and makes possible a turning of their energy to the essentially human task of making their home, their town, their world a gentler, more considerate environment in which children might better be raised and in which they might with more peace and greater reward live out their lives.

He is generally suspicious of contented men, but he is stirred to a therapeutic ardor by contented blacks, convinced as he is that a black man contented with his circumstances in America is very sick indeed.

He validates other healers similarly in terms of patients and he asks not how militant the therapist is but to what extent he has freed his patients for that vital social activity in behalf of all blacks. He wastes no time in the petty internecine struggle between professionals which in any event he considers an unworthy exercise in jealousy and rivalry. For it is apparent to him that some essentially conservative colleagues, when frightened by change, flee, terrified into a pseudo-militant posture, and spend their days scared, crouched, and witless, critically calibrating the blackness of wiser and more courageous men.

The black therapist considers himself primarily a healer and is content with such a definition, knowing that black people need healers.

As a good therapist, he never ignores the most pressing issue of the moment. If a patient's house is aflame, he puts it out. If his patient has a physical ailment, he sees that it is cared for. If his patient is hungry, he sees that he is fed; if he is cold, he sees that he is warmed; and if his patient is threatened, he extends a shield-arm of protection, knowing that these are the sets which define one human's benevolent involvement with another, and convinced that only within such a matrix of love and concern can any psychological treatment flourish.

It is true that black patients have had little reason to trust healers. And it is equally true that they have been singled out as one group offered by society as a universal victim. The result, as we have written in *Black Rage,* is a suspiciousness—a *black norm* of distrust and circumspection which is in fact not only appropriate but life-preserving and life-sustaining.

If, therefore, one asks a black man to set aside his armor and to come *unarmed* into a house of healing, one can at best expect to be ignored and, at worst, rudely dealt with. So long as a reasonable man has the option he will decline to place himself in the hands of his enemy.

The therapist must therefore be prepared for a period in which his words, "I am not as the others who injure you," are measured against his acts. Such testing is prudent, and wise, and adaptive, and speaks well for the survival instincts of the patient.

It is necessary for that involvement to come. If the initial encounter works, then the patient must be willing to show the therapist his favorite psychological strategems and he must identify which of his basic styles of operating are more and which are less effective.

For here in the vital center of his person he must allow the therapist to see all and to render judgment on which of the structures are sound and which are puffed-up, illusory armaments aimed like the great guns of Singapore out to sea when there is no naval threat.

If both the therapist and patient are serious and well-intentioned, the result is bound to be of help. Useless, energy-consuming defensive structures are abandoned. The energy involved in supporting these is shifted to other psychological functions more important to survival and well-being.

The result might be, could be, should be, a highly efficient reassignment of priorities, and a much greater efficiency in the use of, what is for us all, a limited fund of energy.

For all patients the issue is grave; for blacks it is of overriding critical importance. They, after all, face greater danger. Their senses, over a lifetime, have been sharpened to a point at least perceptive enough to have kept a man alive. He wants his functioning made more efficient, but, to repeat, he can tolerate no mistakes, for any decrease in his effectiveness may be literally fatal. Because of all these elements, the engagement between the black patient and the therapist bears the seeds of both magnificence and disaster and nothing can be of greater importance to the patient. We would hope that it would be seen by the therapist as a responsibility of the greatest importance.

But for the therapist even to *begin* by considering his involvement with a black patient to be of special significance is already to assume that the latter is a special kind of person who has been left sufficiently untouched by national attitudes to make such an approach possible. The truth is that such people are in short supply, black or white.

The therapist must be willing to learn all he can, in and out of the consultation room, about his patient's world. Again, this seems to be good practice, no matter what the race of the patient or therapist, but, however casually observed with others, with blacks it is crucial.

*   *   *

A 2.3 million dollar grant was obtained by a white hospital located in the black community. The directors arranged for the white therapists each to be assigned a black "cultural guide" to facilitate his dealing with black children and parents.

*   *   *

Such planning strikes the authors as an obscene violation of the most rudimentary principles governing human relationships, not to mention the impossible setting it provides for therapeutic assistance.

Those administrators who are seriously interested in bringing services to blacks must make certain that therapists either know the community or are taught thoroughly about it *before* they begin their assignments.

We cannot long avoid the central issue. Black patients do not long abide any therapist who is short in essential ingredients.

The patient requires that the therapist have courage, honor, and a highly developed moral sense. In the case of the last-named, the fact is that patients require only that the therapist declare some things to be so right and others so wrong that neutrality is ridiculous.

Courage, on the other hand, is more difficult to come by. In terms of the black experience, courage is there if you have been *literally* willing to die for an ideal, *frequently* enough for it not to be new. To be able to reduce a chance encounter with a murderous policeman to the three tactical questions: *Can* I avoid death? *Should* I avoid death? If I cannot or should not, then how can I accomplish the greatest good by my death? At such a point one has achieved courage.

And, finally, honor. Black people respect honorable men and are sensitive judges of honor as a trait of character. They are not only concerned that a man have ideals but are interested in their quality.

"When do you take a stand—and why—and how firm are you—and how much have your ideals cost you—and how vulnerable are you—and how sensitive—and how much pain can you stand—and what exactly are these convictions for which *you say* you would suffer so much?"

We have a special knowledge of honor and white America. The country is intolerant of rectitude but is most unable to bear the presence or existence of an honorable black. He is threatened, and tempted, and tested, and forced often to abandon his idealism.

So when a black man has retained his honor it is no mean prize and he will be raised up by his fellow men.

How can one trust his mental life to one other than an honorable, courageous, moral man? Black patients are careful about the selection; they cannot afford mistakes.

Whites might ask themselves if they, in all their affluence, can themselves afford a lesser man.

VIII.

The Only Game in Town

1*♪♪*

> "The only thing wrong with Jews is that they just ain't Jewish enough."

The speaker is a black laborer who looks on the conflict between blacks and whites with the objectivity of a casualty, removed from the struggle but bringing to his criticism an intimate knowledge of the fight. This wise man must now accommodate himself to a back injury, a pension and semi-invalidism, and people who *think* he needs psychiatric help.

> "If they wore fur hats and beards and long coats and spoke Jewish, then they'd know what the honky will do to you. As long as they act white and other white folks accept them, then they can't possibly know what we're up against."

Having delivered himself of this wisdom, he turned to other matters, but we wrote down his words—he had said it well.

Blacks *do* have a gripe against Jews. It is the same damning indictment they have against the rest of white Americans—all of them have committed a hideous act against black people solely for profit and solely because it was possible to do. We cannot be expected to uncritically extend the hand of brotherhood to Jews who have so uncritically embraced the whiteness of America, when it is the whiteness of America that has all but crushed the life from us. The color bar included them and excluded us and if, perhaps understandably, they did not jeopardize their opportunities for *our* sake, then we cannot sacrifice our children's future for *their* sake.

Nothing can ever "turn us around." The liberalizing, the reforming, the freeing of America from bigotry and racial hatred have become for us a sacred mission and we will not be turned aside.

We have found however that our mightiest weapon is the truth, and we lay it aside at our peril. We know some truths about the American white man that most others do not know. And we know a great deal about Jews.

We know for example that Jews are 98 percent white and that it is *that* critical 2 percent of mistreatment that keeps them from completely identifying with the white majority, and which reminds them of Europe, and which stimulates compassion which might otherwise be withheld. We know that it is the above together with the memory of their past which allows for that partial identification with the black cause and which moves them to allow blacks more of a chance than do other white men.

*   *   *

A Jewish man entered psychiatric treatment with a black therapist several years before "black anti-Semitism" was an issue.

His problem was phobias. He was afraid of everything: blood, sharp objects, bridges, heights, distances, motion, quiet, and, of course, the dark.

He was well-paid but managed to squander money so wildly that it scarcely lasted from one payday to the next. In treatment, he made much of his being free even of the *awareness* of racial differences. He had more in common, he said, with his black therapist than with his co-workers downtown, and he imagined himself a spy in the Anglo-Saxon world of big business.

Time passed, and as the discussion wandered across other aspects of his life, he took pains to conceal how much he earned. He acted ashamed of his high income and was certain that the therapist earned much less.

He identified himself with Jewish shopowners who he thought had exploited blacks in the past. To him, most Jewish wealth was tainted, since in his mind it had been stolen from hardworking, naive blacks. He was terrified that the therapist would punish him for all the wrongs he imagined Jews had visited on blacks.

It further developed that he was re-experiencing the feelings of superiority and vulnerability which had first involved his father. The ease with which he saw his problems in terms of a Jewish-black-WASP triad is a common occurrence when the Jewish patient is coupled with a black therapist. This man was willing to assume within the therapeutic setting the burden of all the real and fancied wrongs done to blacks by Jews even though he had never personally been a party to any such action.

The news told of warlike activity by surrounding Arab countries toward Israel, and this made him feel *personally* surrounded and threatened. As he waited for the next Arab attack, he likened the Israeli situation to that of American blacks, far outnumbered and therefore doomed.

He so identified with the Israelis that the surface of his body came to be coterminous with the geographic outline of that country. If the nation were attacked on the northeast border, his left shoulder felt "shooting pains."

A thrust in the narrowed midsection of Israel caused pain in his side.

It was in the midst of this suffering that he spoke with unusual candor. He was glad his doctor was black; such a man he said, knows what it is to be attacked on all sides, to be overwhelmed, and to fight to the death with no alternative.

It was the first time he spoke as a brother and with trust, and it marked the beginning of his recovery.

*   *   *

In Europe, the most important aspect of Jewishness was religion; in America, it is of overriding importance that Jews are white.

Anti-Semitism, still a problem in America, has never approached its bloody European dimensions, and so the Jew can understandably be a grateful and eager American white man and only historically admit membership in a persecuted swarthy minority.

To place a firmer hold on his fundamental self, our phobic friend had to turn away from the whiteness of his world, not because his is black, but because those who despise him are white, and he was wise enough to know that one cannot identify with those who hate him. The only direction for him to take was toward becoming more Jewish, and that led him closer to blacks.

He found that this movement toward blacks was in the interest of survival and we know that a similar movement by blacks has a similar purpose.

Our black patients are most emphatic and insist that in all areas of American life the door to black participation was cracked by a Jew—that however unequal was the sharing of the purse, blacks would never have been in the ring were it not for the Jew.

And so, in spite of the widespread newspaper reports of

black anti-Semitism, the truth, as seen through the eyes of patients and through the eyes of millions of other black Americans—the truth is that the overwhelming majority of blacks would rather deal with Jews, work for Jews, yes, would surely rather trust Jews than other American whites. The black genius for survival has been to spot the slimmest of chances and make the most of it.

But the moment such a statement is framed we hear vigorous objections from the white Anglo-Saxon, Protestant spokesmen for middle- and upper-class white America (our untitled peerage).

They complain that America is essentially a good land, that its people are essentially fair—that honesty and hard work pay, and that the important differences are individual, and we are therefore individually accountable.

When reminded of the barbarism visited on blacks, he hangs his head and, struggling with the burden of guilt, states, "We're not all bad—and things *are* getting better!"

He recites the civil rights laws passed, school desegregation, fair employment and fair housing acts now on the books. He says that he and his people did those things and simply short-sightedness, blindness, and an ignorance of current affairs make blacks act as if he were unworthy of their confidence. He is likely to end his statement with words that suggest his superiority to Jews.

If the above fairly expresses the feelings of economically secure WASPs (and we think it does), then they will probably never understand how every black man in this nation was hunted down in Philadelphia, Mississippi. How caught, pinned in the lights, we were all terrified as they called us (we were all named James Chaney) and how the only human beings in all this creation who cared enough to share the misery and who were now also trapped in the final hour of life were two young men, Andrew Goodman and Michael Schwerner—two Jewish boys from New York.

You can't make any greater commitment than that—and we remember.

There is another body of criticism heard when blacks who deal with the establishment state a preference for Jews. These nineteenth-century radical revolutionaries criticize us not because we prefer to deal with Jews but because we have not joined *them* (the mid-Victorian revolutionaries) in a blind furor designed to *smash the system!* They see problems through class-oriented lenses and say that our troubles are due to capitalism. They insist that we are poor, helpless, and persecuted because the rich barons of property are sucking dry our class and they tell us that our miserable situation here has *nothing to do with race!!* They say we should therefore abandon our attacks on racism and abandon hope for any relief of our grievances under the present capitalist system—only revolution will get us out of the rat-infested tenements of the ghetto.

The answer to this criticism is that blacks know how white people act. We know that Mississippi is a society of dedicated bigots who abuse blacks and we know that this abuse is sanctioned because of the race of the victim. It would remain unchanged under *any* political system, no matter how the wealth might be distributed, so long as the community-at-large condoned the abuse of blacks.

We have no starry-eyed, uncritical vision of democracy, United States style, but neither do we have an unrealistic vision of any other system of political organization. Few revolutions and fewer revolutionaries are willing to guarantee *our* safety from predatory whites *anywhere* in America. Democracy could work for blacks—it is not the political system, it is the people.

We know of individuals of all political persuasions who out of personal commitment have contributed to improvement in housing, education, and employment for blacks. We know further that, despite the mouthings of the left, right, and everything in between, the majority of whites have done nothing.

There are two groups which oppose the black-Jew coalition which ought to cancel each other out but instead enhance one another. We speak of the *irrational* black radicals, fortunately few in number, who want to (1) "destroy the system"; (2) "kill all the honkies"; (3) "seize the Southern states and set up a black republic"; and (4) "demand money from rich whites."

Their hate-filled opposite number, the blue-collar, pick-up truck driver with an "outlaw" sign on the bumper and a rifle in the cab is a true killer of blacks. He wants complete segregation and is convinced that the vague "heritage of white America" needs a Wallace to save it.

From the far right, we hear strident objections to the linking of Jews and blacks. These people who have such morbid personal lives, seem determined to cure themselves of their ills by shifting their misery from inside onto an external group— and they then try to destroy the ideas and feelings which have tormented them.

They attack Communists and leftists and New Dealers and Jews and "traitors" and anyone else with whom they disagree. They engage in a holy war "to rid this sacred soil of scum."

In any event, these rabid folk are particularly distressed by a Black-Jew coalition since it is a union in which both parties are considered the enemy.

The dilemma is resolved by "protecting" those they consider weaker from an alliance with those they see as stronger —so blacks are warned against becoming the dupes of the "Jewish-Communist conspiracy."

It is easy to think that this super-patriotism has grown out of the disappointing and confusing world of World War II and since. Lest we be tempted, remember that it was these same super-patriots who, prior to all the shooting of World War II could see only the legality of hearings and the pseudo-formality of process designed to keep the Scottsboro boys incarcerated.

It took Sam Liebowitz, a New York Jew, to remind this nation that the whole purpose of the courts is to safeguard justice—and for his pains he was called a meddling outsider, dabbling in the internal affairs of a sovereign state; cross-burners threatened his life.

These conservatives conserve their own substance but are profligate with the goods and even lives of others. We could not be expected to submit to their mercies—surely even *they* can understand why we prefer the Jews to them.

The irrational radical black and the blue-collar Wallaceite are cut from the same cloth—they both hate blacks.

We might add one factor to close the matter and that has to do with what began as the Civil Rights struggle and has lately become a broadly based social reform movement encompassing the poor and the powerless of every color. It was funded from the beginning primarily by donations from Jews. Without their support of this unlikely movement, it would have died in its cradle.

It is therefore difficult to judge what aspect of America or of their own conscience has made Jews more responsive to the oppressed. Of all the persecuted minorities which fled Europe for America—Irish, French, Sicilians, Greeks, Poles, Ukrainians—most were persecuted ethnic minorities fleeing Europe, and most adopted the posture of white reactionary upon reaching these shores. One could perhaps make a case that it was *those* minorities which were so harshly treated who now develop such deep-seated resentment toward blacks in the New World.

On the other hand, one might say that, to the extent that Jews *remembered* what it was like in the Old World, they were inclined to turn a more benign face to the sufferer in the New World.

Where other immigrants forgot the past and seized the opportunity to sit in the tyrant's seat, the very presence of a memory of bad times and the compulsion to act on that memory might be called a profoundly significant morality.

Blacks do not require that acts which are of benefit to them be consonant with a theoretical notion of how minority groups should get along. They take the position that it makes no sense to analyze the motivation of Jews who offer jobs, however menial, when no one else is offering any jobs at all.

Blacks may seem to agree with the occasional anti-Semite, but, in their actions, and in the quiet of the consultation room there is to be found a pragmatism which admits that all whites are racist, but Jews have more compassion. And, as a result, blacks would rather have Jews as social workers, employers, lawyers, physicians, and, yea, as teachers, than have other whites.

It seems important for Jews to know this and to recognize that a local skirmish over schools should be no occasion for aligning themselves with the forces of bigotry which have in other times made *them* its victims.

Above and beyond all the problems, Jews are an incredibly yeasty addition to America. They have left their mark on everything they have touched. Their course in America has been that of white men who are labeled white and treated that way most of the time. But it was whispered in their ear that the label could be removed.

*   *   *

A prominent Jewish scholar had a long-standing reputation as a liberal thinker. The public positions he assumed were generally sympathetic to the cause of minorities. He was, in fact, often called upon as an intellectual resource by minority groups. It came then as a surprise when he described himself as not being a "progressive Jew." He explained that he thought of himself as an academician without ethnic identity.

He actually seemed to think that the degree of his Jewishness was a matter which *he* could decide. He was also blind to the fact that America considers a man Jewish or it does not, and anything the *individual* does is of no consequence.

*   *   *

Jews came to America at a time when millions of white men were roaring across a continent, piling up enormous wealth. Blacks by the millions were moving slowly away from the longest, most hideous slavery known to the modern world.

In a nation orbiting around these two great populations, Jews were positioned near the bottom of the white group. Viewed by the latter as distinctly inferior, they could feel a kinship with blacks who defied the nether social pole. But they were white and they tried to become even whiter.

We agree with the statement which began this chapter. Jews *should* be more Jewish. The most complete Jews have always been more compassionate; we could always recognize them; they have soul.

The black movement has had as its purpose a determination that blacks are to find their own destiny. To do so, America must change its way so that pathways to material and human rewards do not lie through aspiring to be white.

We have no intention of ever again being ashamed of how we are or of how our parents were. We will live in dignity, love with a great heart, and work, creating beauty and magnificence for all of mankind to enjoy.

Black Americans have begun by forging powerful instruments for social reform—civil dissent, protest, and demonstrations—American-style—black-style.

The new laws have benefited all Americans, and Jews have been among the beneficiaries. Barriers to Jews evaporated swiftly and silently before the black marchers. The Jewish problem could be settled immediately—"Let them in the schools, drop the quotas, surrender on the anti-Semitic front while we consolidate our forces for a major battle against the blacks."

Like it or not we are fighting for Jews to have accents, to be clannish, to summer in the Catskills and winter in Miami, and to love New York. We know that as we make room for *our* broader lives, Jews can more openly relish being Jewish.

If ever a Jewish woman sits in the highest councils of the nation, mark clearly it will be due directly to the strong fresh winds of the black movement.

For too many years we sat and dealt the cards with them and in all that time it was the only game in town.

IX.
Testified, Sanctified, and Saved

1ᶠᶠᶠ

Melba was a school teacher. At twenty-nine, she was dark-skinned, awkward, loose-jointed, with too long legs. She was plain, tearful, and self-conscious. Her fifth-graders made her laugh but rarely. For the most part she simply worked so hard that nothing made sense except the children and their occasional light of understanding.

She was born in a Southern town where her father and grandfather had been school principals and her mother an English teacher. Melba had been a comfortable only child, aimed for college.

The family went to church, but she never thought them "overly religious." If she thought about it at all, she accepted simply that all the people she knew intended to do the right thing. She lived a life of restraint and virtue and duty and that was that. At college she was rarely tested and remained chaste. There were no affairs, no serious loves.

After graduation she moved north, in part for the adventure and in part to be more than "Professor Ferguson's daughter." In her new city, there seemed no place for her; she was alone and isolated. She tried activities, clubs, sororities, but felt welcome nowhere and miserable everywhere.

Through it all her conscience guided her. She knew right from wrong and acted on it. What few men she met wanted only to take her to bed and she was determined to remain virginal. At a time when she was most lonely she met a salesman, who touched her in a special way. He was the first to talk of marriage and when he turned away she desperately gave herself to him. Following their only night together, she became pregnant.

When he learned of it he fled, and Melba never saw him again. The pregnancy and his abandonment left her stunned, depressed, and paralyzed with indecision. Each time she thought of a way out she turned a renewed attack on herself.

All the horrors of hell and her child's vision of sin came back to haunt her. Her conscience had become her enemy. She was promiscuous, a child-killer, a whore, unfit to teach innocent children, and a blight on her parents who had spent years working for her.

Melba came unhinged with endless obsessional thought. She acted more childlike and each day moved about more and more slowly, remembering only to telephone school to report her absence.

A neighbor brought the only food she was willing to eat. She slept most of the day and was tortured throughout the night with self-recrimination. One moment she reached to turn on the gas and in another she would have slashed her wrists. But she was too weak to carry through either gesture.

After two months of this she called a hospital aide whom she had once heard speak of abortions. The aide talked to her, but was suspicious and gave no help.

As she thought more about an abortion, her mind was haunted by sayings of her youth which spoke of pregnancy as "God's will" and abortion as a dreadful sin. She resolved to have the baby. But as she settled on this course, she saw herself as a slut who had "birthed a bastard" and *this* seemed the penultimate sin.

Her ideas were confused, but finally a day of persistent telephoning uncovered another abortionist—a woman who came and did the painful thing there in Melba's apartment—and who took the money and left.

The doctors later told her how close she had come to death, and she thought of her parents and wondered if they had been told—and if so, how *much* they had been told. A neighbor had found her unconscious and called for help; it seemed that the secret was safe.

Her brush with death made her more reflective. Convinced she had experienced the ultimate degradation, she had nothing to hide from a psychiatrist. Life had asked too much of her and she felt she had given too much. She dwelt on her imperfections. She had never lived up to her ambitions. Professionally, she admitted some success. She was a good teacher, but she had always dreamed of marriage, a home, children, and now all of this was impossible. No one wanted her. The abortion had ruined her and she was too foul to even teach the children of others.

In other sessions she berated herself. She spoke of her family and their disappointment that she had not been so fair as her mother. She had always been awkward and lacking in confidence. But her parents had been most concerned that she never "act like a nigger."

"Niggers did shameful things. They fucked like animals . . . lustful . . . uncontrolled . . . with casual partners . . . one-night stands. They got pregnant and had abortions or bastards . . ." and now she, God knows, had "acted like a nigger."

Each visit opened up another part of her life. Her overactive conscience and her own feeling of worthlessness were troublesome discoveries. She felt that there was nothing lovable about her. During her childhood, her parents showed little love and in so doing challenged her to do better and earn more. She never knew what more she could do to win their love. She was polite, respectful of her elders, avoided "trouble," and worked hard in school. And still she was made to feel she could do better.

It was in her adolescence that she first thought her parents' love was limited because she was black. The idea returned as she put her life together again after the abortion.

During one visit she spoke rapidly, lisping and mouthing her words in baby-talk. She tied it to a rebellious regression into messy infancy—something she had done often growing up. Her world demanded of blacks that they disguise aggression and hostility toward whites and that they appear nice, proper, highly controlled, virtuous super-humans. She had not always wanted to comply.

To survive, she denied strong feelings, and grew up convinced that any emotion was forbidden. Under great pressure, however, she on occasion had to express some feeling and it was then she became a baby, expressive, spontaneous, and irresponsible. During her only sexual experience, she had regressed this way. If losing control was bad, then losing control of sexual feelings was doubly so, and to protect herself she became an infant who had no control over the external world.

Melba had a great sense of duty. Rarely spontaneous, she was greatly concerned that she not neglect her obligations. She enjoyed teaching and in the classroom was relatively free and uninhibited. Most things she did seemed onerous, no doubt because she rarely did anything that was not felt to be obligatory. Her inhibition of feeling was strong and linked with an inhibition of curiosity. As a result she performed far below her superior intellectual capacity.

She was a hypochondriac and magnified every ache. Under stress, she developed physical symptoms grave enough to occupy her attention. She retired to her room, brooding, literally grieving over her physical condition —having successfully diverted herself from the real crisis and focused rather on inner suffering. She could remain in her room for days, lonely, sick, craving for someone's, anyone's, interest in her and her sufferings.

Overriding everything and reinforcing every inhibition was her unbending moral code. Even when she left the home and the hovering presence of her family, it persisted. Being good, virtuous, responsible, and controlled obsessed her and consumed her energy. At the most troubled time of her life, she was handicapped by what she had always considered virtues. When she needed a benign conscience most, it failed her.

She embraced white ideals and rejected blackness; she renounced herself and found herself worried about blacks and uncomfortable around them.

Once driving home, she saw a crowd of young blacks, raucous, loud, laughing, and later at home she vomited in reaction to the sight.

She was once enveloped by a crowd of demonstrating militants. She looked at their bushy hair and African dress and felt faint. Anything equatable with "low-class niggers"—emotional, demonstrative black people—any such thing caused her to recoil and turn away.

This extended to other parts of her life. Some of her students were from big families, whose mothers had never married, and this bothered her. She had visions of bearing children herself and having no husband and thereby being all the more black, dirty, and disheveled.

She thought her family had worked too hard for her to be just another "anonymous nigger."

And now, after three generations of respectability, she might have this baby, and having it would mean welfare and a grubby, marginal life.

Two classmates had dropped out of college, pregnant and abandoned, and were now barely getting by on public assistance. In such a reflective mood, she recognized for the first time the fragility of her family's station, and how easily everything might all crash.

She spoke of the suffering of blacks and of their justifiable anger—and finally her own anger appeared. The thought occurred of killing her ex-boyfriend—but she laughed at the strangeness of the idea of murder. Since early childhood she had heard of Saturday night cuttings and most of her life had wondered why black people seemed to hurt mainly blacks. She had never understood it—even now wanting to send her lover to his reward— she thought there were white men who deserved it more; it was all a puzzle.

Before the abortion, Melba had enrolled in night school and developed a friendship with Virginia, a white classmate. The young woman worked as a receptionist for a gynecologist and spoke openly of the affair they were having. He had performed an abortion on her some months earlier and she said laughingly that in the future she planned to go out only with doctors, it made things so much easier. With this in mind, Melba arranged to see the doctor without her friend's knowledge.

Standing by the examining table, a disapproving look on his face, he told Melba that she was pregnant and he could not do an abortion. He preached about professional ethics and, as a final touch, added that he would not do an abortion even if his own daughter had been raped and impregnated.

Melba might have been furious or cynical, but being Melba, she *defended* him. She thought him a good man with good intentions, and the hypocritical double standard on which he based his acts seemed to escape her entirely. She had a host of rationalizations with which to justify his pseudo-morality. He could perform an abortion on his receptionist, piously explain his refusal to even consider Melba's condition, and yet she exempted him from criticism. All her troubles stemmed from her own shortcomings, not from the defects of others.

Her feelings were frozen but her thoughts moved from the consultation room back to the black militants. They talked ferociously about "the Man" and "protecting black women." The thought had never occurred to her that black women needed protection, but maybe they did. Maybe this was why her mother had been determined that she avoid certain sections of town and teachers always made a special effort to praise her for being such a *nice* girl. Now she felt she had heard only half the story.

If the doctor saved his protection for her white classmate, maybe *only* the black militants would protect her. All her life she had avoided everything which even appeared improper and now she thought of needing the protection of an obscene, disreputable band, and of her own obscenity and disrepute.

In her life who had protected her? The family had partially shielded her, but their protection seemed designed for a world much different from the one in which she lived. At home and in college, the world was small and predictable and she was prepared for it. As a teacher she kept her world small and was, for a time, successful. She had rarely ventured beyond self-imposed boundaries, but the abortion had changed everything and had thrust her into a world for which she had no preparation.

She had known few white people save an occasional Virginia. Her activities placed her close to whites, but there was rarely open, free exchange. She had been to cocktail parties where she was the only Negro, but those were not occasions for intimacy. She had dated white men, but there was rarely a second date. Her parents and, in fact, the small society from which she came held to the strict requirement that she please grownups.

Melba was now surrounded by people from whom she was alienated and her inner self had become her worst enemy.

Isolated, America had denied her the ordinary social defenses, and of all Americans she was most needful of protection. With this thought a fundamental change began and for the first time in twenty-nine years she began to examine herself and her origins. She read everything obtainable about black people and soon saw things in a clearer light. Daily she felt herself more free and sought ways to express this new freedom.

She was drawn to the militants who originally had aroused in her such antipathetic feelings. While she never became an admirer of their harsh rhetoric and could never bring herself to adopt an Afro hair style, she felt important inner changes. She became first an apologist for them and later searched the mood and thought of the militants for those things she could support.

She felt them to be a vital part of herself which she must accept; they were her black despised part and her interest in them was a significant sign of health.

And in a quiet gathering together of her resources she forgave her parents for loving her less because she was less white.

She forgave herself for being foolish enough to try to earn their love.

She forgave herself for reaching for love and she forgave a man for responding.

She forgave the doctor and her friend and the countless people who had withheld themselves from her when she needed them.

There was no changing the past but she could now forgive, knowing that no one felt more hate for her than she felt for herself. And who could assign blame for something so deep and personal and bitter as Melba's hatred for Melba.

2✓✓✓

In January, 1968, Reverend Larry Potts, a white Baptist minister of Cairo, Illinois, battered a seventy-two-year-old black gardener to death with a baseball bat. Potts said he caught the gardener raping his wife. The state's attorney promptly ruled the killing justifiable homicide, and Potts returned to his pulpit.

At the 16th Street Baptist Church in Birmingham, Alabama, in September, 1963, three little black girls were blown to bits while attending Sunday School. Their killers were never found.

Memphis, Tennessee, has 575 churches, which, like Birmingham, comes to more than one church per thousand citizens. It was in Memphis that Martin Luther King, Jr., ended his long, glorious march to martyrdom. One must think that the silent white churchmen of Memphis knew not who had been among them nor what they had lost when he was killed.

In Cairo, blacks' anger rose with the acquittal of Reverend Potts and against the white vigilantes who sprang up to support him. These night-riders wore white plastic construction "hard hats" and came to be known as "white hats."

Much of the conflict in Cairo crystallized around their activities—these violent men who described themselves as defenders of the white community and who terrorized blacks.

The imprint of the Ku Klux Klan on the "white hats" was clearly recognizable. And although "responsible" white observers prefer to minimize its influence, blacks know that the KKK and its local offspring reflect the white community's final line of defense. They know how desperate and determined this group can be and how easily they find protection in clean, all-American cities, north and south.

Cairo, Birmingham, and Memphis all are cities which have felt the strong influence of the Klan and cities in which the citizenry has either actively supported it or averted its eyes, to be occupied with other business.

The Klan reached its peak of 6 million members in 1924. There were 60 million Americans of voting age at that time.

Twenty million were either black, Jewish, or Catholic, and one-half of the remaining 40 million were women. Since the Klan accepted only white, Protestant, Anglo-Saxon males, it would appear that one out of every three or four such men embraced the principles of the Klan vigorously enough to pay the ten-dollar initiation fee and sign or "X" the dotted line.

There were surely at least as many sympathizers as "card-carrying" KKK's and it is the progeny of this bestiary of the twenties with which we now contend as the "white backlash." It is not surprising that they and their new-found converts comprise a sizable fraction of American voters.

Up to the advent of Martin Luther King, Jr., the often violent white churchman has been matched by a passive, law-abiding, black co-religionist. At best, white preachers have ignored the psychic and physical murder of their black Christian brothers; at worst, fundamentalist churches have been the seed of virulent race hatred, infecting the community with the notion that all would be right with the world if "the niggers were kept in their place."

Black religionists on the other hand have been meek, forgiving, non-violent, law-abiding, and willing to wait through unspeakable misery on earth for a reward in heaven. In our defense, it must be said that many parts of our fair land have harbored white hatred of such an intensity that the meek, accepting posture has been the only one a prudent black man might adopt had he hopes of staying alive.

As organized American religion oscillates between silence and ineffective murmuration on the vital social matters of our time, it is a puzzlement that troubled whites find anything at all helpful in their church.

And, aside from the spiritual sunburst of Selma, it defies reason that black men can find in religion a living institution to which they may bind themselves and from which they gain strength to guard the precious things of life.

Martin Luther King, Jr., found his white brethren of the cloth too confused to know right from wrong and, when instructed in the right, too frightened to act on its behalf.

It seems that here the black revolution has exposed another rotting beam in the nation's house. Religion has done little to proclaim injustice where it flourishes and less to combat it.

When black leadership begins with a preacher, spreads to other preachers, and is for years borne on the shoulders of black preachers, these events suggest that black heroes march to the beat of a different drum, for who would believe that Christianity inspires only black men. Their dedication to righteousness must have another base.

The words of the Bible may be the same, but blacks have given it new meaning and even those who turn away from the church altogether share a morality which is by now more *black* than religious.

A deeply religious black mother voiced *her* concern.

*   *   *

Rodney's got a gun and he joined this group. All of them have guns. They say they want to defend us against the police. He goes to meetings and I never know where he is.

I wish you could talk to him, doctor. I have almost stopped praying . . . I don't know what to pray for. I don't want Rodney to kill nobody . . . but the police shot and killed a boy the other day and he was only 14 years old. . . . They said he stole a car and ran away when they told him to stop.

The police kill somebody every few days or so . . . for no reason at all.

I can't blame Rodney for wanting to protect himself. I don't want him to get killed . . . and I don't want him to kill nobody.

It don't seem enough just to pray for the right anymore . . . because I know it isn't right for anything to happen to Rodney. But it's like if I pray for the right thing, God's will, I'm praying against Rodney, and if I pray for Rodney, I'm praying against God's will.

I've stopped praying and stopped going to church. Maybe after a while I'll go back. Right now I just don't know what to do.

*   *   *

At the outset, religion defined right and wrong—it embodied a set of moral imperatives rooted in Southern fundamentalist tradition. It was and is a basic element of black culture and life-style and is a heavy contributor to the essence of black life. But its origins were in slavery and its first purpose was psychological bondage.

Now we face a dilemma. Religion, of such deep emotional importance and sustenance to so many blacks for hundreds of years, is now seen by more and more of us as hypocritical and capable of only the feeblest moral leadership, and even that, in its own interest and on its own terms. The psychological consequences of such a shift are extreme and profound. A massive ethical upheaval is in progress. It will provide fuel to either cleanse the nation or reduce it to rubble.

3✓✓

The derivatives of religion permeate black life, touching every act and defining the "Christian" response. The network of derivatives form a matrix, an ethic which is bought whole and undivided by the faithful.

When you "get religion" you get an attitude toward dancing (generally don't dance); you get an attitude toward George Wallace (he is not for us to punish, God will take care of him);

you get an attitude toward eating (gluttony is a sin); you get an attitude toward the space race (men ought to be as occupied with the salvation of their souls as they are with landing on the moon); and a limitless set of like commandments.

The black religionist, like many other pious men, is careful, and suspicious of too much pleasure. He distrusts good feelings outside of church and urges an anhedonic posture on others of the faith.

Like co-religionists elsewhere, he feels an abiding distrust of new things. If they save time, he challenges the need for speed; if they save labor, he extols the virtue of hard work; and, when all else fails, he retreats to the innate goodness of old things.

On social matters he appears to be strongly conservative and as distrustful of innovations here as anywhere else in his life. But the similarities end here. He is, for example, determined that his children will have a better life than he had and *prays* for a revolutionary social reform in America.

Pious black folk are urged to yield to God's will. Men everywhere have found that, for religion to be an effective pacifying instrument, it must include such teaching. Piety becomes tightly bound to passivity and an additional teaching becomes inevitable:

"Render unto Caesar that which is Caesar's and to God that which is God's."

Circumstances in other parts of the world have no doubt at times required soothing religious tones to keep the peasantry in harness, and the Christian teachings have probably survived because they have been helpful to rulers when the mood of the serfs turned ugly.

We submit, however, that it would be difficult to find any

modern people who should be more suspicious of the above passage than blacks. It has meant for us, "Give the white man whatever he *says* he wants." And, in America, when theft of labor and goods hangs so darkly between the races, it takes a special kind of misguided piety for a black man to yield to God's will, when that means a surrender to the white man.

The faithful are further urged not to set store in worldly goods, and, in fact, the lusting after material things is considered a major sin.

They are urged to confine their ambition to affairs of the soul and forget earthly power and position.

The words are portentous:

> "It is as difficult for a rich man to enter the kingdom of heaven as for a camel to pass through the eye of a needle."

This is a particularly interesting pillar of belief, since it is in some form shared by most other sects and seems not to inhibit any of *their* members from gathering as much money and power as luck and a strong right arm will allow.

It could be argued that black religionists are the only Americans who take this Biblical admonition seriously, but such would be facetious. The fact is that white people *keep* blacks "pious" on this score. If a black man does pile up wealth through some miscalculation of his white neighbors, they are quick to relieve him of it, thus making it easier for him to commune with God with clean and empty hands.

Traditionally, religion's strongest censure has been against violence. Black Americans hear more than their share of such abjurations in religious teachings.

They are urged to relinquish hostility and to place their faith in God. The urging is strong but admits openly that blacks have much to be enraged about. It goes no further than such an admission however, since,

"Vengeance is mine, sayeth the Lord."

Obviously one would be better off occupied with personal salvation than trying to bring justice to a neighbor whom the Lord has on His list anyway.

Adherence to such teaching requires great faith for black men, considering that any examination of history shows that bastards, far from being punished, seem to flourish.

The teachings further urge believers to view all rewards and punishments as flowing from God. Thus, on the occasion of good or bad fortune, the cause lies directly with God and is the outcome of some issue between the individual and God.

If there is a human intermediary involved, he is ignored in favor of the more important dialogue with the Originator of the deed.

Such a position has had great psychological import for blacks. It has allowed them to deal with impossible situations and maintain some spiritual equanimity. A cruel attack by a Southern sheriff on a black family, once it had passed, could be thought of as simply a puzzling example of God's will.

The theft of patrimonial lands by dishonest local officials could be afterward thought of as "God working in mysterious ways."

Similarly, assigning good fortune and wise decisions to God made it unlikely that the successful but vulnerable black man need ever be accused of hubris and subjected to the jealous attacks of white neighbors.

We are defining those ways in which the black man's religious life inhibits and compromises his relationship with the wider world.

*   *   *

A black preacher, talented and well-trained, felt his career was heading nowhere. He doubted the depth of his own belief—he doubted that his natural impulses reflected faith and holiness—he doubted that his preaching reflected the piety it ought to reflect.

Inhibited and paralyzed by such doubt he could only conclude that personal deficiencies lay at the root of his troubles. He could not see that his white colleagues blocked his promotions.

*   *   *

His religious life imposes a humble posture on him and discourages ambition or even rightful aggression. It insists that *God* makes life miserable, not his neighbors, and that he *never helps himself,* but is only the recipient of God's bounty.

It provides, in other words, a religious rationale for a circumscribed life which has been imposed on him by fellow Americans, not by God. And he remains in his small space *because the white man will not let him out;* it has nothing to do with modesty or meekness, however much he is told that such attitudes will make him heir to the earth.

4↗↗

Religion was originally imposed from without for the purpose of keeping the slave enslaved and to safeguard the property of the master.

First, it had to be set down that conversion did not involve a risk to the slaveholder or the possible loss of his property. By 1706, six of the colonies had passed laws perpetuating slavehood even though the slave had been converted to Christianity.

Thus, as tobacco became an important export in 1700, and the need for field labor jumped, the instrument of slavery was ready with the bodies. For the next hundred years, slaveowners considered the religious conversion of slaves to be a danger to their tranquil containment.

By the end of the eighteenth century, cotton had become the favored cash crop in the South. And with the invention of the cotton gin and the resulting ease of harvesting, slaves were in greater demand than ever.

Great numbers of slaves made the maintenance of physical control a primary concern of slaveholders. Torture and carefully dosed cruelty were dependable as controls and posed a problem only when the necessity of too many guards made it uneconomical. Obviously, anything which reduced the manpower required to manage slaves was welcomed by the planters. They therefore reexamined the matter of religion as *slaveholders* with specific management problems.

There were lengthy discussions on the proper content of religious instruction and how it should be offered. Most agreed that slaves should not share the same religious instruction as whites. This would encourage a feeling of egalitarianism by placing blacks on an equal footing and make it impossible to censor what they heard.

Some considered a special sermon by the white minister to the slaves. But this was time-consuming and troublesome and in no way relieved the concern of the owners regarding what the blacks might be taught.

It settled finally on two possibilities; either the owner or his overseer delivered the sermon, or, if this were not possible, one slave was chosen and given the task of preaching.

As regards content, slaveowners had always been careful to select those passages in the Bible which emphasized a servant's duty and which criticized rebellious bondsmen, but their uneasiness was put to rest when bowdlerized slave Bibles were published. In these editions, all passages which might stimulate rebels were removed. Only "safe" material was left.

By 1830, the economic and social structure of the South was completely dependent on the slave system and the religionists were quick to develop a pro-slavery philosophy which justified their profits.

The importation of slaves was made illegal in 1808, but a high birth rate and illegal slave-trading swelled the black population to 2½ million by 1830. In Southern states, blacks were everywhere and whites were terrified.

In this climate of white terror and reaction, the religion of frontier America, the emotional and highly personalized liturgy of the evangelical sects, found its greatest use not as a body of theological thought, but as a psychological straitjacket designed to harness black yearnings for freedom.

When, finally, slavemasters observed that their best, most controlled slaves were religious, religion for slaves became a necessity. It had become an *undisguised* instrument for their control.

The white man had no way to predict how deadly this religious device was to be. It came to exert a profound inner control. It gave justification to the hard work slaves otherwise had reason to avoid. It encouraged honesty and caused the slave to expose deficiencies in himself and made his previously helpful pseudo-stupidity more difficult to accommodate. It elevated theft to one of life's greatest sins.

The slavemaster had found his means of control. Not even the bloody slave revolt in 1831 led by Bible-reading Nat Turner could change the use to which religion was now put.

The slave had been converted to a religion of death-row— while comforting the condemned it did nothing to smash his chains.

*   *   *

A poor, sick man, slightly beyond his prime, was struggling to make ends meet for his family on $170 per month. The ailments of his wife and children together with his own chronic illness made for massive medical bills.

He and his family were ill-housed, ill-fed and ill-clothed. Against all reality, being a pious man, he prayed for relief and, believing deeply in sin, blamed himself and his sinful ways for his plight.

*   *   *

The moral slave worked hard, accepting his lot in life as ordained by God. Sex existed, not for pleasure, but to create more slaves for the use of the master. He was instructed to cultivate personal virtues and to ignore completely the oppressive environment. The slave was to build moral credits to be cashed in heaven but not on earth.

Ambition made a poor slave, so religion required that he bridle ambition. Learning made him more rebellious, so the new religion made learning a dangerous thing.

Where effective, it converted blacks to perfect slaves and destroyed their determination to survive. In its demand for honesty, it opened their innermost thoughts to the master, and, preaching as it did against violence, it bound their hands from being lifted in rebellion. It even provided a motivation in the after-life for slaves to work themselves to death in this one. What better way to ensure passive and compliant slaves than by this use of religion?

Christianity in the hand of the slaveowner held a potentiality for wickedness that is terrifying, and one is awed by its perfection for evil purposes.

In hard cold truth it was against this perfect instrument that blacks were required to wage a successful struggle for survival or else abandon their hopes once and forever.

X.

The Jesus Bag

1*✓✓✓*

America is a powerful nation, with a sophisticated technology, gigantic corporations, and staggering wealth.

Standing thus at the height of its powers, its details etched clear, it is on public view. That vicious strain of racial hatred which might have been excused in a rapidly growing youth looks ugly and ominous in the mature giant.

America has come to the place of Rome in the fourth century—arrogant, vulnerable, and possibly on the verge of a mulish, obstinate death.

Like Rome, America has had a failure of leadership as the gap has widened between haves and have-nots. Then, as now, there was endless war and a corrupt bureaucracy. Terrorism and repression reached excesses previously unknown.

Neither the rulers of Imperial Rome nor the dominant figures in contemporary America ever learned that ethical responsibility accompanies political power.

In the end, the Roman Empire became a military aristocracy which spoke and acted independently of the people and which thrust aside the ancient ideals.

The autocratic military moved toward tyranny when during the massive urban riots of the third and fourth centuries the army chose to protect the Empire *against the people, at any cost.*

The Romans looked to the aristocracy for answers which in truth lay with the peasants. Nowadays, as America does likewise, who can deny that it has at hand a *black method* of survival. This proud land now must find a rejuvenating experience to escape the fate of Rome and make a new life. To do less is to ensure disaster.

We submit that if America is to discover that new experience, it must look to those who have survived its cruelty and must learn from them. The black capacity for converting weakness into strength needed for survival is nowhere more evident than in religion. It was thrust upon us to make us docile and it focused on the life hereafter. It gave little spiritual sustenance for life on earth and it left an unyielding conscience which is yet a barrier containing our rage.

For blacks, the misery of life was too much and they reached into the religious experience to extract a black mystique—"soul."

Soul is the toughness born of hard times and the compassion oppressed people develop after centuries of sharing a loaf that is never enough. It is a special brotherhood of those set apart from their fellows, made visible by physical appearance, and different customs. Soul is the *graceful* survival under impossible circumstances.

From the beginning, there were some black converts who found support in the Bible for their unwavering hatred of American oppression. They became our earliest agitators for radical social reform.

Religion made most blacks patient, but this patience wore thin under the grossness of their mistreatment. For most of our history in America, the churches counseled reliance on the law and on the good intention of whites and only recently have many churches supported organized protest. At last, blacks have psychologically untangled themselves from whites religiously and found a flowering of racial pride and a growth of black identity.

Religion lost its hold on some of us and the rage-binding conscience was no longer effective. In a fury, we burst into the streets. We had survived the oppression and we now have survived the riots. Where we once were ashamed of the scars we now see them as badges of honor. We looked into ourselves and, even more, looked deep into white America. *Our* flaws, which we were taught to hide in shame, were in fact the flaws of this nation. The hatred we had of ourselves was minor placed alongside whites' hatred of us. Where once we saw ourselves as deformed and debased, we now see how much more deformed and debased is the white bigotry which has so hurt us.

Black people who all that time had tried futilely to turn themselves inside out have now opened the festering wound of America and see that it is *America* which has most need of healing.

2↗↗↗

The lot of black Americans has been undeniably harsh, but we have survived.

From slavery on, for example, passivity was forced on us

and we came to use it as a protective shield. We hid passively, in full view, and lulled the white man into thinking we were harmless enough to be allowed to live. In time, we knew more about him than he knew about us.

This same passivity, while it eats at a man's insides, has checked our rage and kept us from an open battle which we could not win.

With the odds being what they are, if we have not prevailed, the miracle is that we have endured. Friends and critics, and at times they have been the same, have seen what they wanted to see in black families and in their myopia have overlooked the simple fact that the black family has sustained us.

To those who attribute the miseries of blacks to a "weak family structure," or those who chauvinistically applaud our every act, wise or foolish, we commend our experience. It is the experience of ordinary, undistinguished blacks who daily gather their resources, and go to do battle with America. Whatever the failure of their families, it is of no consequence when set beside the failures of the nation, now modern, urban, still squandering resources, crushing people, and polluting the earth.

Blacks have seen good men rise from mediocre families. They have also seen great men come from shattered homes. They have seen Malcolm X risen to world statesmanship from the filth that America offers blacks. We are not sure whites have much to teach us on *further* strengthening the black family.

That family as a matter of fact has played an important part in producing a revolutionary black churchman. Blacks, having used religion, but most particularly having used *religionists* as instruments of survival, invite white America to consider our solution. They must look not to Reverend Larry Potts but to Martin Luther King, Jr.

What was the nature of King, in whom were joined such great powers of intellect and persuasion? What meanings can we draw from his life and from his impact on his times?

Is he to be defined as a great preacher who pushed his calling to its grandest limits? Or should he be seen as a man who transcended the religious medium and invested ordinary struggles with grandeur and timelessness?

There are those of us who are convinced that the grand march of blacks has deserved better than traditional religion has offered. But none can obscure the massive investment of black genius in that pedestrian ritual.

King exemplifies the fury of a dedicated life which galvanizes all that it touches. From our psychological vantage point we are awed by the intensity and overpowering passion of his commitment.

We have spoken elsewhere of the hallmark of genius—the capacity to focus great intellectual powers on a single problem for a great period of time. King had this capacity and more. He was able to mount an impassioned, crusading, olympian zeal, pinpoint-focused on the cause, and maintain it at the peak until the cause was won.

Further, his was the genius of the shared emotional experience. He was unique in the completeness of his commitment. Let us not in our time be guilty of weighing our gifts before we commit them. We all have more to give than we think.

We have further conclusions regarding the importance of King's life. He lived in a manner which illustrates certain hard psychological truths.

From the moment he came on stage, King's was the classic struggle of the American black man. From the beginning, he was condemned to death—death at the hands of the meanest, most capricious of men. And he knew that nothing he did could block, nor speed, nor slow the killer's hand. There was, in fact, nothing he could do. Had he retired from public view immediately after the Montgomery bus boycott he was still marked for death. He knew that a killer waited and that he, King, could invoke no protective forces in his own behalf.

It was his nobility in the face of death that caught the imagination of black men. King lived out publicly the private hell of black America. It has been our fate to be hounded by the predator and to stand ever in jeopardy of our lives with no shield to protect and no sword to strike back.

The unbelievable reality has been for us the most dangerous of lives, the most unpredictable of worlds drawn in the heavy lines of "apparently" ordered Western determinism. Ours is a world where all things *ought to be* orderly and predictable but where social organization *seeks* to protect only white people against untoward malignity. Closing their eyes to the system they are truly *convinced* that their actions determine their future.

Social structures are so built as to wage war on blacks and to impress all with the unpredictable deadliness of life. Blacks must learn to live with the immediate prospect of death, to face death every day. There is no rhyme or reason to the danger save that they are black. The danger has no relation to their goodness or wickedness. It has nothing to do with their adoption of either the sense or the letter of the law. And this fact is not accepted by whites as reality. Whites would have a black believe that his life experience is no different from theirs—that he faces no special dangers.

But black life *is* dangerous and unpredictable and the black must adapt himself to that fact. He must do as all men do— pretend that life is orderly and meaningful and at the same time respond to its disorder and its meaninglessness.

It is not that blacks are concerned only with the realities of today. It is rather that the white world has deliberately made tomorrow so chancy and unreliable a thing that reasonable men can occupy themselves only with today. If one is black, to be "present-day oriented" is to be *reality-oriented*.

Walking always in the shadow of death, a black man finds that when he conquers that fear he has conquered much more. He observes that white people have preferred to see blacks as easily frightened. They laughed as they fantasied blacks, bug-eyed, running through cemeteries, turning white, terrified of ghosts.

Whites are *supposed* to frighten blacks and blacks are *supposed* to be easily frightened. That is how it is *still* supposed to be.

But we rise now unafraid, with a new morality, a new religion, willing to die for principles we hold dearer than life. We have suffered hideous mistreatment and are determined that neither we nor anyone else is to suffer anything like it in America ever again.

The serenity of our confidence grows out of two elements. We are weaponed finally with fearlessness and we know there is no deadlier foe than that man without fear of suffering or death.

Those who were once the lowliest are now noblest and say that, for America to fulfill a sanguine expectation of democracy, it must travel the path of the oppressed and frame for itself a new definition.

3

We blacks remain ever crucial to all definitions of America. We have been thrust to the bottom and others assume a position at greater or less distance from us, but always "above" us. For white America, only one element is necessary for the social situation to be termed essentially stable—the inferiority of blacks. For blacks, only one thing is certain—that their social and economic and political oppression must cease. And this is the essential confrontation and struggle of America today. This is the entrenched custom which requires radical change but which is so central to all other social functioning that there is no fixed point in the system free of its influence.

This nation has never supported an important group of radical leftists, primarily because the struggle has never been of the European peasant versus aristocracy, or laborer versus landowner.

It began and remains a slave versus master society. For a model we should look beyond the struggle of darker peoples to throw off colonial domination. America, in its white-black relations, has never progressed to so modern a style. We would do better to look back to Spartacus and ancient Rome, to an oppressed people who had no alternative.

"Liberty or death!" might better have been the cry of modern blacks and Roman slaves than the slogan of American revolutionaries. It is a bestial system of cruelty out of antiquity that blacks are determined to reform, and we seek the aid of every true patriot.

Our white fellow citizens must learn that the hatred of injustice unites all blacks. We have no Uncle Toms, only those of us who have been tortured beyond our capacity. The fact is that there are millions of white men who are more deadly enemies than the most malignant Tom. If we are serious about priorities, we at least ought to confront a brace of Southern governors and Northern police chiefs before we turn on some wretched black casualty of the racial wars who is now so confused that he does not know to which side he belongs. He has become a true black racist—one who is convinced of the inherent superiority of the white man!

From a psychological point of view, the Tom is a casualty. He who began with the spirit, the courage, the ideals, indeed the nobility that we all share—born with this, he has had it crushed within his living body. We must conclude that those who vilify him cannot see him as one of our own, wounded, to be cared for.

We are drawing closer together; our casualties do not typify us. We are essentially a people of love and dignity—unified on the matter of this nation's mistreatment—unified in a determination to rid this land of bigotry and hateful, murderous, race-determined criminality.

*   *   *

A sainted grandmother, gentle, long-suffering, ambitious for her children, considerate of strangers, compassionate toward neighbors, had a stock response when told of an accident.

"Anybody hurt?"

"Yes, a (man, woman, child)."

"White or colored?"

If the answer was "white," she continued her sewing, missing not a stitch, idly closing the conversation with, "Oh."

If the answer was "colored" (we are not antiquarians; this antedated the general use of "black"; she now corrects anyone caught using any word other than black), she would spring to her feet and race to the side of the wounded, bearing liniment, iodine, and bandages.

*   *   *

No one knew anybody black whose sole concerns were piety and the hereafter. Even the sweetest old lady had enough real dangers, crises, humiliations, and hairbreadths— all at the hands of white folks—to take her mind off heaven occasionally, and to cause her to hate white folks, and wish them dead.

But, in spite of the mistreatment and the resulting hatred, blacks continue to show more love for fellow humans than white Americans can muster.

4↗↗↗

The new America must remove the onus from the slave and the privileges from the slaveowner. History's greatest black bank robber is a piker compared to his white counterpart. A white bank president may embezzle millions and, when his face smiles from the morning newspaper, show a security born of the knowledge that prison can be avoided and with luck he may even get rehired at the bank. A black adolescent caught stealing from a parking meter can be equally certain that he will go to jail and that the record will never be expunged.

Compare two men, similar in many ways, but different in one important way.

*   *   *

Mr. B. was a black banker, highly regarded and active in civic and charitable causes. He participated in politics and he might have expected to have friends in high places. He was involved in a minor scandal related to a real estate transaction. Most of his colleagues of whatever color agreed that what he did was by no means uncommon and that men were rarely jailed for it. But B. was caught, and, after embarrassing publicity and trial in court, was sentenced to a jail term. He was removed from all seats of influence and status, and, when he returned to his community, he was consigned to live out his life a symbol of crime discovered and punished. He cannot work in any of the businesses he helped to found and build, and is welcomed by few of his friends.

*   *   *

Mr. L., a white banker, was also widely known in his home town. At one time he held an important political office, and most of his constituents would say he did a good job. He became a high bank official and seemed to enjoy being in the public eye. When he was accused of bribing a federal official, he fielded questions with aplomb. Sometime later he was embroiled in a messy divorce suit that was reported deliciously by the press. Following the divorce he was involved in another matter which received even wider coverage. In a rather conventional community, he and his new mistress were arrested for possession of narcotics. But the charges were dismissed, the judge berated the arresting officers, and, when last seen, L. was still enjoying his high bank position.

*   *   *

These two cases are not intended to wish anyone ill. The white banker may well have been innocent of all charges. But that is beside the point. To attribute the difference in the treatment of the two to guilt or innocence, good lawyers, or just plain good luck is to misperceive the essence of America. To be black is to be allowed only one turn at bat. Any error, small or large, is enough to be tossed out of the game. To be caught in a transgression of whatever importance is to step into that bottomless pit America reserves for less favored citizens.

The solution to all of this must be preceded by actions which make a solution possible—dynamics which could now be at work and which could play a crucial role in that solution. America has always rushed into meretricious solutions, preferring the excitement of ecological politics to the humane task of relieving human hunger.

The dynamics and the solution they might produce in a future America require the statement of certain assumptions.

We assume that America will continue essentially on its present course. It will find its inner affairs ever more complex, requiring greater controls. And this we assume will continue to be called "free" enterprise. "Rugged individualism" will be praised even as giant corporations become the sole means by which individuals transact business with one another.

We assume that America will continue its disastrous foreign adventures and that these will either verge on war or explode into open and protracted conflict.

We further assume that the country will be blessed with a small number of brilliant private citizens and public administrators who by force of will and genius make an unworkable bureaucracy work.

We assume that technological advances will continue, making us capable of doing more and more of the impossible and widening the "wisdom gap" whereby we have not the sense to ask for the bountiful gifts of which our hands are capable.

And we can safely assume that in all other ways public affairs will grow further in complexity beyond any man's control as those of us survivors who have not been slain gradually suffocate in an environment made unfit for life.

It is for an America of this kind that we propose a solution —a solution which comes of the black experience and which is a healing *black morality,* psychologically profound and true.

We have said that the black religious experience grew out of the imposition of a bastardized Christianity by slave masters, the environment in which slaves and subsequently freed men lived, and the creative use black people put it to. The brotherhood, the generosity, the sensory and sensual involvement with life, the humility before life, and the grand courage in its defense—America has need of these.

We do not propose a nationwide "mock soul-fest." We suggest rather that America turn in a direction of a *new ethic*. Such a direction is the only way left for a nation so powerful it cannot be subjected to external control and so at war with itself that it cannot yield to intellect.

If the nation looks for a way of life that is keyed to survival it will find the *black morality*. This has guided our lives, given us strength, and sustained a moral stance for blacks when the world around was immoral.

Unlike the morality of "white killers" who give only enough to slow down starvation, the black morality is generous, full-bosomed, and bountiful. It has played an important role as we developed a reverence for life and a capacity for waiting on life's unfolding. We have come to respect each man's encounter with the world and to stand by, neither passive nor fatalistically helpless, but reverently, watching a holy thing.

We love the land which tries each man, which stands like the great brooding eternal protagonist, testing each, trying him, and determining his worth. We could not befoul this earth, the place where men are made. We would be careful husbanders of the air and the waters and the land.

We are the few Americans who truly believe in democracy—which means (and we tremble to say it) that even now we would want to trust our fellow Americans and would be willing, given some sign, to be guarded by their consciences. That seems incredible but it is true. Black America still devotes itself to democracy, to equality, to equal representation and equal protection. It is an astonishing thing when most other Americans seem so distrustful of the system. Others are eager to tamper with the mechanism, making it yield a larger pay-off. It is no doubt dangerous for us to trust people who do not trust us, but, dangerous or not, that is how it is.

We truly believe that all men are brothers and that we all here bear a responsibility for one another. Lacking the unfortunate conviction white people have of innate superiority, we could not possibly have made the blunders with other peoples that white America has made. This nation has wretched relations with the people of Africa, Asia, South America, in fact with all the world save those few areas populated by whites. And even there all is not calm.

How can there be any doubt that the white man's contempt for his darker brother lies at the bottom of this tragic situation?

We will share our bread with a neighbor and we will not kill him to take that which is his. The now deeply ingrained feeling of brotherhood and love is a permanent thing available to be seeded throughout the society. These are the moral riches which reside in black America.

We see black morality as a style of living developed under pressure. It is a highly beneficial structure and we are convinced that it has much less to do with Christianity than Christians think. It is rather the creative response of a tortured, driven people. Indeed the genius would seem to be the grafting of such a high order of humanity onto a religious structure heretofore characterized more by warfare and simony than saintliness.

So we look past the oppression and the religion to what blacks have made of their lot. And we find a body of ethical standards which are desperately needed.

But, let it be clear, any thoughtful observer must gravely

mistrust religion. It has been used to doubly enslave blacks and at best has raised only a feeble hand in their defense. Moreover it is not lost on us that some of the most ferocious bigots are scrupulous churchgoers and manage to make their hatred of blacks an expression of religious zeal.

So we speak of people, not religion, and we speak of their capacity for greatness.

There have been, no doubt, heroes who died never having seen the dragon. Heroism is surely as much a function of chance as it is of courage.

The enemy must be big enough to set the stage for greatness. Great issues must hang in the balance. Brave men must have fallen in full cry. The fate of generations must rest on the outcome.

On such a stage a million anonymous black men have stepped. They have survived an attack aimed at their lives with guns and at their secret selves with the weapon of religion. They have refined and built a morality on that which had been their greatest danger. And they stand now the most moral of Americans, the most humane of Americans, the most democratic of Americans, and surely the most courageous of Americans.

They have taken a Jesus Bag shaped like a noose and refashioned it into a black cornucopia of spiritual riches.

They are determined to reform the nation and if need be, the world.

It all hangs in the balance.

It all depends on them.

Appendix

I. Hypertension and Blacks

II. General Bibliography

I.

Hypertension and Blacks

This bibliography is drawn largely from the work of Dr. Jan Howard of the University of California Medical Center at San Francisco. It covers the results of research on the relationship between hypertension (high blood pressure) and race, undertaken primarily during the last decade and published in English-language journals.

Abrahams, D. G., and Alele, C. A. "A Clinical Study of Hypertensive Disease in West Africa," *W Afr Med J,* IX (October, 1960), 183–93.

Abrahams, D. G., Alele, C. A., and Barnard, B. G. "The Systemic Blood Pressure in a Rural West African Community," *W Afr Med J,* IX (April, 1960), 45–58.

Abrahams, D., and Brigden, W. "Syndrome of Mitral Incompetence, Myocarditis, and Pulmonary Hypertension in Nigeria," *Brit Med J,* II (July 15, 1961), 134–39.

Abramson, J. H., *et al.* "Observations on the Epidemiology of Hypertension in an Urban Zulu Community," in preparation. Cited in

Scotch, N. A. "A Preliminary Report on the Relation of Socio-cultural Factors to Hypertension Among the Zulu," *Ann NY Acad Sci,* LXXXIV, Art. 17 (December 8, 1960), 1000–09.

Acheson, R. M. "Mortality from Cerebrovascular Accidents and Hypertension in the Republic of Ireland," *Brit J Prev Soc Med,* XIV (July, 1960), 139–47.

Achor, R. W. P., Hanson, N. O., and Gifford, R. W. Jr. "Hypertension Treated with Rauwolfia Serpentina (Whole Root) and with Reserpine: Controlled Study Disclosing Occasional Severe Depression," *JAMA,CLIX* (October 29, 1955), 841–45.

Ackerman, J. L., and Lee, A. J. "Hypertension in Young Negro Males," *Industr Med Surg,* XX (October, 1951), 463–64.

Adkins, G. H., Fahr, G., and Bernstein, I. C. "Hypertensive Encephalopathy Versus Schizophrenia," *Minnesota Med,* XXXVIII (September, 1955), 636.

Alimurung, M. M., *et al.* "Heart Disease in the Philippines; Seven-Year (1947–1953) Postwar Survey of Four Manila General Hospitals," *Amer Heart J,* L (August, 1955), 293–302.

Altman, H., and Wayburne, S. "Hypertensive Cardiac Failure Due to an Aberrant Renal Artery: Report of a Case in an African Child," *S Afr Med J,* XXX (September 15, 1956), 896–98.

Altschule, Mark D. "Emotion and the Circulation," in Blumgart, H. L. (ed.) *Clinical Progress in Cardiovascular Disease.* New York: Grune and Stratton, 1952, 118–36.

Altschule, M. D., and Shah, M. H. "Effect of Breath Holding on Arterial Pressure in Patients with Mental and Emotional Disorders," *AMA Arch Neural,* LXVIII (September, 1952), 318–20.

Alvarez, Walter C. *How to Live With Your Blood Pressure.* Chicago: Wilcox and Follett, 1951.

Andersen, R. S., Ellington, A., and Gunter, L. M. "The Incidence of Arteriosclerotic Heart Disease in Negro Diabetic Patients," *Diabetes,* X (March-April, 1961), 114–18.

Anderson, M., et al. "Chemical and Pathological Studies on Aortic Atherosclerosis. A Comparative Study of One Hundred Twenty-eight Aortas in South African Bantu and White Subjects," *AMA Arch Path,* LXVIII (October, 1959), 380–91.

Anderson, W. F., and Cowan, N. R. "Arterial Pressure in Healthy Older People," *Clin Sci,* XVIII (February, 1959), 103–17.

Apter, N. S., and Halstead, W. C. "The Psychiatric Manifestations of Early Cerebral Damage in Essential Hypertension," *Med Clin N Amer*, XXXV (January, 1951), 133–42.

Arenberg, H. "Hypertension Among Seamen," *New York J Med*, LII (July 1, 1952), 1663–66.

"Arterial Hypertension and Ischemic Heart Disease: Comparison in Epidemiological Studies," *Canad Med Ass J*, 88:1218, 15 Jun 63.

Askar, O. "Portal Hypertension in Egyptian Splenomegaly," *J Egypt Med Ass*, XLIII (1960), 32–42.

Ayman, D. "Hereditary and Constitutional Factors: Specific Mendelian Trait or Non-Specific Predisposition?" in The Commonwealth of Massachusetts. *A Symposium on Essential Hypertension.* Boston: Wright and Potter, 1951, 234–38.

Babow, I. "Minority Group Integration in Hospitals: A Sample Survey," *Hospitals* XXXV (February 1, 1961), 47–48.

Backer, M. "Essential Hypertension: Birth of Its Concept Two Hundred Years Ago," *Angiology*, IV (June, 1953), 207–209.

Backer, M. "Whither Hypertensive Research?" *Conn Med*, XX (September, 1956), 687–92.

Balme, H. W., and Cole, L. "Heredity of Hypertension in Diabetes Mellitus," *Quart J Med*, XX (October, 1951), 335–51.

Barker, N. W. "Hypertension and Unilateral Renal Disease," *Med Clin N Amer*, XXXV (July, 1951), 1041–50.

Bauer, J. "Pathogenesis and Clinical Significance of Constitutional Hypertension," *Angiology*, XI (December, 1960), 499–507.

Bays, R. P., and Scrimshaw, N. S. "Facts and Fallacies Regarding the Blood Pressure of Different Regional and Racial Groups," *Circulation*, VIII (November, 1953), 655–63.

Beach, S. A.: "Heredity in hypertension," *Lancet* 1: 1269–70, 8 Jun 63.

Bell, E. T. (ed.) *Symposium on Hypertension.* Minneapolis: University of Minnesota, 1951.

Bell, M. E., and Wills, L. "Racial Differences in Incidence of Pre-Eclampsia and Eclampsia in Fiji," *J Obstet Gynaec Brit Emp.* LXII (December, 1955), 917–21.

Bello, C. T., and Turner, L. W. "Resperine As An Antihypertensive in the Outpatient Clinic: A Double-Blind Clinical Study," *Amer J Med Sci,* CCXXXII (August, 1956), 194–97.

Bello, C. T., *et al.* "Renal Hemodynamic Responses to Stress in Normotensive and Hypertensive Subjects," *Circulation,* XXII (October, 1960), 573–82.

Benedict, Ruth B. "Onset and Early Course of Essential Hypertension," *J Chron Dis,* IV (September, 1956), 221–30.

Benedict, R. B. "Psychiatric Concepts in Essential Hypertension." *Med Ann DC,* XXIII (April, 1954), 197–99.

Berkson, D. M., *et al.* "Socioeconomic Correlates of Atherosclerotic and Hypertensive Heart Diseases," *Ann NY Acad Sci,* LXXXIV, Art. 17 (December 8, 1960), 835–50.

Bernardis, L. L., and Skelton, F. R., "Effect of Crowding on Hypertension and Growth in Rats Bearing Regenerated Adrenals. *Proc. Soc. Exp. Biol.* New York: 1963, 113/4 (952–954).

Bersohn, I., and Wayburne, S., "Serum Cholesterol Concentration in Newborn African and European Infants and Their Mothers," *Amer J Clin Nutr,* IV (March-April, 1956), 117–23.

Bertrand, A., and Storla, C. A. *Lay Attitudes and Opinions About Heart Disease.* New Orleans: Louisiana Heart Association, 1955.

Binger, C. "On So-Called Psychogenic Influences in Essential Hypertension," *Psychosom Med,* XIII (September-October, 1951), 273–76.

Binger, C., "Psychogenic Influence as Initiating and Sustaining Factors in Essential Hypertension in Man," in The Commonwealth of Massachusetts. *A Symposium on Essential Hypertension.* Boston: Wright and Potter, 1951, 193–200.

Bisgeier, G. P., "Comparison of Three Health Test Survey Programs," *J Med Soc New Jersey,* 61:413–6, Sept. 64.

Blackburn, H. W., Taylor, H. L., Puchner, T. C. and Keip, A.: "Relationship of Resting and Postexercise Electrocardiographic Abnormalities to Obesity, Hypertension, and Hypercholesteremia in Working Men." (887–888). Abstract of paper delivered at the 34th Scientific Session of the American Heart Association (Bal Harbour, Miami Beach, Florida, Oct 1961) *Circulation* 1961, 24/4, Part 2.

Bloomberg, B. M., *et al.* "Serum Lipids in South African Bantu and White Subjects," *Circulation,* XVII (June, 1958), 1021–28.

Boines, G. J., "Emotional Stress and Hypertension," *Med Times,* LXXXVI (July, 1958), 855–59.

Boines, G. J., "The Problem of Emotional Stress in Hypertension," *Delaware Med J.*, XXIX (May, 1957), 116–18.

Boles-Carenini, B., *et al.* "Comparative Tonographic Study of Normotensive Eyes of White and Negro Persons," *Amer J Ophthal*, XL (August, 1955), 224–27; *Science*, CXXII (November 11, 1955), 923–24.

Bolt, W., Bell, M. F., and Harnes, J. R. "Study of Mortality in Moderate and Severe Hypertension," *Trans Ass Life Insur Med Dir Amer*, XLI (1957), 61–100.

Bonar, J., *et al.*, "Plasma Renin Concentration in American Negro Women with Hypertensive Disease of Pregnancy." *J Obstet Gynaec Brit Comm*, 73: 418–20, Jun 66.

Bordley, J. III, *et al.* "Recommendations for Human Blood Pressure Determinations by Sphygmonanometers," *JAMA*, CXLVII (October 13, 1951), 632–36.

Borhani, N. O., *et al.*, "Report of a Ten-year Follow-up Study of the San Francisco Longshoremen; Mortality from Coronary Heart Disease and from All Causes," *J Chronic Dis*, 16: 1251–66, Dec. 63.

Borhani, N. O., *et al.*, "Recent Changes in CVR Disease Mortality in California." *Public Health Rep*, 79:147–60, Feb. 64.

Bourne, G., "Some Cardiological Problems of Life Assurance," *Practitioner*, 194:240–3, Feb. 65.

Breslin, D. J., *et al.*, "Essential hypertension. A twenty-year follow-up study," *Circulation* 33:87–97, Jan. 66.

Brest, A. N., and Moyer, J. H., "The Etiology and Therapy of Essential Hypertension: A Review," *J S Carolina Med Ass*, LVI (May, 1960), 171–75.

Brink, A. J., "Normal Electrocardiogram in Adult South African Bantu," *S Afr J Lab Clin Med*, II (June, 1956), 97–123.

Brock, J. F., and Bronte-Stewart, B., "Arteriosclerosis in African Populations," *Minnesota med*, XXXVIII (December, 1955), 852–63.

Brod, J., "Influence of Environmental Factors on the Pathogenesis of Hypertension," *Cardiologia*, XXXI (Number 5, 1957), 500–08.

Brod, J., *et al.*, "Circulatory Changes Underlying Blood Pressure Elevation During Acute Emotional Stress (Mental Arithmetic) in Normotensive and Hypertensive Subjects," *Clin Sci*, XVIII (May, 1959), 269–79.

Brodman, K., *et al.,* "The Cornell Medical Index—Health Questionnaire: VI. The Relation of Patients' Complaints to Age, Sex, Race, and Education," *J Geront,* VIII (July, 1953), 339–42.

Bronte-Stewart, B., *et al.,* "The Health and Nutritional Status of the King Bushmen of South West Africa," *S Afr J Lab Clin Med,* VI (December, 1960), 187–216.

Brouha. L., and Harrington, M. E., "Heart Rate and Blood Pressure Reactions of Men and Women During and After Muscular Exercise," *J Lancet,* LXXVII (March, 1957), 79–80.

Browne, F. J., and Sheumack, D. R. "Chronic Hypertension Following Pre-Eclamptic Toxemia. Influence of Familial Hypertension on Its Causation," *J Obstet Gynaec Brit Emp,* LXIII (October, 1956), 677–79.

Brozek, J. "Personality of Young and Middle-Aged Normal Men: Item Analysis of Psychosomatic Inventory (Study on Development of Hypertension)," *J Geront,* VII (July, 1952), 410–18.

Bruce, J. M., Jr., and Thomas, C. B., "A Method of Rating Certain Personality Factors as Determined by the Rorschach Test for Use in a Study of the Precursors of Hypertension and Coronary Artery Disease," *Psychiat Quart* (Suppl), XXVII (Number 2, 1953), 207–38.

Brunner, D., and Lobl, K., "Serum Cholesterol, Electrophoretic Lipid Pattern, Diet, and Coronary Artery Disease: A Study in Coronary Patients and in Healthy Men of Different Origin and Occupations in Israel," *Ann Intern Med,* LXIX (October, 1958), 732–50.

Bryans, C. I., Jr., Southerland, W. L., Zuspan, F. P., "Eclampsia: a Long Term Follow-up Study," *Obstet Gynec,* 21:701–7, Jun 63.

Burch, G. E., and Depasquale, N., "The Value of Home Recordings of Blood Pressure in the Management of Patients with Arterial Hypertension," *Amer J Med Sci,* CCXL (September, 1960), 273–79.

Burch, G. E., Phillips, J. H., and Wood, W., "The High-Pork Diet of the Negro of the Southern United States," *Arch Intern Med* (Chic), C (December, 1957), 859–61.

Burgess, A. M., "Benign Essential Hypertension: Follow-up of 100 Patients Under Observation for from 18 to 34 Years," *Ann Intern Med,* XLIII (October, 1955), 740–44.

Canadian Life Insurance Medical Officers Association, "Morality Trends in Relation to Blood Pressure and Build," *Canad Med Ass J,* LXXXII (May 14, 1960), 1033.

Cantow, L. A., and Weil, R. J., "Some Clues to an Integrative Study of Hypertension," *J Mich Med Soc,* LII (December, 1953), 1316–19; passim 1384.

Cardon, P. V., Jr., "The Relationship of Life Stress to Essential Hypertension," *Mississippi V Med J,* LXXV (July, 1953), 111–14.

Carter, E. T., Hunt, J. C., Tillisch, J. H., "Evaluation of Flying Personnel with Persistent Hypertension," *Aerospace Med,* 33:1206–10, Oct. 62.

Chambers, H. D., "A Clinical Type of Hypertension Observed in Jamaica—Illustrated by the Most Outstanding of the Cases Observed," *W Indian Med J,* IX (March, 1960), 67–72.

Chapman, J. M., *et al.,* "Epidemiology of Vascular Lesions Affecting the Central Nervous System: the Occurrence of Strokes in a Sample Population Under Observation for Cardiovascular Disease," *Amer J Public Health,* 56: 191–201, Feb. 66.

Chazan, J. A., *et al.,* "Household Aggregation of Hypertension: Report of a Preliminary Study," *J Chronic Dis,* 17:9–18, Jan. 64.

Clark, E. G., and Morsell, J. A., "An Epidemiologic Approach to the Study of High Blood Pressure," *Amer J Public Health,* XLII (May, 1952), 542–48.

Clark, E. G., Glock, C. Y., and Vought, R. L., "An Epidemiologic Approach to the Study of the Natural History of Essential Hypertension," *J Chron Dis,* IV (September, 1956), 231–39.

Clark, E. Gurney, *et al.,* "Studies in Hypertension: Analysis of Individual Blood Pressure Changes," *J Chron Dis,* IV (November, 1956), 477–89.

Clark, E. G., "Modern Concepts of Epidemiology," *J Chron Dis,* II (November, 1955), 593–96.

"Classification of Types of Hypertension," *JAMA,* CLXVI (February 8, 1958), 640–41.

Clifford, N. J., *et al.,* "Coronary Heart Disease and Hypertension in the White Mountain Apache Tribe," *Circulation,* 28: 926–31, Nov. 63.

Cobb, S., *et al.,* "Some Psychological and Social Characteristics of Patients Hospitalized for Rheumatoid Arthritis, Hypertension, and Duodenal Ulcer," *J Chronic Dis,* 18: 1259–78, Dec. 65.

Cohen, A. M., Neumann, E., and Michaelson, I. C., "Involutionary

Sclerosis and Diastolic Hypertension. Effect of Environmental Change," *Lancet,* 1960, 2/7159 (1050–1051).

Cohen, B. M., "Arterial Hypertension Among Indians of the Southwestern United States," *Amer J Med Sci,* CCXXV (May, 1953). 505–13.

Cohen, S. I., and Silverman, A. J., "Psychophysiological Investigations of Vascular Response Variability," *J Psychosom Res,* III (Number 3, 1959), 185–210.

Cohen, S. I., Silverman, A. J., and Zuidema, G., "Physiologic Stress Response Evaluation by Focused Interviewing," *Arch Neurol* (*Chic*), LXXVI, (December, 1956), 670–74.

Collier, H. N., "Hypertension and Life Assurance," *Practitioner,* CLXVI (June, 1951), 577–82.

The Commonwealth of Massachusetts. *A Symposium on Essential Hypertension.* Boston: Wright and Potter, 1951.

Comstock, G. W., "Mortality of Persons with Photofluorograms Suggestive of Cardiovascular Disease," *New Engl J Med,* CCXLVIII (June 18, 1953), 1945–50.

Comstock, G. W., and Kendrick, M. A., "Blood Pressure and the Weather," *Amer Heart J,* LIII (June, 1957), 825–28.

Comstock, G. W., "An Epidemiologic Study of Blood Pressure Levels in a Biracial Community in the Southern United States," *Amer J. Hyg,* LXV (May, 1957), 271–315.

Conn, J. H., "The Psychiatric Aspects of Hypertension," *Sinai Hosp J* (Balt), II (May, 1953), 29–33.

Corcoran A. C., "Changing Status of Sodium Restriction in Therapy of Hypertension," *Amer J Cardiol* 8: 887–9, Dec. 61.

Corcoran, A. C., "Concepts of 'Primary Hypertension' and Their Epidemiological Significance," *Amer Heart J,* 69: 137–9, Jan. 65.

Corcoran, A. C., Dustan, H. P., and Page, I. H., "The Evaluation of Antihypertensive Procedures, with Particular Reference to Their Effects on Blood Pressure," *Ann Intern Med,* LXIII (December, 1955), 1161–77.

Dahl, L. K., "Chronic Excess Salt Consumption as an Etiologic Factor in Human Hypertension," *Heart Bull,* 11: 61–5, Jul–Aug. 63.

Dahl, L. K., "Possible Role of Chronic Excess Salt Comsumption in the Pathogenesis of Essential Hypertension," *Amer J Cardiol* 8: 571–5, Oct. 61.

Dahl, L. K., Heine, M., "The Enhanced Hypertensogenic Effect of Sea Salt Over Sodium Chloride," *Amer J Cardiol* 8: 726–31, Nov. 61.

Dahl, L. K., Heine, M., Tassinari, L., "High Salt Content of Western Infant's Diet: Possible Relationship to Hypertension in the Adult," *Nature* (London), 198: 1204–5, 22 Jun 63.

Dahl, L. K., "Salt, Fat and Hypertension: The Japanese Experience," *Nutr Rev,* XVIII (April, 1960), 97–99.

Dahl, L. K., Heine, M., Tassinari, L., "Effects of Chronic Excess Salt Ingestion. Evidence that Genetic Factors Play an Important Role in Susceptibility to Experimental Hypertension," *J Exp Med,* 115: 1173–90, 1 Jun 62.

Dahl, L. K., Heine, M., Tassinari, L., "Role of Genetic Factors in Susceptibility to Experimental Hypertension Due to Chronic Excess Salt Ingestion," *Nature (Lond),* 194: 480–2, 5 May 62.

Dahl, L. K., *et al.,* "Effects of Chronic Salt Ingestion. Further Demonstration that Genetic Factors Influence the Development of Hypertension: Evidence from Experimental Hypertension Due to Cortisone and to Adrenal Regeneration," *J Exp Med,* 122: 533–45, 1 Sep. 65.

D'Alonzo, C. A., Densen, P. M., and Munn, M. G., "Hypertension in Industry: Inquiry into the Influence of Familial Factors," *Industr Med Surg,* XXIII, (November, 1954), 491–96.

D'Alonzo, C. A., Fleming, A. J., and Gehrmann, G. H., "Role of Heredity in the Problem of Hypertension in Industrial Workers," *JAMA,* CLVII (February 19, 1955), 631–33.

D'Alonzo, C. A., *Heart Disease, Blood Pressure and Strokes*. Houston: Gulf, 1960.

Damon, Albert, "Constitution and Smoking," *Science,* 1961, 134, 339–340.

Danaraj, T. J., *et al.,* "Ethnic Group Differences in Coronary Heart Disease in Singapore: An Analysis of Necropsy Records," *Amer Heart J,* LVIII (October, 1959), 516–26.

Davies, R. R., Marvel, R. J., and Genovese, P. D., "Heart Disease of Unknown Etiology," *Amer Heart J,* XLII, (October, 1951), 546–65.

DeNyse, D. L., "Clinical Observations with Phenaglycodol in Hypertension with Anxiety States," *Rhode Island Med J,* XL (September, 1957), 514–15; passim.

Department of Nutrition, Pretoria, "The Role of Fat in Causing Disease of the Heart and Arteries," *S Afr Med J,* XXX (March 17, 1956), 276.

"Desegregation: Its Implications for Orthopsychiatry; Round Table, 1955," *Amer J Orthopsychiat,* XXVI (July, 1956), 445–70.

De Takats, G., "The Phenomenon of Stress in Relation to Human Essential Hypertension," *Angiology,* II (December, 1951), 461–75.

De Takats, G., "Ten-Year Follow-Up Study of Surgically Treated Hypertensive Patients," *Geriatrics,* XIV (June, 1959), 361–66.

Dickson, H. E., "The Management of Hypertension and 'Low Blood Pressure' in the Employee," *Industr Med Surg,* XXX (May, 1961), 195–99.

Dotto, B. B., "An All-India Survey of Normal Blood Pressure Range in Males. (A Study Based on 66,000 Subjects Between the Ages of 10 to 80 Years)," *Med Dig* (Bombay), XXVI (Number 10, 1958), 448–64.

Douglas, Donald B., and Hoch, Paul H., "Blood Pressure Studies in Schizophrenia: Atropine and Saline," *Psychiat Quart,* XXX (April, 1956), 204–10.

Doyle, A. E., and Fraser, J. R., "Essential Hypertension and Inheritance of Vascular Reactivity," *Lancet,* II (September 2, 1961), 509–11.

Dreger, R. M., and Miller, K. S., "Comparative Psychological Studies of Negroes and Whites in the United States," *Psychol Bull,* LVII (September, 1960), 361–402.

Dreyfuss, F., and Hamosh, P., "A Coronary Disease Study Among Cochin Jews in Israel," *Amer J Med Sci,* CCXL (December, 1960), 769–75.

Droller, H., *et al.,* "High Blood Pressure in the Elderly," *Brit Med J,* II (November 1, 1952), 968–70.

Dykman, R. A., and Gantt, W. H., "Experimental Psychogenic Hypertension: Blood Pressure Changes Conditioned to Painful Stimuli (Schizokinesis)," *Bull Johns Hopkins Hosp,* CVII (August, 1960), 72–89.

Eagles, J. B., "Blood Pressures and Cold Pressor Tests in Psychoneurotic Patients," *J Roy Army Med Corps,* XCIX, (October, 1953), 245–49.

Earle, Anne, and Earle, Brian Vigors., "The Blood Pressure Response to Pain and Emotion in Schizophrenia," *J Nerv Ment Dis,* CXXI (February, 1955), 132–39.

Edington, G. M., "Cardiovascular Disease as a Cause of Death in the Gold Coast African," *Trans Roy Soc Trop Med Hyg,* XLVIII (September, 1954), 419–25.

Edwards, F., McKeown, T., and Whitfield, A. G. W., "Arterial Pressure in Men Over Sixty," *Clin Sci,* XVIII (Number 2, 1959), 289–300.

Edwards, J. C., *Management of Hypertensive Diseases.* St. Louis: C. V. Mosby, 1960.

Elsherif, A., Sorour, A., and Ibrahim, M., "Heart Disease in Essential Hypertension," *J Egypt Med Ass,* XXXIV (1951) 509–21.

"Enigma of hypertension." *Brit Med J,* 5469: 1011–2, 30 Oct 65.

El-Wakil, I., "The Surgical Treatment of Portal Hypertension in Egypt," *J Egypt Med Ass,* XLII (1959), 405–11.

"Emotional Factors in Hypertension," *Heart Bull,* I (November–December, 1952), 82–84.

"Epidemiology of Cardiovascular Diseases: Methodology. Hypertension and Arteriosclerosis," *Amer J Public Health,* L (October, 1960, Suppl.), 1–124.

Epstein, F. H., *et al.,* "The Epidemiology of Atherosclerosis Among a Random Sample of Clothing Workers of Different Ethnic Origins in New York City," *J Chron Dis,* V (March, 1957), 300–41.

Epstein, F. H., Simpson, R., and Boas, E. P., "Relations Between Diet and Atherosclerosis Among Working Population of Different Ethnic Origins," *Amer J Clin Nutr,* IV (January–February, 1956), 10–19.

"Epidemiology of Hypertension," *Brit Med J,* (May 3, 1952), 962–63.

Evans, W., "Hypertonia or Uneventful High Blood Pressure," *Lancet,* II (July 13, 1957), 53–59.

Evelyn, K. A., "The Natural Course of Essential Hypertension in Man," in The Commonwealth of Massachusetts. *A Symposium on Essential Hypertension.* Boston: Wright and Potter, 1951, 63–71.

Evelyn, K. A., *et al.,* "Effect of Thoracolumbar Sympathectomy on the Clinical Course of Primary (Essential) Hypertension. A Ten-Year Study of 100 Sympathectomized Patients Compared with Individually Matched, Symptomatically Treated Control Subjects," *Amer J Med,* XXVIII (February, 1960), 188–221.

Faucett, Robert L., Litin, Edward M., and Achor, Richard W. P., "Neuropharmacologic Action of Rauwolfia Compounds and Its Psychodynamic Implications," *AMA Arch Neurol,* LXXVII (May, 1957), 513–18.

Ficca, Sylvester Charles. *Relationship of "Autonomic" Blood Pressure Pattern Type of Subject's Performance on the Wechsler-Bellevue and Rorschach Test.* Pennsylvania State College, 1950. (Ph.D. Thesis).

Finnerty, F. A., Jr., "Toxemia of Pregnancy as Seen by an Internist: An Analysis of 1,081 Patients," *Ann Intern Med,* XLIV (February, 1956), 358–75.

Fishberg, A. M., *Hypertension and Nephritis,* Edition 5. Philadelphia: *Clin N Amer,* XXXVIII (May, 1954), 753–64.

Fishberg, A. M., "Differential Diagnosis of High Blood Pressure," *Med Clin N Amer,* XXXVIII (May, 1954), 753–64.

Fitzpatrick, William H., and DeLong, Chester W. (eds), U.S. Health, Education, and Welfare Dept., National Library of Medicine. *Soviet Medical Research Related to Human Stress, Review of Literature.* Washington 25, D.C.: U.S. Government Printing Office, 1961, 121 pages.

Fleishman, S. J., and Gelfand, M., "The Electrocardiogram in Apparently Healthy African Men," *Cent Afr J Med,* VI, (August, 1960), 356–59.

Flynn, J. T., and Wolf, S., "Variations in the Hyperdynamic Cardiovascular Response to Stress Among Hypertensive Subjects," *Bull NY Acad Med,* XXVII (June, 1951), 382. (Abstract).

Forbes, J. I., and Carter, T. D., "A Short Trial of Darenthin in the Treatment of Hypertension in the African," *Cent Afr J Med,* VI (May, 1960), 191–96.

Fraser, B. N., "Manifestations and Aetiology of Hypertension in the Coloured and Bantu," *Brit Med J,* I (March 21, 1959), 761–64.

Fraser, B. N., and Hart, D., "A Blood-Volume Study in the Non-European Patient with Hypertension," *S Afr J Lab Clin Med,* VII (June, 1961), 77–80.

Fraser, B. N., and Kavin, H., "The Management of Hypertension in the Bantu," *Cent Afr J Med,* VI (November, 1960), 481–84.

Fregly, M. J., "Relationship Between Ambient Temperature and the Spontaneous Running Activity of Normal and Hypertensive Rats," *Amer J Physiol,* CLXXXVII (November, 1956), 297–301.

Freis, Ed., "The Role of Hypertension," *Amer J Public Health*, L (March, 1960; Part 2), 11–13.

Funkenstein, Daniel H., "The Role of Ordinary Epinephrine and Nor-Epinephrine in the Elevation of Blood Pressure During Stress," *J Nerv Ment Dis*, CXIII (February, 1951), 177–78.

Funkenstein, D. H., Greenblatt, M., and Solomon, H. C., "Nor-Epinephrine-Like and Epinephrine-Like Substances in Psychotic and Psychoneurotic Patients," *Amer J Psychiat*, CVIII (March, 1952), 652–62.

Funkenstein, Daniel H., and Meade, Lydia W., "Nor-Epinephrine-Like and Epinephrine-Like Substances and the Elevation of Blood Pressure During Acute Stress," *J Nerv Ment Dis*, CXIX (May, 1954), 380–97.

Furman, K. I., "Nephritis in the Bantu," *S Afr Med J*, XXIX (June 18, 1955), 590–93.

Gampel, B., Slome, C., Scotch, N., Abramson, J. H., "Urbanization and Hypertension Among Zulu Adults," *J Chron Dis*, 15:67–70, Jan. 62.

Gearing, F. R., Clark, E. G., Perera, G. A., and Schweitzer, M. D., "Hypertension Among Relatives of Hypertensives. Progress Report of a Family Study," *Amer J Publ Hlth*, 1962, 52/12 (2058–2065).

Geiger, H. J., *et al.*, "The Epidemiology of Essential Hypertension. A Review with Special Attention to Psychologic and Sociocultural Factors. I. Biologic Mechanisms and Descriptive Epidemiology," *J Chronic Dis* 16: 1151–82, Nov. 63. (125 ref.).

Gelfand, M., "Recent Advances in Tropical Medicine; Cardiac and Vascular Disorders in the African," *W Afr Med J*, I (July–August–September, 1952), 91–101.

Giovacchini, Peter L., "Somatic Symptoms and the Transference Neurosis," *International Journal of Psycho-Analysis*, 1963, 44 (2), 143–150.

Giovacchini, P. L., "Coexisting Organ Neuroses: A Clinical Study," *Psychosom Med*, XVIII (January–February, 1956), 84–89.

Glock, Charles Y., and Lennard, Henry L., "Studies in Hypertension: Psychologic Factors in Hypertension," *J Chron Dis*, V (February, 1957), 174–85.

Glock, Charles Y., *et al.*, "Studies in Hypertension: Comparison of Reaction of Three Tests for Hyperreactivity Among 204 Volunteers," *J Chron Dis*, IV (November, 1956), 490–98.

Glock, Charles Y., et al., "Studies in Hypertension: Variability of Daily Blood Pressure Measurements in the Same Individuals Over a Three-Week Period," *J Chron Dis*, IV (November, 1956), 469–76.

Goldring, W., et al., "Reassurance in the Management of Benign Hypertensive Disease," *Circulation*, XIV (August, 1956), 260–64.

Goldstein, M. S., "Longevity and Health Status of Whites and Non-Whites in the United States," *J Nat Med Ass*, XLVI (March, 1954), 83–104.

Gordon, H., et al., "A Prospective Interracial Study of Hypertensive Toxaemia of Pregnancy," *S Afr Med J*, 38: 829–30, 17 Oct. 64.

Gordon, T., "Some Observations on the Epidemiology of Heart Disease," *Public Health Rep*, LXXIII (April, 1958), 321–28.

Gore, I., Hirst, A. E., Jr., and Koseki, Y., "Comparison of Aortic Atherosclerosis in the United States, Japan, and Guatemala," *Amer J Clin Nutr*, VII (January–February, 1959), 50–54.

Gottschalk, L. A., et al., "Some Psychophysiologic Relations in Hypertensive Women; Effect of Hydrochlorothiazide on the Relation of Affect to Blood Pressure," *Psychosom Med*, 26: 610–7, Sep–Oct 64.

Graham, D. T., Kabler, J. D., Graham, F. K., "Physiological Response to the Suggestion of Attitudes Specific for Hives and Hypertension," *Psychosom Med* 24:159–69, Mar–Apr. 62.

Grant, F. W., and Groom, D., "A Dietary Study Among A Group of Southern Negroes," *J Amer Diet Ass*, XXXV (September, 1959), 910–18.

Greene, C. R., and Kelly, J. J., Jr., "Electrocardiogram of the Healthy Adult Negro," *Circulation*, XX (November, 1959), 906–09.

Griep, A. H., et al., "Prognosis in Arterial Hypertension: Report on 117 Patients Under 53 Years of Age Followed 8 to 10 Years," *Amer J Med Sci*, CCXXI (March, 1951), 239–49.

Griffith, J. Q., Jr., "The Treatment of Hypertension," *Med Clin N Amer*, XXXVIII (November, 1954), 1717–31.

Groen, J. J., Tijong, K. B., Koster, M., Willebrands, A. F., Verdonck, G., Pierloot, M., "The Influence of Nutrition and Ways of Life on Blood Cholesterol and the Prevalence of Hypertension and Coronary Heart Disease Among Trappist and Benedictine Monks," *Amer J Clin Nutr*, 10: 456–70, June, 62.

Groen, J., van der Valk, J. M., and Bastiaans, J., "A Case of Malignant Hypertension, Treated with Prefrontal Leucotomy and Psychotherapy, Followed for Over Eight Years," *J Psychosom Res,* II (Number 2, 1957), 120–33.

Grollman, A., "The Relationship of Salt and Diet to Diastolic Hypertension," *Amer J Cardiol,* 9:700–3, May, 62.

Grollman, Arthur, and Furness, Franklin N., "New Diuretics and Antihypertensive Agents," *Ann NY Acad Sci,* LXXXVIII, Art. 4 (October 11, 1960), 771–1020.

Groom, D., *et al.,* "Coronary and Aortic Atherosclerosis; Comparative Incidence in the Negro Race in Haiti and the United States," *Circulation,* XVI (October, 1957), 888–89.

Groom, D., *et al.,* "Coronary and Aortic Atherosclerosis in the Negroes of Haiti and the United States," *Ann Intern Med,* LI (August, 1959), 270–89.

Groom, D., *et al.,* "Coronary Disease in the Negroes of Haiti and the United States," Abstract in Proceedings of the Thirty-First Scientific Sessions (October 24–26, 1958). San Francisco: American Heart Association, 729–30.

Groom, D., *et al.,* "Developmental Patterns of Coronary and Aortic Atherosclerosis in Young Negroes of Haiti and the United States," *Ann Intern Med,* 61:900–13, Nov. 64.

Groom, D., *et al.,* "A Comparative Study of Coronary Disease in Haitian and American Negroes," *Southern Med J,* LII (May, 1959), 504–10.

Grusin, H., "Pecularities of Heart Disease in the Bantu," *Leech,* XXVIII (Number 2, 1958), 76–80.

Grusin, H., "Pecularities of the African's Electrocardiogram and the Changes Observed in Serial Studies," *Circulation,* IX (June, 1954), 860–67.

Hagans, J. A., and Brust, A. A., "The Natural History of Hypertension," *Amer J Med,* XXVIII (June, 1960), 905–12.

Hahn, L., "Blood Pressure Changes in Adolescent Girls: A Follow-Up Study in 60 Girls Attending a Secondary Modern School in the City of Leicester," *Med Offr.,* C (August 8, 1958), 97–99.

Hall, C. E., and Hall, O., "Enhancement of Somatotrophic Hormone-Induced Hypertensive Cardiovascular Disease by Stress," *Amer J Physiol,* CXCVII (September, 1959), 702–04.

Hall, C. E., *et al.,* "Augmented Salt Ingestion and Its Effect Upon Salt Hypertension and Adrenal-Regeneration Hypertension," *Lab Invest,* 13: 1471–83, Nov. 64.

Hall, C. E., *et al.,* "Hypertension and Hypersalimentation. I. Aldosterone Hypertension," *Lab Invest* 14: 285–94, Mar. 65.

Hambling, John, "Psychosomatic Aspects of Arterial Hypertension," *Brit J Med Psychol,* XXV (Part 1, 1952), 39–47.

Hambling, J., "Emotions and Symptoms in Essential Hypertension," *Brit J Med Psychol,* XXIV (Number 4, 1951), 242–53.

Hamilton, M., *et al.,* "The Etiology of Essential Hypertension. (II. Scores for Arterial Blood Pressures Adjusted for Differences in Age and Sex)," *Clin Sci,* XIII (Number 1, 1954), 37–49.

Hamilton, M., Pickering, G. W., Roberts, J. A., Sowry, G. S., "Arterial Pressures of Relatives of Patients with Secondary and Malignant Hypertension," *Clin Sci,* 24: 91–108, Feb. 63.

Hammer, E. F., "Frustration-Aggression Hypothesis Extended to Socioracial Areas: Comparison of Negro and White Children's H-T-P-'s," *Psychiat Quart,* XXVII (October, 1953), 597–607.

Handler, F. P., Blache, J. O., and Blumenthal, H. T., "Comparison of Aging Processes in the Renal and Splenic Arteries in the Negro and White Races," *AMA Arch Path,* LIII (January, 1952), 29–53.

Harburg, E., Julius, S., McGinn, N. F., McLeod, J., and Hoobler, S. W., "Personality Traits and Behavioral Patterns Associated with Systolic Blood Pressure Levels in College Males." *Journal of Chronic Diseases,* 1964, 17 (5), 405–413.

Harburg, E., *et al.,* "Recalled Treatment by Parents Among College Males and Blood Pressure Levels vs. Variability," *J Psychosom Res,* 9: 173–83, Oct. 65.

Hardyck, Curtis, Singer, Margaret Thaler, and Harris, Robert E., "Transient Changes in Affect and Blood Pressure," *Arch Gen Psychiat,* 1962, 7 (7), 15–20.

Harlan, W. R., Osborne, R. K., Graybiel, A., "A Longitudinal Study of Blood Pressure," *Circulation,* 26: 530–43, Oct. 62.

Harlan, William R., Osborne, Robert K., and Graybiel, Ashton, "A Longitudinal Study of Blood Pressure," *USN Sch Aviat Med Res Rep,* 1962, Proj. MR005.13-3001, Subtask 2, Rep. No. 4, 19p.

Harrington, M. (ed), "Symposium on Hypotensive Drugs and the Control of Vascular Tone in Hypertension," *Hypotensive Drugs.* London and New York: Pergamon, 1956.

Harris, R. E., *et al.,* "Response to Psychologic Stress in Persons Who are Potentially Hypertensive," *Circulation,* VII (June, 1953), 874–79.

Hartroft, W. S., "The Nutritional Aspects of Hypertension and Its Reversibility," *Amer J Public Health,* 56: 462–8, Mar. 66. (40 ref.)

Hartroft, W. S., "Symposium: Studies on Arteriosclerosis; Experimental Renal Hypertension of Dietary Origin (Choline Deficiency)," *J Geront,* VI (April, 1951), 154–59.

Hastings, D. W., "Psychologic Factors in Hypertension," *Lancet,* 1961, 81/9 (366–367).

Hayes, J. A., *et al.,* "Heart Weight of Jamaicans. Autopsy Study of Normal Cases and Cases of Hypertension and Chronic Lung Disease," *Circulation,* 33: 450–4, Mar. 66.

Heijtmancik, M. R., and Herrmann, G. R., "The Electrocardiographic Syndrome of Short P-R Interval and Broad QRS Complexes. A Clinical Study of 80 Cases," *Amer Heart J,* LIV (November, 1957), 708–21.

Hennis, Gail M., and Ulrich, Celeste, "Study of Psychic Stress in Freshmen College Women," *Res Quart,* XXIX (May, 1958), 172–79.

Henricks, F. H., "Hypertension—Its Importance in Insurance Examinations," *J Nat Med Ass,* XLIII (September, 1951), 305–07.

"Heredity and Hypertension," *Lancet,* 1: 643–4, 23 Mar 63.

Heseltine, W. W., and Campbell, P. J. (eds.), "Symposium on the Use of Modern Diuretics in the Control of Hypertension, Liverpool, 1959." Symposium Held at the University of Liverpool, November 25, 1959. Liverpool: Birchall, 1959.

Higginson, J., "World Trends in Cardiology: I. Cardiovascular Epidemiology. Atherosclerosis, Diet and Serum Cholesterol in the South African Bantu," in *Selected Papers from Second World Congress of Cardiology and Twenty-Seventh Annual Scientific Sessions of the American Heart Association Held in Washington, D.C.* New York: Hoeber-Harper, 1956, 34–41.

Higginson, J., and Pepler, W. J., "Fat Intake, Serum Cholesterol Concentration, and Atherosclerosis in the South African Bantu. Part II. Atherosclerosis and Coronary Artery Disease," *J Clin Invest,* XXXIII (October, 1954), 1366–71.

Hill, M., and Hugge, R., "Syphilis Prevalence as Related to Social Factors in a Negro Subcommunity," *Am J Syph,* XXXVIII (November, 1954), 583–92.

Hilleboe, H. E., James, G., and Doyle, J. T., "Cardiovascular Health Center. I. Project Design for Public Health Research," *Amer J Public Health,* XLIV (July, 1954), 851–63.

Hines, E. A., Jr., "The Effects of Tobacco On Blood Pressure and In Peripheral Vascular Diseases," *Proc Mayo Clin,* XXXV (June 22, 1960), 337–43.

Hirsch, E. F., "The Hospital Care of Negroes and the Appointment of Negro Physicians to Medical Staffs of Hospitals in Chicago," *Proc Inst Med Chicago,* XXIII (November 15, 1960), 156–59.

Hokanson, Jack Eric, "Some Physiological and Behavioral Concomitants of Experimentally Aroused Anger," *Dissertation Abstr.,* XX (December, 1959), 2375 (Abstract).

Hokanson, Jack E., Burgess, Michael, and Cohen, Michael F., "Effect of Displaced Aggression on Systolic Blood Pressure," *J Abnorm Soc Psychol,* 1963, 67 (3), 214–218.

Hokanson, Jack E. and Edelman, Robert, "Effects of Three Social Responses on Vascular Processes," *Journal of Personality and Social Psychology,* 1966, 3 (4), 442–447.

Hoobler, S. W., *Hypertensive Disease,* New York: Hoeber-Harper, 1959.

Hoobler, S. W., *et al.,* "Hypertension, Pregnancy Toxemia and Renal Disease—Community Services," *Nat Conf Cardiov Dis,* 2: 735–47, 1964.

Howard, J., "Race Differences in Hypertension Mortality Trends. Differential Drug Exposure as a Theory," *Milbank Mem Fund Quart,* 43:202–18, Apr. 65.

Hudak, W. J., and Buckley, J. P., "Production of Hypertensive Rats by Experimental Stress," *J Pharm Sci,* L (March, 1961), 263–64.

Humphries, S. V., "Study of Hypertension in the Bahamas," *S Afr Med J,* XXXI (July 13, 1957), 694–99.

Hutcheson, J. M., Jr., Maijtmancik, M. R., and Herrmann, G. R., "Changes in the Incidence and Types of Heart Disease; A Quarter-Century Follow-Up in a Southern Clinic and Hospital," *Amer Heart J,* XLVI (October, 1953), 565–75.

Hyman, A. S., "The Cardiac Athlete. Recent Studies in Sports Medicine," *Texas J Med,* 60:571–6, Jul, 64.

"Hypertension and Hypertensive Heart Disease in Adults. United States: 1960–1962," *Vital Health Statist,* 11:1–62, May, 66.

"Hypertension, Salt, and Genetics—Animal Studies," *Nutr Rev,* 22: 152–5, May, 64.

Igersheimer, Walter W., and Stevenson, James A. F., "Effect of Electroshock on the Blood Pressure in Psychotic Patients," *AMA Arch Neurol*, LXV (June, 1951), 740–51.

Innes, George, Millar, W. Malcolm, and Valentine, Max, "Emotion and Blood Pressure," *J Ment Sci*, CV (July, 1959), 840–51.

Isaacson, L. C., Modlin, M., Jackson, W. P., "Sodium Intake and Hypertension," *Lancet*, 1:946, 27 Apr 63.

Ives, E. R., "Vasospasm of the Retinal Arteries, Association with Psychiatric Manifestations and Focal or General Neurological Signs and Symptoms," *Bull Los Angeles Neurol Soc*, XXV (June, 1960). 100–05.

Ivy, A. C., "Physiological Differences Produced by Race and Diet Other Than Vitamin and Mineral Deficiencies," *Hawaii Med J*, XVI (September–October, 1956), 21–25.

James, G., *et al.*, "Cardiovascular Health Center: II. First Year's Operation: General Observations and Hypertension," *New York J Med*, LV (March 15, 1955), 774–78.

Johnson, B. C., and Remington, R. D., "A Sampling Study of Blood Pressure Levels in White and Negro Residents of Nassau, Bahamas," *J Chron Dis*, XIII (January, 1961), 39–51.

Jones, E. W., *et al.*, "Diet and Hypertension," *Practitioner*, 193: 50, 6 Jul 64.

Jones, H. H., Jr., "Reversible Depression and Parkinsonian Occurring During Treatment of Hypertension with Rauwolfia, *J Okla Med Ass*, XLVIII (November, 1955), 380–81.

Jost, H., *et al.*, "Studies in Hypertension: I. Technics and Control Data, Central and Autonomic Nervous System Reactions of Normal Adults to Sensory and Ideational (Frustration) Stimulation," *J Nerv Ment Dis*, CXV, (January, 1952), 35–48.

Jost, H., *et al.*, "Studies in Hypertension: II. Central and Autonomic Nervous System Reactions of Hypertensive Individuals to Simple Physical and Psychologic Stress Situations," *J Nerv Ment Dis*, CXV (February, 1952), 152–62.

Judson, A. J., and Katahn, M., "The Relationship of Autonomic Responsiveness to Process-Reactive Schizophrenia and Abstract Thinking," *Psychiatric Quart*, 1963, 37 (1), 19–24.

Julius, S., *et al.*, "Relation Between Casual Blood Pressure Readings in Youth and at Age 40: A Retrospective Study," *J Chronic Dis*, 17: 397–404, May, 64.

Kalis, B. L., *et al.*, "Personality and Life History Factors in Persons Who Are Potentially Hypertensive," *J Nerv Ment Dis*, CXXXII (June, 1961), 457–68.

Kalis, B. L., *et al.*, "Response to Psychological Stress in Patients with Essential Hypertension," *Amer Heart J*, LIII (April, 1957), 572–78.

Kaltreider, D. F., and Gilbert, R. A., "Unexpected Hypertension in the Early and Late Puerperium," *Amer J Obstet Gynec*, LXI (Number 1, 1951), 161–66.

Kaminer, B., and Lutz, W. P. W., "Blood Pressure in Bushmen of the Kalahari Desert," *Circulation*, XXII, (August, 1960), 289–95.

Kaplan, S. M., *et al.*, "Hostility in Verbal Productions and Hypnotic Dreams of Hypertensive Patients. Studies of Groups and Individuals," *Psychosom Med*, XXIII (July–August, 1961), 311–22.

Karpinos, B. D., "Blood Pressure and Its Relation to Height, Weight, Race and Age: World War II," *Amer J Hyg*, LXVIII (November, 1958), 288–311.

Kass, I., and Brown, E. C., "Treatment of Hypertensive Patients with Rauwolfia Compounds and Reserpine. Depressive and Psychotic Changes," *JAMA*, CLIX (December 17, 1955), 1513–16.

Kawahata, A., and Adams, T., "Racial Variations in Sweat Gland Distribution," *Proc Soc Exp Biol Med*, CVI (April, 1961), 862–65.

Keaney, F. P., *et al.*, "A Hypertension and Diabetes Detection Program," *US Armed Forces Med J*, IV (November, 1953), 1613–21.

Keil, P. G., and McVay, L. V., Jr., "A Comparative Study of Myocardial Infarction in the White and Negro Races," *Circulation*, XIII (May, 1956), 712–18.

Kepecs, Joseph G., Robin, Milton, and Munro, Clare, "Responses to Sensory Stimulation in Certain Psychosomatic Disorders," *Psychosom Med*, XX (September–October, 1958), 351–65.

Keys, A., "World Trends in Cardiology: I. Cardiovascular Epidemiology. Field Studies in 1955," in *Selected Papers from Second World Congress of Cardiology and Twenty-Seventh Annual Scientific Sessions of the American Heart Association Held in Washington, D.C.*, New York: Hoeber-Harper, 1956, 175–86.

Kirkendall, W. M., "Current Concepts of the Mechanisms of Hypertension," *Ann NY Acad Sci*, LXXXVIII, Art. 4 (October 11, 1960), 922–26.

Knight, A. M., "Psychosomatic Aspects of Essential Hypertension," *J Med Ass Georgia,* XLIX (July, 1960), 369–70.

Kohlstaedt, K. G., *et al.,* "Panel Discussion on Genetic and Environmental Factors in Human Hypertension," *Circulation,* XVII (April, 1958, Part 2), 728–42.

Koletsky, S., "Pathogenesis of Experimental Hypertension Induced by Salt," *Amer J Cardiol,* 8: 576–81, Oct. 61.

Koller, E. K., and Katz, J. (eds.), *A Bibliography of the World Literature on Blood Pressure,* 1920–1950, I-III. The Commonwealth of Massachusetts, the Recess Commission on Hypertension, 1952.

Kooperstein, S. I., Schifrin, A., and Leahy, T. J., "Level of Initial Blood Pressure and Subsequent Development of Essential Hypertension. A Ten and Fifteen Year Follow-Up Study," *Amer J Cardiol,* 1962, 10/3 (416–423).

Korhonen, J., and Koskinen, P., "Acute Myocardial Infarction. A Study of the Sex Distribution, Immediate Mortality, Age Distribution, Incidence of Hypertension and Diabetes, and the Effect of the Seasons in a Series of 376 Cases," *Ann Med Intern Fenn,* XLIX (1960), 247–54.

Krautheimer, S., Moynier, R., and Soula, C., "Determination of the Period of 'Recuperation' After Work by Measurement of Arterial Pressure by Means of a New Automatic and Continuous Recorder," *J Physiol Path Gen,* XLVII (1955), 821–28.

Kurlander, A. B., Hill, E. H., and Enterline, P. E., "An Evaluation of Some Commonly Used Screening Tests for Heart Disease and Hypertension," *J Chron Dis,* II (October, 1955), 427–39.

Lamb, L. E., "The Problem of Elevated Blood Pressure or Hypertension in the Pilot," *Amer J Cardiol.* VI (July, 1960), 30–34.

Lambo, T. A., "Further Neuropsychiatric Observations in Nigeria with Comments on the Need for Epidemiological Study in Africa," *Brit Med J,* II (December 10, 1960), 1696–704.

Lambo, T. A., "The Concept and Practice of Mental Health in African Cultures," *E Afr Med J,* XXXVII (June, 1960), 464–71.

Lambo, T. A., "Psychiatric Syndromes Associated with Cerebrovascular Disorders in the African," *J Ment Sci,* CIV (January, 1958), 133–43.

Lambo, T. A., "The Influence of Cultural Factors on Epidemiological Surveys in Africa," *W Afr Med J,* X (April, 1961), 87–92.

Lampe, J. M., "Questions About Salt," *J Sch Health* 34:36–7, Jan. 64.

Larsen, N. P., and Bortz, W. M., "Atherosclerosis: A Comparative Study of Caucasian and Japanese Citizens in the Hawaiian Islands —1959," *J Amer Geriat Soc,* VIII (November, 1960), 867–72.

Lasser, R. P., and Master, A. M., "Observation of Frequency Distribution Curves of Blood Pressure in Persons Aged 20 to 106 Years," *Geriatrics,* XIV (Number 6, 1959), 345–60.

Laurie, W., Woods, J. D., and Roach, G., "Coronary Heart Disease in the South African Bantu," *Amer J Cardiol,* V (January, 1960), 48–59.

Laurie, W., and Woods, J. D., "Atherosclerosis and Its Cerebral Complications in the South-African Bantu," *Lancet,* I (February 1, 1958), 231–32.

Lavernhe, J., and Granotier, E., "The Medical Examination of Navigating Personnel: The Problem of Arterial Hypertension," *Rev Corps Sante Armees,* I (October, 1960), 681–90.

Leather, H. M., "Hypertension in Adult Africans in Uganda," *Trans Roy Soc Trop Med Hyg,* LV (January, 1961), 89–97.

Leather, H. M., "Portal Hypertension and Gross Splenomegaly in Uganda," *Brit Med J,* I (January 7, 1961), 15–18

Lee, K. T., Shaper, A. G., Scott, R. F., Goodale, F., Thomas, W. A., "Geographic Studies Pertaining to Arteriosclerosis. Comparison of Fatty Acid Patterns of Adipose Tissue and Plasma Lipids in East Africans With Those of North American White and Negro Groups," *Arch Path* (Chicago), 74: 481–8, Dec. 62.

Lee, R. E., and Schneider, R. F., "Hypertension and Arteriosclerosis in Executive and Nonexecutive Personnel," *JAMA,* CLXVII (July 19, 1958), 1447–50.

Leishman, A. W. D., "Hypertension—Treated and Untreated: A Study of 400 Cases," *Brit Med J,* I (May 30, 1959), 1361–68.

Lemieux, G., Davignon, A., and Genest, J., "Depressive States During Rauwolfia Therapy for Arterial Hypertension. A Report of 30 Cases," *Canad Med Ass J,* LXXIV (April 1, 1956), 522–26.

Lennard, H. L., and Glock, C. Y., "Studies in Hypertension; Differences in the Distribution of Hypertension in Negroes and Whites: An Appraisal," *J Chron Dis,* V (February, 1957), 186–96.

Leonard, J. C., "Treatment of Hypertension: Fifteen-Year Follow-Up," *Yale J Biol Med,* XXIV (June, 1952), 506–17.

Levan, J. B., "Effect of Race, Diet, and Climate on Cardiovascular Diseases," *Hawaii Med J,* XVI (September–October, 1956), 30–31.

Levin, A. R., and Yoffe, Y., "Acute Nephritis in Non-European Children, with Special Reference to the Treatment of Hypertension With Magnesium Sulphate," *S Afr Med J,* XXXIV (October 29, 1960), 921–24.

Levine, Maurice (Chairman), and Ackerman, N. W. (Reporter), "Problems of Hypertension," *J Amer Psychoanal Ass,* I (Number 3, 1953), 562–74.

Lew, E. A., "Some Implications of Mortality Statistics Relating to Coronary Artery Disease," *J Chron Dis,* VI (September, 1957), 192–209.

Lewinsohn, P. M., "Personality Correlates of Duodenal Ulcer and Other Psychosomatic Reactions," *J Clin Psychol,* XII (July, 1956), 296–98.

Lillienfeld, A. M., "Variation in Mortality From Heart Disease–– Race, Sex, and Socioeconomic Status," Public Health Rep, LXXI, (June, 1956), 545–52.

Lin, T. Y., *et al.,* "A Study of Normal and Elevated Blood Pressures in a Chinese Urban Population in Taiwan (Formosa)," *Clin Sci,* XVIII, (May, 1959), 301–12.

Lipman, D. G., "Stress and Hypertension: Use of Antistress Diet and Antihistamine," *J Amer Geriat Soc,* VIII (March, 1960), 177–84.

Litin, E. M., Faucett, R. L., and Achor, R. W. P., "Depression in Hypertensive Patients Treated with Rauwolfia Serpentina," *Proc Mayo Clin,* XXXI (April 18, 1956), 233–37.

Love, W. D., and Burch, G. E., "Plasma and Erythrocyte Sodium and Potassium Concentrations in a Group of Southern White and Negro Blood Donors," *J Lab Clin Med,* XLI (January–June, 1953), 258–67.

Lovell, H. G., *et al.,* "Arterial Blood Pressure in Jamaican Women with and without Uterine Fibroids," *W Indian Med J,* 15:45–51, Mar. 66.

Lovell, R. R., "The Relationship Between Blood Pressure and Age in Various Races of Mankind," *Gerontologist,* 1966, 6(2), 111–115.

Lowe, C. R., "Arterial Pressure, Physique and Occupation," *Brit J Prev Soc Med,* 1964, 18/3 (115–124).

Lowe, C. R., McKeown, T., "Arterial Pressure in an Industrial Population; and Its Bearing on the Problem of Essential Hypertension," *Lancet,* 1:1086–92, 26 May 62.

Lowenstein, F. W., "A Study of Blood Pressure in Relation to Diet in Chinese and Caucasian Students in New York City," *Amer Heart J,* XLIX (April, 1955), 562–80.

Lowenstein, F. W., "Blood-Pressure in Relation to Age and Sex in the Tropics and Subtropics. A Review of the Literature and an Investigation in Two Tribes of Brazil Indians," *Lancet,* I (February 18, 1961), 389–92.

Lowy, S., "A Few Notes on Hypertension," *Amer J Psychother,* V (July, 1951), 362–66.

Luisada, A. A., and Liu, C. K., *Cardiac Pressures and Pulses.* New York: Grune and Stratton, 1956.

MacDonald, I. D., *et al.,* "Hypertension and Life Assurance," *Practitioner,* 193:57–60, Jul. 64.

Macpherson, I., and Peel, A. A. F., "Effects of Dorsolumbar Sympathectomy (for Hypertension) on Peptic Ulceration," *Brit Med J,* I (May 14, 1955), 1185–86.

Maddocks, I., "Possible Absence of Essential Hypertension in Two Complete Pacific Island Populations," *Lancet,* II (August 19, 1961), 396–99.

Malmo, Robert B., Shagass, Charles, and Heslam, R. Murray, "Blood Pressure Response to Repeated Brief Stress in Psychoneurosis: A Study of Adaptation," *Canad J Psychol,* V (Number 4, 1951), 167–79.

Mallov, S., "Effect of Hypertension and Sodium Chloride on Vascular Reactivity in Vitro," *Amer J Cardiol,* 8:542–8, Oct. 61.

Mann, G. V., Roels, O. A., Price, D. L., Merrill, J. M., "Cardiovascular Disease in African Pygmies. A Survey of the Health Status, Serum Lipids and Diet of Pygmies in Congo," *J Chronic Dis,* 15:341–71, Apr. 62.

Marks, John B., *et al.,* "Physiological Reactions and Psychiatric Prognosis," *J Nerv Ment Dis,* CXXX (March, 1960), 217–23.

Master, A. M., Lasser, R. P., and Jaffe, H. L., "Blood Pressure in White People Over 65 Years of Age," *Ann Intern Med,* XLVIII (February, 1958), 284–99.

Master, A. M., "New Definitions of Normal Blood Pressure and Hypertension," *Merck Rep,* LXIII (July, 1954), 12–15.

Master, A. M., Garfield, C. I., and Walters, M. B., *Normal Blood Pressure and Hypertension,* Philadelphia: Lea and Febiger, 1952.

Master, A. M., Goldstein, I., and Walters, M. B., "New and Old Definitions of Normal Blood Pressure: Clinical Significance of the Newly Established Limits," *Bull NY Acad Med,* XXVII (Number 7, 1951), 452–65.

Master, A. M., Lasser R. P., and Donoso E., "Elevated Blood Pressure in Individuals From 20 to 100 Years of Age," (991). Abstract of paper delivered at the 34th Scientific Session of the American Heart Association (Bal Harbour, Miami Beach, Florida, October 1961)," *Circulation,* 1961, 24/4, Part 2.

Matarazzo, J. D., "An Experimental Study of Aggression in the Hypertensive Patient," *J Personality,* XXII (March, 1954), 423–47.

Maxwell, R. D. H., and Maxwell, K. N., "ABO Blood Groups and Hypertension," *Brit Med J,* II (July 16, 1955), 179–80.

McDonough, L. B., "Inhibited Aggression in Essential Hypertension." *Journal of Clinical Psychology,* 1964, 20 (4), 447.

McDonough, J. R., *et al.,* "Blood Pressure and Hypertensive Disease Among Negroes and Whites; A Study in Evans County, Georgia," *Ann Intern Med,* 61: 208–28, Aug. 64.

McGinn, Noel Francis, "Perception of Parents and Blood Pressure," *Dissertation Abstracts,* 1963, 24 (2), 872–Abstract.

McGinn, Noel F., Harburg, Ernest, and Julius, Stevo, "Blood Pressure Reactivity and Recall of Treatment by Parents," *Journal of Personality and Social Psychology,* 1965, 1 (2), 147–153.

McGinn, Noel F., Harburg, Ernest, Julius, Stevo, and McLead, Jack M., "Psychological Correlates of Blood Pressure," *Psychological Bulletin,* 1964, 61 (3), 209–219.

McGovern, V. J., and Greenaway, J. M., "Hypertension: A Survey of Autopsy Findings from Patients Over and Under the Age of Forty Years," *Med J Aust,* II (July 3, 1954), 10–12.

McKeown, T., "Population Study of Arterial Pressure," *Amer Heart J,* 67:569–71, Apr. 64.

McKusick, V. A., "Genetics and the Nature of Essential Hypertension," *Circulation,* XXII (November, 1960), 857–63.

McVay, L. V., Jr., and Keil, P. G., "Myocardial Infarction with Special Reference to the Negro," *Arch Intern Med,* XCVI (December, 1955), 762–67.

Meadow, Arnold, and Funkenstein, Daniel H., "The Relationship of Abstract Thinking to the Autonomic Nervous System in Schizophrenia," in Hoch, Paul H., and Zubin, Joseph (eds.), *Relation of Psychological Tests to Psychiatry,* New York: Grune and Stratton, 1952, 131–49.

Meadow, Arnold, *et al.,* "Relationship Between Capacity for Abstraction in Schizophrenia and Physiologic Response to Autonomic Drugs," *J Nerv Ment Dis,* CXVIII (October, 1953), 332–38.

Meehan, J. P., Jr., "Individual and Racial Variations in a Vascular Response to a Cold Stimulus," *Milit Med,* CXVI, (May, 1955), 330–34.

Meltzer, E., and Ronald, A. C., "Coronary Thrombosis with Cardiac Infarction: Two Probable Cases in Africans," *S Afr Med J,* XXVI (May 24, 1952), 435–41.

Mendlowitz, Milton (ed), *A Mount Sinai Hospital Monograph on Hypertension.* New York: Grune and Stratton, 1961.

Menof, P., "The Cause of Essential Hypertension," *S Afr Med J,* XXVII (October 24, 1953), 968.

Merton, R. K., Morsell, J. A., and Clark, E. G., "A Proposal for Long-Term Community Research in the Epidemiology of Hypertension," in The Commonwealth of Massachusetts. *A Symposium on Essential Hypertension.* Boston: Wright and Potter, 1951, 327–35.

Meyer, B. J., Pepler, W. J., Meyer, A. C., and Theron, J. J., "Atherosclerosis in Europeans and Bantu," *Circulation,* 1964, 29/3 (415–421).

Miall, W. E., and Oldham, P. D., "Factors Influencing Arterial Blood Pressure in the General Population," *Clin Sci,* XVII (August, 1958), 409–44.

Miall, W. E., Oldham, P. D., "The Hereditary Factor in Arterial Blood-Pressure," *Brit Med J,* 5323: 75–80, 12 Jan 63.

Miall, W. E., and Oldham, P. D., "Study of Arterial Blood Pressure and its Inheritance in Sample of General Population," *Clin Sci,* XIV (August, 1955), 459–88.

Milburn, A. A., "Anxiety, Hypertension, Obesity, and Diabetes," *W Virginia Med J,* LIII (October, 1957), 420–21.

Mihaly, J. P., and Whiteman, N. C., "Myocardial Infarction in the

Negro. Historical Survey as It Relates to Negroes," *Amer J Cardiol,* II (October, 1958), 464–74.

Miles, B. E., and De Wardener, H. E., "Effect of Emotion on Renal Function in Normotensive and Hypertensive Women," *Lancet,* II (September 12, 1953), 539–44.

Miles, B. E., De Wardener, H. E., and McSwiney, R. R., "Renal Function During Emotional Diuresis," *Amer J Med,* XII (June, 1952), 659–66.

Miller, D. C., Spencer, S. S., White, P. D., "Survey of Cardiovascular Disease Among Africans in the Vicinity of the Albert Schweitzer Hospital in 1960," *Amer J Cardiol,* 10: 432–46, Sept. 62.

Milliken, Robert L., "Mathematical-Verbal Ability Differentials of Situational Anxiety as Measured by Blood Pressure Change," *Journal of Experimental Education,* 1964, 32 (3), 309–311.

Milling, R. N., "The Physician, the Psyche and Hypertension Today," *J S Carolina Med Ass,* 58:299–301, Aug. 62.

Mills, L. C., "Stress and Hypertension," *Med Rec Ann,* (Houston) 56:48–9, Mar. 63.

Mills, L. C., "Stress As An Etiologic Factor in Essential Hypertension," *Amer J Cardiol,* IV (December, 1959), 711–18.

Milton, G. A., "Changes in Essential Hypertension Over Time: A Factor Analytic Case Study," *Journal of Clinical Psychology,* 1961, 17(3), 322–326.

Monroe, R. R., Heath, R. G., Head, R. G., Stone, R. L., and Ritter, K. A., "A Comparison of Hypertensive and Hypotensive Schizophrenics," *Psychosom Med,* 1961, 23, 508–519.

Moore, P. J., Taylor, R. D., and Corcoran, A. C., "Incidence of Coexistent Essential Hypertension and Malignant Neoplastic Diseases; Study Based on Records of 509 Clinic Patients With and 509 Without Malignant Neoplasms," *Amer J Med Sci,* CCXXXII (November, 1956), 555–59.

Moos, R. H., Engel, B. T., "Psychophysiological Reactions in Hypertensive and Arthritic Patients," *J Psychosom Res,* 6: 227–41, Oct–Dec 62.

Moreno, A. H., Rousselot, L. M., and Panke, W. F., "Studies on Portal Hypertension: II. Correlation Between Severity of Pathologic Involvement of the Portal System and Variations in Tension," *Surg Clin N Amer,* XXXVIII (April, 1958), 421–45.

Moriyama, I. M., and Woolsey, T. D., "Statistical Studies of Heart Disease; Race and Sex Differences in Trend of Mortality from the Major Cardiovascular-Renal Diseases," *Public Health Rep*, LXVI (March 23, 1951), 355–68.

Moriyama, I. M., Woolsey, T. D., and Stamler, J., "Observations on Possible Factors Responsible for the Sex and Race Trends in Cardiovascular-Renal Mortality in the United States," *J Chron Dis*, VII (May, 1958), 401–12.

Morris, J. N., *et al.*, "Coronary Heart Disease and Physical Activity of Work," *Lancet*, II (November 21, 1953), 1053–57.

Morris, Norman F., and Browne, J. C. McClure (eds.), London University Institute of Obstetrics and Gynaecology, *A Symposium on Non-Toxaemic Hypertension in Pregnancy*. Boston: Little, Brown, 1958.

Morrison, S. L., and Morris, J. N., "Epidemiological Observations on High Blood-Pressure Without Evident Cause," *Lancet*, II (November 21, 1959), 864–70.

Morsell, J. A., "The Problem of Hypertension: A Critical Review of the Literature Dealing with Its Extent," in The Commonwealth of Massachusetts. *A Symposium on Essential Hypertension*. Boston: Wright and Potter, 1951, 26–49.

Moser, M., *et al.*, "Acute Psychosis as Complication of Hydralazine (Phthalazine Derivative) Therapy in Essential Hypertension," *JAMA*, CLII (August 1, 1953), 1329–31.

Moser, M., *et al.*, "Epidemiology of Hypertension with Particular Reference to the Bahamas. I. Preliminary Report of Blood Pressures and Review of Possible Etiologic Factors," *Amer J Cardiol*, IV (December, 1959), 727–33.

Moser, M., Harris, M., Pugatch, D., Ferber, A., Gordon, B., "Epidemiology of Hypertension II. Studies of Blood Pressure in Liberia," *Amer J Cardiol*, 10: 424–31, Sept. 62.

Moser, M., "Epidemiology of Hypertension with Particular Reference to Racial Susceptibility," *Ann NY Acad Sci*, LXXXIV, Art. 17 (December 8, 1960), 989–99.

Moser, M., *et al.*, "Epidemiology of Hypertension. II. Blood Pressure in Liberia," (To be published). Cited in Moser, M., "Epidemiology of Hypertension with Particular Reference to Racial Susceptibility," *Ann NY Acad Sci*, LXXXIV, Art. 17 (December 8, 1960), 989–99.

Moses, L., Daniels, G. E., and Nickerson, J. L., "Psychogenic Factors in Essential Hypertension; Methodology and Preliminary Report," *Psychosom Med*, XVIII (November–December, 1956), 471–85.

Moutsos, S. E., Krifchei, E., Miller, R. E., and Shapiro, A. P., "A Study of Conditioning and Reactivity as Determinants of Pressor Responses to Noxious Stimuli," *Psychosomatic Medicine*, 1964, 26(3), 274–286.

Moyer, John H. (ed.), *Hypertension. The First Hahnemann Symposium on Hypertensive Disease*. Philadelphia: W. B. Saunders, 1959.

Mozes, E. B. *High Blood Pressure*. Philadelphia: Lippincott, 1959.

Muir, C. S., "Coronary Heart Disease in Seven Racial Groups in Singapore," *Brit Heart J*, XXII (January, 1960), 45–53.

Muller, J. C., *et al.*, "Depression and Anxiety Occurring During Rauwolfia (Serpentina) Therapy," *JAMA*, CLIX (October 29, 1955), 836–39.

Murphy, F. D., "Hypertension. Types and Treatment," *Med Times*, LXXXVIII (June, 1960), 659–66.

Murray, P. M., "Status of Negro Physician in New York State," *New York J Med*, LV (October 15, 1955), 2980–82.

Nesfield, V. B., *High Blood Pressure; Cause and Treatment*. 145 Upton Court Rd., Slough, Buckinghamshire, England: M. Wood, 1054.

Newman, M. J. D., and Robertson, J. I. S., "Some Aspects of Prognosis in Treated Hypertension," *Brit Med J*, I (May 30, 1959).

Nichaman, M. A., Boyle, E., Jr., Lesesne, T. P., Sauer, H. I., "Cardiovascular Disease Mortality by Race, Based on a Statistical Study in Charleston, South Carolina," *Geriatrics*, 17: 724–37, Nov. 62.

O'Connell, Desmond D., and Lundy, Richard M., "Level of Aspiration in Hypertensive Cardiac Patients Compared with Non-Hypertensive Cardiac Patients with Arteriosclerotic Heart Disease," *J Consult Psychol*, 1961, 25(4), 353–359.

Ochsner, A., Jr., Colp, R. Jr., and Burch, G. E., "Normal Blood Pressure in Superficial Venous System of Man at Rest in Supine Position," *Circulation*, III (May, 1951), 65–66.

Olansky, S., Simpson, L., and Schuman, S. H., "Untreated Syphilis in

Male; Environmental Factors in Tuskegee Study," *Public Health Rep*, LXIX (July, 1954), 691–98.

Olansky, S., *et al.,* "Untreated Syphilis in Male Negro; Twenty Years of Clinical Observation of Untreated Syphilitic and Presumably Nonsyphilitic Groups," *J Chron Dis*, IV (August, 1956), 177–85.

O'Hare, J. P., and Holden, R. B., "Longevity in Essential Hypertension," *Trans Ass Amer Physicians*, LXIV (1951), 378–83.

Orr, K. D., and Fainer, D. C., "Cold Injuries in Korea During Winter of 1950–51," *Medicine* (Balt), XXXI (May, 1952), 177–220.

Osbaldeston, J. B., and Stuart, C. K., "Observations on Blood Pressure Estimation," *Canad Med Ass J*, LXV, (July, 1951), 65–66.

Ostfeld, A. M., Paul, O., "The Inheritance of Hypertension," *Lancet* 1: 575–9. 16 Mar 63.

Ostfeld, A. M., and Lebovits, B. Z., "Personality Factors and Pressor Mechanisms in Renal and Essential Hypertension," *AMA Arch Intern Med*, CIV (July, 1959), 43–52.

Ostfeld, A. M., and Wolf, S., "Synthesis and Perspectives," *Psychosom Med*, 1964, 26 (4, Part 2), 510–537.

Padmavati, S., "The Cardiac Patient in Underdeveloped Countries," *Amer Heart J*, LVIII (Number 3, 1959), 418–24.

Padmavati, S., and Gupta, S., "Blood Pressure Studies in Rural and Urban Groups in Delhi," *Circulation*, XIX, (March, 1959), 395–405.

Padmavati, S., Gupta, S., and Pantulu, G. V., "Dietary Fat, Serum Cholesterol Levels and Incidence of Atherosclerosis and Hypertension in Delhi," *Indian J Med Res*, XLVI (March, 1958), 245–60.

Padmavati, S., Gupta, S., and Pantulu, G. V. A., "Dietary Fat, Serum Cholesterol Levels, and Incidence of Atherosclerosis and Hypertension in Delhi, India," *Amer Heart J*, LVI (July, 1958), 112.

Page, E. W., *The Hypertensive Disorders of Pregnancy*. Springfield, Illinois: C. C. Thomas, 1953.

Page, I. H., "Current Treatment of Arterial Hypertension," *J Chron Dis*, I (May, 1955), 536–45.

Palmer, R. S., "Medical Progress; Essential Hypertension: A Selected Review and Commentary," *New Engl J Med*, CCLII (June 2, 1955), 940–47.

Palmer, R. S., "The Results of Office Treatment in Two Hundred Patients with Hypertension: The Use of Diet Combined with Other Methods Including Psychotherapy," *Amer Practit,* VIII (January, 1957), 33–39.

Palmer, R. S., "Treatment of Hypertension; A 23-Year Follow-Up of 453 Patients With a Selected Review and Report of Current Experience," *J Chron Dis,* X (December, 1959), 500–12.

Palmer, R. S., and Muench, H., "Course and Prognosis of Essential Hypertension; Follow-Up of 453 Patients 10 Years After Original Series was Closed," *JAMA,* CLIII, (September 5, 1953), 1–4.

Parker, Paul A., "Acute Effects of Smoking on Physical Endurance and Resting Circulation," *Res Quart,* XXV, (May, 1954), 210–17.

Patton, E. W., "Symposium on Hypertension: Etiologic Factors in Hypertension," *J Tenn Med Ass,* XLV (December, 1952), 467–69.

Payet, M., *et al.,* "Ecological Factors of Atherosclerosis in Senegalese (With the Exclusion of Dietetic Factors)," *Bull Soc Path Exot,* LIII (November–December, 1960), 1010–23.

Pell, S., D'Alonzo, C. A., and Fleming, A. J., "A Study of the Relation of the ABO Blood Groups to Peptic Ulceration and Hypertension," *Ann Intern Med,* XLVI (June, 1957), 1024–30.

Pell, S., and D'Alonzo, C. A., "Acute Myocardial Infarction in a Large Industrial Population, Report of a 6-Year Study of 1,356 Cases," *J Amer Med Ass,* 1963, 185/11 (831–838).

Pennell, M. Y., and Gover, M., "Negro Mortality. IV. Urban and Rural Mortality from Selected Causes in the North and South," *Public Health Rep,* LXVI (March 9, 1951), 295–305.

Pepler, W. J., "Study of Some of Structural Changes of Bantu Aorta," *S Afr J Lab Clin Med,* I (December, 1955), 203–53.

Perera G. A., "Primary (essential) Hypertension. Epidemiology, Etiology and Pathogenesis," *Nat Conf Cardiov Dis,* 2:333–4, 1964.

Perera, G. A., "Relation of Blood Pressure Lability to Prognosis in Hypertensive Vascular Disease," *J Chron Dis,* I (February, 1955), 121–26.

Perera, G. A., "Hypertensive Vascular Disease; Description and Natural History," *J Chron Dis,* I (January, 1955), 33–42.

Perera, G. A., "Hypertensive Vascular Disease; Description and Natural History," *J Chron Dis,* I (February, 1955), 121–26.

Perera, G. A. "The Life History of One Hundred Patients with Hypertensive Vascular Disease," *Amer Heart J,* XLII (September, 1951), 421–23.

Perera, G. A., *The Natural History of Hypertensive Vascular Disease,* in *Hypertension: A Symposium.* Minneapolis: University of Minnesota, 1951, 363–69.

Perera, G. A., and Adler, G., "ABO Blood Groups in the Accelerated Form of Hypertension," *Ann Intern Med,* LIII (July, 1960), 84–86.

Perera, G. A., "The Unnatural History of (Hypertensive) Disease," *Circulation,* XXI (January, 1960), 1–2.

Perera, G. A., *et al.,* "The Family of Hypertensive Man, Progress Report of a Long-Range Study Program," *Amer J Med Sci,* CCXLI (January, 1961), 18–21.

Peters, J. J., *et al.,* "Untreated Syphilis in the Male Negro. Pathologic Findings in Syphilitic and Nonsyphilitic Patients," *J Chron Dis,* I (February, 1955), 127–48.

Phelan, E. L., and Smirk, F. H., "Cardiac Hypertrophy in Genetically Hypertensive Rats," *J Path Bact,* LXXX (October, 1960), 445–48.

Phillips, H. T., "The Assessment of Blood Pressure at Routine Medical Examinations," *Med Offr,* XCVI, (November 9, 1956), 285–89.

Phillips, John H., and Burch, George E., "A Review of Cardiovascular Diseases in the White and Negro Races," *Medicine* (Balt), XXXIX (May, 1960), 241–88.

Phillips, J. H., Jr., and Burch, G. E., "Cardiovascular Diseases in the White and Negro Races," *Amer J Med Sci,* CCXXXVIII (July, 1959), 97–124.

Picard, R. S., "The Psychosomatic Aspects of Hypertension," *J Louisiana Med Soc,* CX (June, 1958), 199–204.

Pickering, G. W., "The Genetic Component in High Blood Pressure," *Triangle,* III (June, 1957), 59–66.

Pickering, G. W. *High Blood Pressure.* New York: Grune and Stratton, 1955.

Pickering, G. W., "The Concept of Essential Hypertension," *Ann Intern Med,* XLIII (December, 1955), 1153–60.

Pickering, G. W., *The Nature of Essential Hypertension.* New York: Grune and Stratton, 1961.

Pickering, G. W., "The Genetic Factor in Essential Hypertension," *Ann Inter Med,* XLIII (September, 1955), 457–64.

Pickering, G. W., Cranston, William Ian, and Pears, Michael Andrew. *The Treatment of Hypertension*. Springfield, Illinois: C. C. Thomas, 1961.

Pla, J. C., Delbene, R., and Rodrigez, Iribarne L., "Importance of Increased Peripheral Venous Pressure in the Diagnosis and Prognosis of Various Conditions," *Rev Clin Med*, III (Numbers 1–3, 1951), 3–12.

Platt, R., "The Natural History and Epidemiology of Essential Hypertension," *Practitioner*, 193: 5–13, Jul. 64.

Platt, R., "Essential Hypertension. Incidence, Course and Heredity," *Ann Intern Med*, 1961, 55/1 (1–11).

Platt, R., "Genetic Effects in Human Disease," *Trans Med Soc London*, 78: 155–77, 1961–2.

Platt, R., "Heredity in Hypertension," *Lancet* 1: 899–904, 27 Apr 63.

Platt, R., "Essential Hypertension, Incidence, Course, and Heredity," *Ann Intern Med*, LV (July, 1961), 1–11.

Plotkin, Z., "Peptic Ulcer and Hypertension," *Arizona Med*, XI (October, 1954), 359–63.

Poindexter, H. A., "Epidemiologic Survey Among Gola Tribe in Liberia," *Amer J Trop Med*, II (January, 1953), 30–38.

Pollack, A. A., and Gudger, J. R., "Benign Hypertension; a Study on 2,500 Cases," *AMA Arch Intern Med*, CIII (May, 1959), 758–61.

Postell, W. D., "Survey on the Chronic Illnesses and Physical Impairments Among the Slave Population in the Ante-Bellum South," *Bull Med Libr Ass*, LXII (April, 1954), 158–62.

"Psychotherapy of a Psychosomatic Illness: Essential Hypertension," *Amer J Med*, XI (September, 1951), 381–86.

Rasmussen, P., "The Genetics of Essential Hypertension," *Maryland Med J*, 15:99–100, Jan. 66.

Raychadhury, A. K., "A Case of Hypertension; A Study in Psychosomatic Medicine," *Psychosom Med*, XVI (May–June, 1954), 246–51.

"Recent Advances in Hypertension," *Amer J Med*, 39: 616–45, Oct. 65.

Reeder, L. G., "Social Factors in Heart Disease: A Preliminary Research Report on the Relationship of Certain Social Factors to Blood Pressure in Males," *Soc Forces*, XXXIV (May, 1956), 367–71.

Reich, N. E., "Firefighting and Heart Disease," *Dis Chest*, XXIV (September, 1953), 304–09.

Reinhardt, D. J. III, *et al.*, "Symposium on Diabetes and Obesity; Diabetes Mellitus with Diastolic Hypertension; Study of Incidence, Complications and Management," *Med Clin N Amer*, XXXIX (November, 1955), 1361–42.

Reinhardt, D. J. III, "Arterial Hypertension. A Review of the Recent Advances in Evaluation," *Delaware Med J*, XXXIX (January, 1957), 6–12.

Reinhardt, D. J. III, "Essential Hypertension: Classification by Severity Index," *Bull Ayer Clin Lab*, IV (May, 1954), 67–71.

Reiser, M. F., Rosenbaum, M., and Ferris, E. B., "Psychologic Mechanisms in Malignant Hypertension," *Psychosom Med*, XIII (May–June, 1951), 147–59.

Reiser, M. F., *et al.*, "Life Situation, Emotions, and the Course of Patients with Arterial Hypertension," *Psychosom Med*, XIII (May–June, 1951), 133–39.

Reitan, R. M., "Intellectual and Affective Changes in Essential Hypertension," *Amer J Psychiat*, CX (May, 1954), 817–24.

Remington, R. D., *et al.*, "Circulatory Reactions of Normotensive and Hypertensive Subjects and of the Children of Normal and Hypertensive Parents," *Amer Heart J*, LIX (January, 1960), 58–70.

Restrepo, C., and McGill, H. C., Jr., "The Early Lesions of Aortic Atherosclerosis in Cali, Colombia," *AMA Arch Path*, LXVII (June, 1959), 618–23.

Robertson, W. B., "Atherosclerosis and Ischaemic Heart-Disease: Observations in Jamaica," *Lancet*, I (February 28, 1959), 444–46.

Robins, M., and Steinman, A. M., "Methods of Studying the Ecology of Coronary Heart Disease," *Public Health Rep*, LXXIII (April, 1958), 313–21.

Robinson, J. O., "A Study of the Relationship Between Blood Pressure and Certain Aspects of Personality," *Bull Brit Psychol Soc*, XXXVII (1959), 5A(Abstract).

Rose, G., "A Study of Blood Pressure Among Negro School Children," *J Chronic Dis*, 15:373–80, Apr. 62.

Rose, G., "Cardiovascular Mortality Among American Negroes," *Arch Environ Health* (Chicago), 5:412–4, Nov. 62.

Rose, G., "The Distribution of Mortality From Hypertension Within the United States," *J Chronic Dis*, 15:1017–24, Nov. 62.

Ross, D. C., *et al.*, "Precursors of Hypertension and Coronary Disease Among Healthy Medical Students: Discriminant Function Analysis. 3. Using Ethnic Origin as the Criterion, with Observations on Parental Hypertension and Coronary Disease and on Religion," *Bull Hopkins Hosp*, 117:37–57, Jul, 65.

Roth, G. M., and Shick, R. M., "Cardiovascular Effects of Smoking of Tobacco on Normal Persons and Patients with Hypertension," *Penn Med J*, LVIII (March, 1955), 281–83.

Roth, G. M., and Shick, R. M., "The Cardiovascular Effects of Smoking with Special Reference to Hypertension," *Ann NY Acad Sci*, XC, Art. 1 (September 27, 1960) 308–16.

Rowland, H. A., "Cardiovascular Disease in Sierra Leone," *W Afr Med J*, 14: 99–114, Jun. 65.

Rudolf, G. de M., "Clinical Blood-Pressure in Anxiety," *J Ment Sci*, CI (October, 1955), 893–94.

Rueger, D. E., "Hypertensive and Chronic Respiratory Disease Mortality, Confirmation of Trends by Multiple Cause of Death Data," *Public Health Rep*, 81: 197–8, Feb. 66.

Ruskin, A., (ed.), *Classics in Arterial Hypertension*. Springfield, Illinois: C. C. Thomas, 1956.

Sacks, M. I., "Aortic and Coronary Atherosclerosis in the Three Racial Groups in Cape Town," *Circulation*, XXII (July, 1960), 96–109.

Salem, E. El-Din, "Study of Hypertension Over the Age of 40 in Egypt," *J Egypt Med Ass*, XL (Number 2, 1957), 69–82.

Sancetta, S. M., and Rakita, L., "Response of Pulmonary Artery Pressure and Total Pulmonary Resistance of Untrained, Convalescent Men to Prolonged Mild Steady State Exercise," *J Clin Invest*, XXXVI (Number 7, 1957), 1138–49.

Saul, L., and Sheppard, E., "An Attempt to Quantify Emotional Forces Using Manifest Dreams; A Preliminary Study," *J Amer Psychoanal Ass*, IV (July, 1956), 486–502.

Saul, L., *et al.*, "The Quantification of Hostility in Dreams with Reference to Essential Hypertension," *Science,* CXIX (March 19, 1954), 382–83.

Schachter, H., "Pain, Fear, and Anger in Hypertensives and Normotensives; A Psychophysiological Study," *Psychosom Med,* XIX (January–February, 1957), 17–29.

Schilling, R. S. F., Goodman, N., and O'Sullivan, J. G., "Cardiovascular Disease in Cotton Workers. II. A Clinical Study with Special Reference to Hypertension," *Brit J Industr Med,* IX (April, 1952), 146–56.

Schneckloth, R. E., Corcoran, A. C., Stuart, K. L., Moore, F. E., "Arterial Pressure and Hypertensive Disease in a West Indian Negro Population. Report of a Survey in St. Kitts, West Indies," *Amer Heart J,* 63, 607–28, May, 62.

Schneider, R. A., and Zangari, V. M., "Variations in Clotting Time, Relative Viscosity and Other Physiochemical Properties of Blood Accompanying Physical and Emotional Stress in Normotensive and Hypertensive Subject," *Psychosom Med,* XIII (September–October, 1951), 289–303.

Schneider, R. A., *et al.,* "Estimation of Central Sympathetic Reactivity Using the Blood Pressure Response to Methacholine (Mecholyl)," *Psychiat Res Rep Amer Psychiat Ass,* Number 12 (January, 1960), 149–60.

Schreier, P. C., *et al.,* "Estimation of Central Sympathetic Reactivity Using the Blood Pressure Response to Methacholine (Mecholyl)," *Psychiat Res Rep Amer Psychiat Ass,* Number 12 (January, 1960), 149–60.

Schrire, V., "Myocardial Infarction: Its Racial Incidence in Cape Town During 1956," *S Afr Med J,* XXXII (February 15, 1958), 177–78.

Schrire, V., "The Comparative Racial Prevalence of Ischemic Heart Disease in Cape Town," *Amer J Cardiol,* VIII (August, 1961), 173–77.

Schrire, V., "The Racial Incidence of Heart Disease at Groote Schuur Hospital, Cape Town: Coronary Vascular Disease," *Amer Heart J,* LVI (August, 1958), 280–90.

Schrire, V., "The Racial Incidence of Heart Disease at Groote Schuur Hospital, Cape Town: Hypertension and Valvular Disease of the Heart," *Amer Heart J,* LVI (November, 1958), 742–60.

Schrire, V., "The Racial Incidence of Heart Disease at Groote Schuur

Hospital, Cape Town: III. The Less Common Forms of Heart Disease," *Amer Heart J*, LIX (June, 1960), 835–43.

Schroeder, Henry, A., *Hypertensive Diseases: Causes and Control*, Philadelphia: Lea and Febiger, 1953.

Schroeder, H. A., "Pathogenesis of Hypertension," *Amer J Med*, X (February, 1951), 189–209.

Schroeder, Henry A., and Menhard, E. M., "Spontaneous Variations of Blood Pressure in Hypertensive and Normotensive Individuals," *Amer Heart J*, LI (April, 1956), 577–87.

Schroeder, H. A., *Mechanisms of Hypertension, With a Consideration of Atherosclerosis*. Springfield, Illinois: C. C. Thomas, 1957.

Schroeder, H. A., "Degenerative Cardiovascular Disease in the Orient. II. Hypertension," *J Chron Dis*, VIII (Sept, 1958), 312–33.

Schroeder, H. A., "Hypertension in the Orient," In Moyer, John H. (ed.) *Hypertension*. Philadelphia and London: W. B. Saunders, 1959, 84–88.

Schuman, S. H., *et al.*, "Untreated Syphilis in the Male Negro; Background and Current Status of Patients in the Tuskegee Study," *J Chron Dis*, II, (November, 1955), 543–58.

Schweitzer, M. D., Clark, E. G., Gearing, F. R., Perera, G. A., "Genetic Factors in Primary Hypertension and Coronary Artery Disease. A Reappraisal," *J Chronic Dis*, 15: 1093–108, Dec. 62.

Schweitzer, M. D., *et al.*, "Epidemiology of Cardiovascular Disease. Hypertension," *Nat Conf Cardio Dis*, 2:226–9, 1964.

Schweitzer, M. D., *et al.*, "The Epidemiology of Primary Hypertension. Present Status," *J Chronic Dis*, 18:847–57, Aug. 65. (47 Ref.).

Schwob, R. A., *et al.*, "Dynamic Study of Aldosteronuria During Severe Arterial Hypertension with Hypopotassemia After Nervous Exhaustion; Study of Spontaneously Resolvent Functional Conn's Syndrome," *Bull Soc Med Hop Paris*, LXXV (April 24–May 15, 1959), 504–14.

Sclare, A. B., "Cultural Determinants in the Neurotic Negro," *Brit J Med Psychol*, XXVI (1953), 278–88.

Scotch, N. A. *et al.*, "The Epidemiology of Essential Hypertension. A Review With Special Attention to Psychologic and Sociocultural Factors. II. Psychologic and Sociocultural Factors in Etiology," *J Chronic Dis*, 16: 1183–213.

Scotch, N. A., "Sociocultural Factors in the Epidemiology of Zulu Hypertension." *Amer J Public Health,* 53: 1205–13, Aug. 6.

Scotch, N. A., "A Preliminary Report on the Relation of Sociocultural Factors to Hypertension Among the Zulu," *Ann NY Acad Sci,* LXXXIV, Art. 17 (December 8, 1960), 1000–09.

Scotch, N., *et al.,* "Blood Pressure Measurements of Urban Zulu Adults," *Amer Heart J,* LXI (February, 1961), 173–77.

Scott, R. F., *et al.,* "Comparison of the Amount of Coronary Arteriosclerosis in Autopsied East Africans and New Yorkers," *Amer J Cardiol,* VIII (August, 1961), 165–72.

Seedat, Y. K., "Malignant Hypertension in the Natal African and Indian," *S Afr Med J,* 37:655–6, 22 June 63.

Selye, H., "The General-Adaptation-Syndrome in Its Relationships to Neurology, Psychology, and Psychopathology," in Weider, A. (ed.), *Contributions Toward Medical Psychology,* I. New York: Ronald, 1953, 234–74.

Shapiro, A. P., "An Experimental Study of Comparative Responses of Blood Pressure to Different Noxious Stimuli," *J Chronic Dis,* 1961, 13, 293–311.

Shapiro, A. P., "Psychophysiologic Aspects of Blood Pressure Regulation: Methodological Issues," *Psychosomatic Medicine,* 1964, 26 (4, Part. 2), 481–509.

Shapiro, A. P., "An Experimental Study of Comparative Responses of Blood Pressure to Different Noxious Stimuli," *J Chron Dis,* XIII (April, 1961), 293–311.

Shapiro, A. P., "Influence of Emotional Variables in Evaluation of Hypotensive Agents," *Psychosom Med,* XVII (July–August, 1955), 291–305.

Shapiro, A. P., "Psychophysiologic Mechanisms in Hypertensive Vascular Disease," *Ann Intern Med,* LIII (July, 1960), 64–83.

Shapiro, A. P., and Horn, P. W., "Blood Pressure, Plasma Pepsinogen, and Behavior in Cats Subjected to Experimental Production of Anxiety," *J Nerv Ment Dis,* CXXII (September, 1955), 222–31.

Shapiro, Alvin P., and Melhado, Julian, "Observations on Blood Pressure and Other Physiologic and Biochemical Mechanisms in Rats with Behavioral Disturbances," *Psychosom Med,* XX (July–August, 1958), 303–13.

Shapiro, A. P., Rosenbaum, M., and Ferris, E. B., "Relationship Therapy in Essential Hypertension," *Psychosom Med,* XIII (May–June, 1951), 140–46.

Shapiro, A. P., *et al.,* "Comparison of Blood Pressure Response to Veriloid and to the Doctor," *Psychosom Med,* XVI (November–December, 1954), 478–88.

Shipp, J. H., and Hargrove, M. D., "Cardiac Enlargement," *New Orleans M. & S. J.,* CIV (November, 1952), 693–99.

Sigler, L. H., "The Mortality from Arteriosclerotic and Hypertensive Heart Diseases in the United States. I. Possible Relation to Distribution of Population and Economic Status," *Amer J Cardiol,* I (February, 1958), 176–80.

Simonson, E., and Brozek, J., "Russian Research on Arterial Hypertension," *Ann Intern Med,* L (January, 1959), 129–93.

Simpson, F. O., and Gilchrist, A. R., "Prognosis in Untreated Hypertensive Vascular Disease," *Scot Med J,* III (January, 1958), 1–14.

Skelton, F. R., and Hyde, P. M., "Plasma Corticosterone Levels and Salt Intake in Experimental Hypertension in the Rat," *Amer J Cardiol,* 1961, 8/5 (700–704).

Sloane, R. Bruce, Lewis, David J., and Slater, Patrick, "Diagnostic Value of Blood Pressure Responses in Psychiatric Patients," *AMA Arch Neurol,* LXXVII (May, 1957), 540–42.

Slome, C., *et al.,* "Variations in Blood Pressure in the Two Arms of Urban Africans," *Amer Heart J,* LVIII (July, 1959), 41–45.

Smirk, F. H., Veale, A. M. O., and Alstad, K. S., "Basal and Supplemental Blood Pressures in Relationship to Life Expectancy and Hypertension Symptomatology," *New Zeal Med J,* LVIII (December, 1959), 711–35.

Smirk, F. H., *High Arterial Pressure.* Springfield, Illinois: C. C. Thomas, 1958.

Smith, G. S., *et al.,* "Hypertension and Cardiovascular Abnormalities in Starved-Refed swine," *J Nutr,* 82:173–82, Feb. 64.

Smithwick, R. H., *Surgical Measures in Hypertension,* Springfield, Illinois: C. C. Thomas, 1951.

Smithwick, R. H., *et al.,* "Hypertension and Associated Cardiovascular Disease: Comparison of Male and Female Mortality Rates and Their Influence on Selection of Therapy," *JAMA,* CLX (March 4, 1956), 1023–26.

Smithwick, R. H., and Robertson, C. W., "The Phenomenon of Hyperreactivity: Definition and Illustrations," *Angiology*, II (June, 1951), 143–56.

Society of Actuaries, *Build and Blood Pressure Study*, I. II. Chicago: Society of Actuaries, 1959, 1960.

Sokolow, M., and Perloff, D., "The Prognosis of Essential Hypertension Treated Conservatively," *Circulation*, XXIII (May, 1961), 697–713.

Solomon, Harry C., and Greenblatt, Milton, "Physiological Changes Predictive of Clinical Outcome Following Frontal Lobe Surgery: Effect of Frontal Lobe Surgery Upon Systolic Blood Pressure Response to an Autonomic Drug (Mecholyl)," *Res Publ Ass Res Nerv Ment Dis*, XXXI (1951), 328–40.

Somers, K., "Hypertension and Its Management in an African Hospital in Uganda," *J Trop Med Hyg*, LXIII (November, 1960), 260–64.

Somers, K., "Mecamylamine and Reserpine in the Management of Severe and Malignant Hypertension in Uganda," *S Afr Med J*, XXXIII (June 20, 1959), 515–19.

Sowry, G. S. C., "Hypertension. The Coincidence of Conditions," *Postgrad Med J*, XXXIV (January, 1958), 39–48.

Speisman, J. C., and Singer, M. T., "Rorschach Content Correlates in Five Groups with Organic Pathology," *J Project Techn*, XXV (September, 1961), 356–59.

Speransky, I., and Beljaeva, N., "The Influence of Heredity and Environmental Factors on the Course of Hypertensive Disease (On the Basis of Long-Term Observations of Patients)," *Amer Heart J*, LX (December, 1960), 855–62.

Spieth, W., "Cardiovascular Health Status, Age, and Psychological Performance," *J Geront*, 19: 277–84, Jul. 64.

Stamler, J., "Breakthrough Against Hypertensive and Atherosclerotic Diseases? Some Possible Implications and Problems for Cardiovascular Research and Clinical Practice," *Geriatrics*, 17: 31–40, Jan. 62.

Stamler, J., and Stamler, R., "Psychosocial Factors and Hypertensive Disease in Low-Income Middle-Aged Negro Men in Chicago," (790). Abstract of paper delivered at the 16th annual meeting of the American Heart Association Council on Arteriosclerosis. *Circulation*, 1962, 26/4 (II).

Stamler, J., Berkson, D. M., Lindberg, H. A., Miller, W. and Hall, Y., "Racial Patterns of Coronary Heart Disease. Blood Pressure, Body Weight and Serum Cholesterol in Whites and Negroes," *Geriatrics*, 1961, 16 (382–396).

Stamler, J., *et al.*, "Epidemiologic Studies on Cardiovascular-Renal Diseases. I. Analysis of Mortality by Age-Race-Sex-Place of Residence, Including Urban-Rural Comparisons. III. Analysis of Mortality by Age-Sex-Nationality," *J Chron Dis*, XIII (October, 1960), 440–75.

Stamler, J., and Hall, Y. F., "Epidemiologic Analysis of Vital Statistics on the Cardiovascular—Renal Diseases in Chicago," *Circulation*, XIV (October, 1956), 1006 (Abstract).

Stein, S. I., "Treatment of Hypertension in Neuropsychiatric Practice —the Clinical Application of L-Tryptophan," *J Neuropsychiat*, 4: 296–309, Jun. 63.

Stevenson, I. P., *et al.*, "Hypertension as a Reaction Pattern to Stress. Correlation of Circulatory Hemodynamics with Changes in the Attitude and Emotional State," *Amer J Med Sci*, CCXXIV (September, 1952), 286–99.

Stirling, G. A., "Hypertensive Disease in Jamaican Necropsy Material," *Brit Med J*, I (April 16, 1960), 1173–74.

Stirling, G. A., "The Adrenals in Hypertensive Jamaicans," *Trop Geogr Med*, XII (June, 1960), 114–18.

Streeper, R. B., *et al.*, "An Electrocardiographic and Autopsy Study of Coronary Heart Disease in the Navajo," *Dis Chest*, XXXVIII (September, 1960), 305–12.

"Stress and Hypertension," *Triangle*, III (June, 1957), 81–83.

Strong, J. P., *et al.*, "The Natural History of Atherosclerosis. Comparison of the Early Aortic Lesions in New Orleans, Guatemala, and Costa Rica," *Amer J Path*, XXXIV (July–August, 1958), 731–44.

Sussman, I., "About Neurotics," *J Med Soc New Jersey*, 61: 87–92, Mar. 64.

Sutin, G. J., and Schrire, V., "The Electrocardiogram in the First Two Days of Life. An Interracial Study," *Amer Heart J*, 1964, 67–6 (749–756).

Sutley, P. H., "Psychosomatic Approach to Hypertension," *Maryland Med J*, V (December, 1956), 749–51.

Swell, L., Field, H., Jr., and Treadwell, C. R., "Relation of Age and Race to Serum Cholesterol Ester Fatty Acid Composition," *Proc Soc Exp Biol Med*, CV (October, 1960), 129–31.

"Symposium: Management of Patients with Primary (Essential) Hypertension," *J Chron Dis*, I (May, 1955), 471–588.

"Symposium on Hypertension," *J Tenn Med Ass*, XLV (December, 1952), 467–87.

Szent-Gyorgyi, N., "Blood Pressure Studies Among American and Foreign-Born Students," *Circulation*, XIV (July, 1956), 17–24.

Takahashi, E., *et al.*, "The Geographic Distribution of Cerebral Hemorrhage and Hypertension in Japan," *Hum Biol*, XXIX (May, 1957), 139–66.

Tejada, C., and Gore, I., "Comparison of Atherosclerosis in Guatemala City and New Orleans," *Amer J Path*, XXXIII, (September–October, 1957), 887–94.

Tejada, C., *et al.*, "Comparative Severity of Atherosclerosis in Costa Rica, Guatemala, and New Orleans," *Circulation*, XVIII (July, 1958), 92–97.

"The Significance of High Blood-Pressure," *Lancet*, II (July 13, 1957), 81–82.

"The Social Significance of Hypertension and Arteriosclerosis," *Canad Med Ass J*, LXXIX (September 15, 1958), 490.

Thomae, H., "Treatment of a Hypertension Considered as an Example of Biphase Repression," *Evolut Psychiat* (*Par*), Number 3 (July–September, 1953), 443–56.

Thomas, C., "Psychophysiologic Aspects of Blood Pressure Regulation: the Clinician's View," *Psychosom Med* 26: 454–80, Jul–Aug. 64.

Thomas, C. B., *et al.*, "Observations on Some Possible Precursors of Essential hypertension and Coronary Artery Disease. VIII. Relationship of Cholesterol Level to Certain Habit Patterns Under Stress," *Bull Hopkins Hosp*, 113: 225–38, Oct. 63.

Thomas, C. B., *et al.*, "Precursors of Hypertension and Coronary Disease; Among Healthy Medical Students: Discriminant Function Analysis. I. Using Smoking Habits as the Criterion." *Bull Hopkins Hosp*, 115: 174–94, Aug. 64.

Thomas, C. B., "Observations on Some Possible Precursors of Essential Hypertension and Coronary Artery Disease," *Bull Johns Hopkins Hosp*, LXXXIX (December, 1951), 419–41.

Thomas, C. B., *et al.*, "The Precursors of Hypertension and Coronary Disease: Statistical Consideration of Distributions in a Population of

Medical Students. I. Total Serum Cholesterol," *Bull Hopkins Hosp,* 114:290–312, May 64.

Thomas C. B., Bateman, J. L., and Lindberg, E. F., "Observations on the Individual Effects of Smoking on the Blood Pressure, Heart Rate, Stroke Volume and Cardiac Output on Healthy Young Adults," *Ann Intern Med,* XLIV (May, 1956), 874–92.

Thomas, C. B., and Murphy, E. A., "The Circulatory Response to Smoking: The Variation in Ballistocardiographic Smoking Tests in Healthy Young Men," *J Chron Dis,* VIII (August, 1958), 202–29.

Thomas, C. B., Stanley, J. A., and Kendrick, M. A., "Observations on Some Possible Precursors of Essential Hypertension and Coronary Artery Disease, VII. The Subjective Reaction to the Cold Pressor Test as Expressed in the Verbal Response," *J Chron Dis,* XIV (September, 1961), 355–65.

Thomas, C. B., and Cohen, B. H., "The Familial Occurrence of Hypertension and Coronary Artery Disease, with Observations Concerning Obesity and Diabetes," *Ann Intern Med,* XLII (January, 1955), 90–127.

Thomas, J., et al. "The Incidence of Renovascular Lesions in the Hypertensive Negro Patient," *J Nat Med Ass,* 57:121–5, Mar. 65.

Thomas, J., et al., "Acute Myocardial Infarction in Ninety Negro Patients: Clinical Manifestations and Immediate Mortality. Comparison with 229 Similarly Studied White Patients," *Amer J Cardiol,* VIII (August, 1961) 178–83.

Threefoot, H. K., "Response of Man to Hot and Humid Environment," *Amer J Med Sci,* CCXXIV (December, 1952), 643–46.

Titchener, J. L., Sheldon, M. B., and Ross, W. D., "Changes in Blood Pressure of Hypertensive Patients With and Without Group Psychotherapy," *J Psychosom Res,* IV (Number 1, 1959), 10–12.

Tobian, L., Jr., "Seminar on the Role of Salt in Cardiovascular Hypertension. II. Effect of Salt on the Kidney and the Juxtaglomerular Apparatus." *Amer J Cardiol,* 8:684–7, Nov. 61.

Tomasson, R. F., "Patterns in Negro-White Differential Mortality," 1930–1957. *Milbank Mem Fund Quart,* 38: 362–86, Oct. 60.

Townsend, Lance, *High Blood Pressure and Pregnancy*. Carlton: Melbourne University, 1960.

Uys, C. J., "Pathology of Renal Disease in Bantu on Witwatersrand; Glomerulonephritis," *S Afr J Lab Clin Med,* II (September, 1956), 232–50.

Uys, C. J. Pathology of Renal Disease in Bantu on Witwatersrand; Hypertensive Vascular Disease (In Relation to Nephrosclerosis)," *S Afr J Lab Clin Med,* II (March, 1956), 13–28.

Uys, C. J., "Pathology of Renal Disease in Bantu on Witwatersrand with Special Reference to Pyelonephritis and Renal Tuberculosis," *South African J Clin Sc,* V (December, 1954), 206–27.

Uys, C. J., "Tumours of the Kidney in the Bantu Races of South Africa. A Pathological Study Based on 3,707 Consecutive Autopsies," *Brit J Urol,* XXVIII (March, 1956), 75–88.

Van der Valk, J. M., "Blood-Pressure Changes Under Emotional Influences, in Patients with Essential Hypertension, and Control Subjects," *J Psychosom Res,* II (Number 2, 1957), 134–46.

Vogelpoel, L., and Schrire, V., "Myocardial Infarction; Its Racial Incidence in Cape Town," *Lancet,* II (November 26, 1955), 1108–09.

Wadsworth, G. R., "The Height, Weight and Blood Pressure of Healthy African Men on a Known Dietary Intake," *E Afr Med J,* XXXVII (November, 1960), 709–14.

Wahl, C. W., "The Psychodynamics of Hypertension," *Calif Med,* XCII (May, 1960), 336–37.

Wainwright, J., "Atheroma in the African (Bantu) in Natal," *Lancet,* I (February 18, 1961), 366–68.

Walker, A. R. P., "Coronary Heart Disease. Limitations to the Application to White Populations of Lessons Learned from the Underprivileged." *Circulation,* 1964, 29/1 (1–3).

Walker, A. R. P., "Extremes of Coronary Heart Disease Mortality in Ethnic Groups in Johannesburg, South Africa," *Amer Heart J,* 1963, 66/3 (293–295).

Walker, A. R. P., "Mortality From Coronary Heart Disease and From Cerebral Vascular Disease in the Different Racial Populations in South Africa. *S Afr Med J,* 1963, 37/46 (1155–1159).

Walker, A. R. P., and Arvidsson, U. B., "Fat Intake, Serum Cholesterol Concentration, and Atherosclerosis in the South African Bantu. Part I. Low Fat Intake and the Age Trend of Serum Cholesterol Concentration in the South African Bantu," *J Clin Invest,* XXXIII (October, 1954), 1358–65.

Wallace, D. C., "Hypotensive Drugs (Combined Oral Reserpine, Rauwolfia Serpentina Alkaloid, and Pentolinium, Pyrrolidine Derivative) and Mental Changes," *Lancet,* II (July 16, 1955), 116–17.

Wasserburger, R. H., "Observations on the 'Juvenile Pattern' of Adult Negro Males," *Amer J Med*, XVIII (March, 1955), 428–37.

Wear, L. E., "A Hypertensive Family," *Lancet*, I (January 14, 1956), 83.

Weiner, H., Singer, M. T., Reiser, M. F., "Cardiovascular Responses and Their Psychological Correlates. I. A study in Healthy Young Adults and Patients with Peptic Ulcer and Hypertension," *Psychosom Med*, 24: 477–98, Sept–Oct. 62.

Weiss, E., "Emotional Factors in Hypertension," *J Med Ass Georgia*, XLI (March, 1952), 93–97.

Weiss, E. "Psychosomatic Aspects of Essential Hypertension," *Acta Psychother (Basel)*, I (Number 1, 1953), 13–22.

Weiss, E., "Tension and Hypertension," *Amer Practit*, VI (November, 1955), 1690–92.

Weiss, Edward, *et al.*, "The Emotional Problems of High Blood Pressure," *Ann Intern Med*, XXXVII (October, 1952), 677–683.

Weiss, M. M., and Grav, W. R., "Hypertension and Myocardial Infarction in the Negro," *Amer J Med Sci*, CCXXVII (February, 1954), 186–87.

Westman, J. C., "An Appraisal of Home Blood-Pressure Readings in the Management of Hypertension," *Univ Mich Med Bull*, XXIV (November, 1958), 430–34.

Whitaker, P. F., "The Psychosomatic Aspects of Hypertension," *N Carolina Med J*, XIII (June, 1952), 269–73.

White, K. L., Ibrahim, M. A., "The Distribution of Cardiovascular Disease in the Community," *Ann Intern Med*, 58: 627–36, Apr. 63.

White, P. D., "Changes in Relative Prevalence of Various Types of Heart Disease in New England: Contrast Between 1925 and 1950," *JAMA*, CLII (May 23, 1953), 303–04.

White, P. D., "Heart Disease at Mid-Century," *Public Health Rep*, LXXI (August, 1956), 742–44.

Whyte, H. M., "Body Fat and Blood Pressure of Natives in New Guinea: Reflections on Essential Hypertension," *Aust Ann Med*, VII (Number 1, 1958), 36–46.

Whyte, H. M., Graham, I. A. D., and de Wolfe, M. S., "Body Fat, Blood Pressure and Serum Cholesterol of Australian Men," *Aust Ann Med*, VII (Number 4, 1958), 328–35.

Whyte, H. M., and Yee, I. L., "Serum Cholesterol Levels of Australians and Natives of New Guinea from Birth to Adulthood," *Aust Ann Med,* VII (Number 4, 1958), 336–39.

Wilgram, G. F., Ingle, D. J., "Hypertension and Renal Cardiovascular Pathology in Adrenalectomized Salt-Loaded Rats," *Amer J Cardiol,* 8: 582–7, Oct. 61.

Wilhelmj, C. M., *et al.,* "Emotional Elevations of Blood Pressure in Trained Dogs; Possible Relation to Origin of Hypertension in Humans," *Psychosom Med,* XV, (September–October, 1953), 390–95.

Wilkins, R. H., Roberts, J. C., Jr., and Moses, C., "Autopsy Studies in Atherosclerosis: III. Distribution and Severity of Atherosclerosis in the Presence of Obesity, Hypertension, Nephrosclerosis, and Rheumatic Heart Disease," *Circulation,* XX (October, 1959, Part 1), 527–36.

Wilkins, R. W., and Stucki, P., "Hypertension: Review of Significant Publications, July 1, 1950 to Jan 1, 1952." *AMA Arch Intern Med,* XCI (January, 1953), 118–37.

Williams, R. B., Jr., *et al.,* "Psychological Aspects of Hypertension. I. The Influence of Experimental Interview Variables on Blood Pressure," *Yale J Biol Med,* 38: 265–72, Dec. 65.

Wilson, C., "East-West Symposium on Pathogenesis of Essential Hypertension," *Lancet,* II (November 12, 1960), 1077–80.

Wilson, G. W., "Discussion of a Dream Pair Reported by a Patient with Early Essential Hypertension," *Psychoanal Quart,* XXVIII (April, 1959), 183–88.

Wilson, J. M. G., "Arterial Blood Pressure in Plantation Workers in North-East India," *Brit J Prev Soc Med,* XII (October, 1958), 204–09.

Wolf, S., "Psychosomatic Aspects of Hypertension," *Med Clin N Amer,* XLV (March, 1961), 339–47.

Wolf, S. G., *et al., Life Stress and Essential Hypertension.* Baltimore: Williams and Wilkins, 1955.

Wolff, H. G., "Life Stress and Bodily Disease," in Weider, A. (ed.) *Contributions Toward Medical Psychology,* I. New York: Ronald, 1953, 315–67.

Wolff, H. G., *Stress and Disease.* Springfield, Illinois: C. C. Thomas, 1953.

Wolstenholme, G. E. W., and Cameron, Margaret P. (eds.), Ciba

Foundation Symposium. *Hypertension: Humoral and Neurogenic Factors*. Boston: Little, Brown, 1954.

Wooding, N. H., "Cardiovascular Renal Complications of Pregnancy in Negro Women," *Virginia Med Monthly,* LXXXVII (February, 1960), 91–93.

Wyndham, C. H., "Post-Absorptive and Resting Physiological Values of Some Bantu Mine Recruits," *S Afr J Med Sci,* XXV (September, 1960), 41–46.

Young, R. C., and Murray, W. A., "Familial Adrenal Phaeochromo-cytoma With Sustained Hypertension," *Canad Med Ass J,* LXXII (April 1, 1955), 503–09.

Zweifach, B. W., and Shorr, Ephraim (eds.), *Conference on Factors Regulating Blood Pressure*. Transactions of the First-Fifth Conferences, 1947–1951, I–V (1947–1951), New York: Macy, 1949–1951.

II.

General Bibliography

The references are selected to provide a deeper and more specialized examination of some of the major themes of *The Jesus Bag.*

This list should serve most readers as only the first step in developing a collection of references consonant with their own specific interests.

Violence

Adams, James T., "Our Lawless Heritage," *Atlantic Monthly* 142:732–40 (1928)

Axelrad, Sidney, "Negro and White Male Institutionalized Delinquents," *American Journal of Sociology* 62:569–574 (May 1952).

Bacon, Margaret K., I. L. Child, and H. Barry III, "A Cross-Cultural Study of Correlates of Crime," *Journal of Abnormal and Social Psychology* 66:291–300 (April 1963).

Barker, Gordon H., and W. Thomas Adams, "Negro Delinquents in Public Training Schools in the West," *Journal of Negro Education* 32:294–300 (Summer 1963).

Bart, Peter, "Panel on Watts Riots Warns of Further Racial Violence," *New York Times,* December 7, 1965.

Bates, William, "Caste, Class and Vandalism," *Social Problems* 9:349–353 (Spring 1962).

Beattie, R. H., "Criminal Statistics in the United States," *Journal of Criminal Law, Criminology and Police Science* 51:49–65 (May–June 1960).

Bensing, R. C., and O. Schroeder, Jr., *Homicide in an Urban Community.* Springfield, Ill.: Thomas, 1960.

Berkowitz, Leonard, "The Study of Urban Violence: Some Implications of Laboratory Studies of Frustration and Aggression," *American Behavioral Scientist,* March-April 1968.

Bittner, Egon, "The Police on Skid Row: A Study of Peace-Keeping," *American Sociological Review,* October 1967.

Bohannon, P., ed., *African Homicide and Suicide.* Princeton: Princeton University Press, 1960.

Brown, Earl L., *Why Race Riots? Lessons from Detroit.* New York: Public Affairs Committee, 1944.

Brown, L. P., "Black Muslims and the Police," *Journal of Criminal Law, Criminology and Police Science* 56:119–126 (March 1965).

Buss, A., *The Psychology of Aggression.* New York: Wiley, 1951.

Byrn, Robert M., "Urban Law Enforcement: A Plea from the Ghetto," *Criminal Law Bulletin* 5:125–36 (April 1969).

Caldwell, M. G., "Personality Trends in the Youthful Male Offender," *Journal of Criminal Law, Criminology and Police Science* 49:405–416 (January–February 1959).

Cavan, Ruth Shonle, "Negro Family Disorganization and Juvenile Delinquency," *Journal of Negro Education* 28:230–239 (Summer 1959).

Chalmers, David M., *Hooded Americanism: The First Century of the KKK, 1865 to the Present.* Doubleday, 1965.

Chein, Isidor, Donald L. Gerard, Robert S. Lee, and Eva Rosenfeld, *The Road to H: Narcotics, Delinquency and Social Policy.* New York: Basic Books, 1964.

Chwast, Jacob, "Value Conflicts in Law Enforcement," *Crime and Delinquency* 16:151–161 (1965).

Clark, Kenneth B., "Color, Class, Personality and Juvenile Delinquency," *Journal of Negro Education* 28:240–251 (Summer 1959).

Clark, Kenneth B., "Group Violence: A Preliminary Study of the Attitudinal Pattern of its Acceptance and Rejection—A Study of the 1943 Harlem Riots," *Journal of Social Psychology* 19:319–337 (August 1944).

Cloward, Richard A., and Lloyd E. Ohlin, *Delinquency and Opportunity: A Theory of Delinquent Gangs.* Glencoe, Ill.: Free Press, 1960.

Cohen, A. K., *Delinquent Boys: The Culture of the Gang.* Glencoe, Ill.: Free Press, 1955.

Cohen, A. K., and J. F. Short, Jr., "Research in Delinquent Subcultures," *Journal of Social Issues* 14:20–37 (Summer 1958).

Cohen, A. K. and J. F. Short, Jr., "Juvenile Delinquency," in R. K. Merton and R. A. Nisbet, eds., *Contemporary Social Problems,* New York: Harcourt, Brace, 1961.

Coles, Robert, "The Question of Negro Crime," *Harper's Magazine* 228:134–136, 139 (April 1964).

Conot, Robert, *Rivers of Blood, Years of Darkness.* New York: Bantam, 1967.

Cray, Ed, *The Big Blue Line.* New York: Coward-McCann, 1967.

Cressey, Donald R., "Epidemiology and Individual Conduct: A Case from Criminology," *Pacific Sociological Review* 3:47–58 (Fall 1960).

Cressey, Donald R., "Crime," in R. K. Merton and R. A. Nisbet, eds. *Contemporary Social Problems.* New York: Harcourt, Brace, 1961.

Cross, G. J., "Negro, Prejudice and the Police," *Journal of Criminal Law, Criminology and Police Science* 55:405 (September 1964).

Curry, J. E., and Glen D. King, *Race Tensions and the Police.* Springfield, Ill.: Thomas, 1962.

Daniel, Walter G., "The Role of Youth Character-Building Organizations in Juvenile Delinquency Prevention," *Journal of Negro Education* 28:310–317 (Summer 1959).

Diggs, Mary H., "Some Problems and Needs of Negro Children as Revealed by Comparative Delinquency and Crime Statistics," *Journal of Negro Education* 19:290–297 (Summer 1950).

Dobbins, D. A., and B. M. Bass, "Effects of Unemployment on White and Negro Prison Admissions in Louisiana," *Journal of Criminal Law, Criminology and Police Science* 48:522–525 (January-February 1958).

"Does Anyone Really Care? Negroes Who Rioted in Los Angeles," *Christian Century* 82:1148 (September 22, 1965).

Douglass, Joseph H., "The Extent and Characteristics of Juvenile Delinquency Among Negroes in the United States," *Journal of Negro Education* 28:214–229 (Summer 1959).

Elliott, Mabel A., "Crime and the Frontier Mores," *American Sociological Review* 9:185–192 (1944).

Epstein, Charlotte, *Intergroup Relations for Police Officers*. Baltimore: Williams & Wilkins, 1962.

"F.B.I. Report on Racial Disturbances During the Past Summer," *America* 111:414–415 (October 10, 1964).

Federal Bureau of Investigation, *Uniform Crime Reports, 1960–1961*. Washington, D.C.: GPO, 1961–1962.

Federal Bureau of Investigation, *Uniform Crime Reports, 1965*. Washington, D.C.: GPO, 1965.

Federal Bureau of Prisons, *National Prisoner Statistics: Prisoners in State and Federal Institutions, 1950*. Leavenworth, Kan.: U.S. Penitentiary, 1954.

Federal Bureau of Prisons, *National Prisoner Statistics: Prisoners Released from State and Federal Institutions, 1951*. Atlanta, Ga.: U.S. Penitentiary, 1955.

Federal Bureau of Prisons, *National Prisoner Statistics: Prisoners Released from State and Federal Institutions, 1952 and 1953*. Atlanta, Ga.: U.S. Penitentiary, 1957.

Federal Bureau of Prisons, "Executions, 1961," in *National Prisoner Statistics*, No. 28 (April 1962).

Finestone, Harold, "Cats, Kicks, and Color," *Social Problems* 5:3–13 (July 1957).

Foote, Joseph, ed., "Crime and Justice in America," *Congressional Quarterly Service*, 2nd ed., December 1968.

Fox, Vernon, and Joann Volakakis, "The Negro Offender in a Northern Industrial Area," *Journal of Criminal Law, Criminology and Police Science* 46:641 (January–February 1956).

Franklin, J. C., "Discriminative Value and Patterns of the Wechsler-

Bellevue Scales in the Examination of Delinquent Negro Boys," *Educational and Psychological Measurement* 5:71–85 (Spring 1945).

Geis, Gilbert, "Statistics Concerning Race and Crime," *Crime and Delinquency* 11:142–150 (April 1965).

Glueck, Sheldon, and Eleanor T. Glueck, *Unraveling Juvenile Delinquency*. New York: Commonwealth Fund, 1950.

Gold, M., "Suicide, Homicide, and the Socialization of Aggression," *American Journal of Sociology* 63:651–661 (May 1958).

Goldstein, Joseph, "Police Discretion Not to Invoke the Criminal Process: Low Visibility Decisions in the Administration of Justice," *Yale Law Journal*, March 1960.

Goodman, George W., Jr., "Watts, U.S.A.: A Post Mortem," *Crisis* 72:487–492, 532 (October 1965).

Gosset, William T., "Law in a Changing Society: The Promise of Order," *New York State Bar Journal* 41:182–8 (April 1968).

Grimshaw, Allen D., "Lawlessness and Violence in America and their Special Manifestations in Changing Negro-White Relations," *Journal of Negro History* 44:52–72 (January 1959).

Grimshaw, Allen D., "A Study in Social Violence: Urban Race Riots in the United States," unpub. doc. diss., University of Pennsylvania, 1959.

Grimshaw, Allen D., "Urban Racial Violence in the United States: Changing Ecological Considerations," *American Journal of Sociology* 66:109–119 (September 1960).

Grimshaw, Allen D., "Relationships Among Prejudice, Discrimination, Social Tension and Social Violence," *Journal of Intergroup Relations* 2:302–310 (Fall 1961).

Grimshaw, Allen D., "Negro-White Relations in the Urban North: Two Areas of High Conflict Potential," *Journal of Intergroup Relations* 3:146–158 (Spring 1962).

Grimshaw, Allen D., "Factors Contributing to Colour Violence in the United States and Great Britain," *Race* 3:3–19 (May 1962).

Grimshaw, Allen D., "Three Major Cases of Colour Violence in the United States," *Race* 5:76–87 (July 1963).

Grimshaw, Allen D., "Police Agencies and the Prevention of Racial Violence," *Journal of Law, Criminology and Police Science* 54:110 (March 1963).

Grimshaw, Allen D., "Actions of Police and the Military in American Race Riots," *Phylon* 26:271–289 (Fall 1963).

"Harlem Diary," *Ramparts* 3:14–28 (October 1964).

Henry, A. F., and J. F. Short, Jr., *Suicide and Homicide*. Glencoe, Ill.: Free Press, 1954.

Henton, Comradge L., and Charles Washington, "Differential Studies of Recidivism Among Negro and White Boys," *Journal of Genetic Psychology* 98:247–253 (June 1961).

Hill, Mozell C., "The Metropolis and Juvenile Delinquency Among Negroes," *Journal of Negro Education* 28:277–285 (Summer 1959).

Hypps, Irene C., "The Role of the School in Juvenile Delinquency Presentation (with Especial Reference to Pupil Personnel Services)," *Journal of Negro Education* 28:318–328 (Summer 1959).

Jenkins, Herbert T., "Police, Progress, and Desegregation in Atlanta," *New South* 17:10–13 (June 1962).

Johnson, Guy B., "The Negro and Crime," in Martin E. Wolfgang, Leonard Savitz, and Norman Johnston, *The Sociology of Crime and Delinquency*, New York: Wiley, 1962.

Kephart, William M., "The Negro Offender," *American Journal of Sociology* 60:46–50 (July 1954).

Kephart, William M., "Integration of Negroes into the Urban Police Force," *Journal of Criminal Law, Criminology and Police Science* 45:325–333 (September–October 1954).

Kephart, William M., *Racial Factors and Urban Law Enforcement*. Philadelphia: University of Pennsylvania Press, 1957.

Klein, Malcolm W., *Juvenile Gangs in Context*. Englewood Cliffs: Prentice-Hall, 1967.

Kramer, S. A., "Predicting Juvenile Delinquency Among Negroes," *Sociology and Social Research* 48:478–489 (July 1964).

Kvaraceus, William C., "The Nature of the Problem of Juvenile Delinquency in the United States," *Journal of Negro Education* 28:191–199 (Summer 1959).

LaFave, Wayne R., *Arrest*. Boston: Little, Brown & Co., 1965.

Lewis, Hylan, "Juvenile Delinquency Among Negroes: A Critical Summary," *Journal of Negro Education* 28:371–387 (Summer 1959).

Lohman, Joseph D., *The Police and Minority Groups.* Chicago, 1947.

Lohman, Joseph D., "Juvenile Delinquency: A Social Dimension," *Journal of Negro Education* 28:286–299 (Summer 1959).

London, Nathaniel J., and Jerome K. Myers, "Young Offenders: Psychopathology and Social Factors," *Archives of General Psychiatry* 4:274–282 (March 1961).

McCloskey, Mark A., "State and Municipal Youth Authorities or Commissions and Their Role in Juvenile Delinquency Prevention," *Journal of Negro Education* 28:339–350 (Summer 1959).

McCormick, Ken, *Sprung: The Release of Willie Calloway.* New York: St. Martin's, 1964.

McManus, George P., "Human Relations Training for Police," *Interracial Review* 35:98–99 (April 1962).

McMillan, George, "Racial Violence and Law Enforcement," *New South* 15:4–32 (November 1960).

McWilliams, Carey, "Watts: The Forgotten Slum," *Nation* 201:89–90 (August 30, 1965).

Maccoby, Eleanor E., Joseph P. Johnson, and Russell M. Church, "Community Integration and the Social Control of Juvenile Delinquency," *Journal of Social Issues* 14:38–51 (Summer 1958).

Mailer, Norman, "Talking of Violence," *20th Century* Vol. 173 (Winter 1964–65).

Matza, David, *Delinquency and Drift.* New York: Wiley, 1964.

Mays, Benjamin E., "The Role of the 'Negro Community' in Delinquency Prevention Among Negro Youth," *Journal of Negro Education* 28:366–370 (Summer 1959).

Miller, Alexander, "Crisis Without Violence," Anti-Defamation League, 1964.

Miller, Carroll L., "Educational Level and Juvenile Delinquency Among Negroes," *Journal of Negro Education* 28:268–276 (Summer 1959).

Miller, Walter, "Lower Class Culture as a Generating Milieu of Gang Delinquency," *Journal of Social Issues* 14:5–19 (1958).

Miller, Walter, "Violent Crimes in City Gangs," *Annals of the American Academy,* Vol. 364 (March 1966).

Morgan, Charles, Jr., "Integration in the Yellow Chair," *New South* 18:11–16 (February 1963).

National Advisory Commission on Civil Disorders, "America's Racial Crisis: The Riot Commission Report: Making America Whole," *Current* 94:32–39 (April 1968).

National Advisory Commission on Civil Disorders, *Supplemental Studies*. Praeger, 1968.

"Negro After Watts" *Time* Essay, *Time* 86:16–17 (August 27, 1965).

Nieburg, H. L., "The Threat of Violence and Social Change," *American Political Science Review* 56:865–873 (December 1962).

Parnas, Raymond I., "The Police Response to the Domestic Disturbance," *Wisconsin Law Review* 914–960 (1967).

Pettigrew, Thomas F., and Rosalind B. Spier, "The Ecological Structure of Negro Homicide," *American Journal of Sociology* 67:621–629 (May 1962).

Porterfield, Austin L., and Robert H. Talbert, "Crime in Southern Cities," in Rupert B. Vance and Nicholas J. Demerath, eds., *The Urban South*. Chapel Hill: University of North Carolina Press, 1954.

President's Commission on Law Enforcement and Administration of Justice, *The Challenge of Crime in a Free Society*. Washington, D.C.: G.P.O., 1967.

President's Commission on Law Enforcement and Administration of Justice, *Task Force Report: The Police*. Washington, D.C.: G.P.O., 1967.

Reiss, Albert J., and Albert Lewis Rhodes, "Are Educational Norms and Goals of Conforming, Truant and Delinquent Adolescents Influenced by Group Position in American Society?" *Journal of Negro Education* 28:252–267 (Summer 1959).

Robin, Gerald D., "Justifiable Homicide by Police Officers," *Journal of Criminal Law, Criminology and Police Science* 54:225–231 (1963).

Robinson, Sophia M., "How Effective are Current Delinquency Preventive Programs?" *Journal of Negro Education* 28:351–365 (Summer 1959).

Roebuck, Julian B., "The Negro Drug Addict as an Offender Type," *Journal of Criminal Law, Criminology and Police Science* 53:36–43 (March 1962).

Roebuck, Julian B., "Negro Numbers Man as a Criminal Type: The Construction and Application of a Typology," *Journal of Criminal Law, Criminology and Police Science* 54:48–60 (March 1963).

Roebuck, Julian B., and M. L. Cadwallader, "The Negro Armed Robber as a Criminal Type: The Construction and Application of a Typology," *Pacific Sociological Review* 4:21–26 (Spring 1961).

Rudwick, Elliott M., "Police Work and the Negro," *Journal of Criminal Law, Criminology and Police Science* 50:596–599 (March–April 1960).

Rudwick, Elliott M., "Negro Policemen in the South," *Journal of Criminal Law, Criminology and Police Science* 51:273 (July–August 1960).

Rudwick, Elliott M., "Negro Police Employment in the Urban South," *Journal of Negro Education* 30:102–108 (Spring 1961).

Rudwick, Elliott M., "The Southern Negro Policeman and the White Offender," *Journal of Negro Education* 30:426–431 (Fall 1961).

Rudwick, Elliott M., *Race Riot at East St. Louis, July 2, 1917*. Carbondale: Southern Illinois University Press, 1964.

Salisbury, Harrison, *The Shook-Up Generation*. New York: Harper, 1958.

Samuels, Gertrude, "Who Shall Judge a Policeman?" *New York Times Magazine*, August 2, 1964.

Sanders, Stanley, "Riot as a Weapon: The Language of Watts," *Nation* 201:490–493 (December 20, 1965).

Savitz, Leonard, *Delinquency and Migration*. Philadelphia: Commission on Human Relations, 1960.

Schmid, C. F., "Urban Crime Areas, Part I," *American Sociological Review* 25:527–542 (August 1960); "Part II", *ibid.* 25:655–678 (October 1960).

Schneidman, Edwin, ed., *Essays in Self-Destruction*. New York: Science House, 1967.

Schnessler, Karl, "Components of Variation in City Crime Rates," *Social Problems* 9:314–323 (November 1962).

Schultz, Leroy G., "Why the Negro Carries Weapons," *Journal of Criminal Law, Criminology and Police Science* 53:476–481 (December 1962).

Scott, J. P., "Anatomy of Violence," *Nation* 200:662–666 (June 21, 1965).

Shapiro, Fred C., and James W. Sullivan, *Race Riots New York 1964*. New York: Crowell, 1964.

Sherif, Muzafer, and Carolyn Sherif, *Reference Groups: Explorations in Conformity and Deviance of Adolescents.* New York: Harper, 1964.

Short, James F., Jr., and Fred L. Strodtbeck, *Group Process and Gang Delinquency.* Chicago: University of Chicago Press, 1965.

Skolnick, Jerome A., *Justice Without Trial.* New York: John Wiley & Sons, 1966.

Spergel, Irving, "Male Young Adult Criminality, Deviant Values, and Differential Opportunities in Two Lower Class Negro Neighborhoods," *Social Problems* 10:237–250 (Winter 1963).

"A Statement of Recommended Police Policy Resulting from the New York University Graduate School of Public Administration Conference on 'The Challenge of Desegregation for the American Police Executive,' " *Interracial Review* 35:115 (May 1962).

Stone, Alfred H., "Is Race Friction Between Blacks and Whites Growing and Inevitable?" *American Journal of Sociology* 13:676–697 (1907–1908).

Strongfellow, William, "The Violence of Despair," *Notre Dame Lawyer,* Vol. 40, No. 5, 1965.

Supplemental Studies for the National Advisory Commission on Civil Disorders. New York: Praeger, 1968.

Teeters, Negley K., and David Matza, "The Extent of Delinquency in the United States," *Journal of Negro Education* 28:200–213 (Summer 1959).

Thomas, Rose C. "Family and Child Welfare Agencies and Juvenile Delinquency Prevention," *Journal of Negro Education* 28:300–309 (Summer 1959).

Towler, Juby E., *The Police Role in Racial Conflicts,* Springfield, Ill.: Charles C. Thomas, 1965.

Tufts, Edith Miller, "The Role of the Children's Bureau and Other Federal Agencies in Juvenile Delinquency Prevention," *Journal of Negro Education* 28:329–338 (Summer 1959).

United States Congress, House, "Memphis Riots and Massacres," 39th Congress, 1st session, Report 101, Archives Series 1274, Washington, D.C.: G.P.O., 1867.

United States National Commission on the Causes and Prevention of Violence, *Progress Report,* January 9, 1969.

Vickers, George, ed., *Dialogue on Violence*. Bobbs-Merrill, 1968.

Violence in the City—An End or a Beginning? A Report by the (California) Governor's Commission on the Los Angeles Riots (December 2, 1965).

"Violence Sends a Message," *Ebony* 19:140–141 (September 1964).

"Violence" (symposium), *Nation* 205:101–107 (August 14, 1967).

Vontress, Clemmont E., "Patterns of Segregation and Desegregation: Contributing Factors to Crime Among Negroes," *Journal of Negro Education* 31:108–116 (Spring 1962).

Waskow, Arthur L., *From Race Riot to Sit-In, 1919 and the 1960's*. Garden City, N.Y.: Doubleday, 1966.

Weaver, Robert C., "Challenges to Democracy," paper given at a symposium in Chicago and published in *The Negro as an American*, Santa Barbara, Calif.: Center for the Study of Democratic Institutions, 1963.

Westley, William A., "The Escalation of Violence Through Legitimation," *Annals of the American Academy* 364:120–126 (March 1966).

"What 'Massive Resistance' Costs Norfolk and Its Businessmen," *Business Week* 1518:32–34 (October 4, 1958).

Wilson, James, Q., "Generational and Ethnic Differences among Career Police Officers," *American Journal of Sociology* 69:522–528 (March 1964).

Wilson, James Q., *Varieties of Police Behavior*. Cambridge, Mass.: Harvard University Press, 1968.

Witcover, Jules, "Rochester Braces for Another July," *Reporter* 33:33–35 (July 15, 1965).

Wolfgang, Marvin E., *Patterns in Criminal Homicide*. Philadelphia: University of Pennsylvania Press, 1958.

Wolfgang, Marvin E. "Uniform Crime Reports: A Critical Appraisal," *University of Pennsylvania Law Review* 109:708–738 (April 1963).

Zeitz, L., "Survey of Negro Attitudes Toward Law," *Rutgers Law Review* 19:288–316 (Winter 1965).

The Consequences of Poverty

Adams, M. S., et al., "Iron-Deficiency Anemia in Negro Infants and Children in the Metropolitan Area of the District of Columbia," *Medical Annals of the District of Columbia* 32:391–393 (October 1963).

Adams, Paul L., and N. F. McDonald, "Clinical Cooling Out of Poor People," *American Journal of Orthopsychiatry* 38:457–463 (April 1968).

Alinsky, Saul, "The Poor and the Powerful," *International Journal of Psychiatry* Vol. 4 (October 1967).

Alsop, J., "No More Nonsense About Ghetto Education," *New Republic,* July 22, 1967.

Altenderfer, Marion E., and Beatrice Crowther, "Relationship Between Infant Mortality and Socio-economic Factors in Urban Areas," *Public Health Reports* 64:331–339 (March 18, 1949).

Alter, S. M. "Multiple Sclerosis in the Negro," *Archives of Neurology* 7:83–91 (August 1962).

Anderson, R. S., and Laurie M. Gunther, "Sex and Diabetes Mellitus: A Comparative Study of 26 Negro Males and 26 Negro Females Matched for Age," *American Journal of the Medical Sciences* 242:481–486 (October 1961).

Babow, Irving, "Minority Group Integration in Hospitals: A Sample Survey," *Hospitals* 35:47–48 (February 1961).

Bagdikian, Ben H., *In the Midst of Plenty: The Poor in America.* Boston: Beacon, 1964.

Baldwin, James, "The Harlem Ghetto: Winter 1948," *Commentary* 5:165–170 (February 1948).

Banfield, Edward C., *The Case of the Blighted City.* Chicago: American Foundation for Continuing Education, 1959.

Batchelder, Alan, "Poverty: The Special Case of the Negro," *American Economic Review* 55:530–540 (May 1965). Bibliography.

Baumgartner, Leona, "Urban Reservoirs of Tuberculosis," *American Review of Tuberculosis* 79:687–689 (May 1959).

Bayley, Nancy, "Comparisons of Mental and Motor Test Scores for Ages 1–15 Months by Sex, Birth Order, Race, Geographical Location and Education of Parents," *Child Development* 36:379–411, 1965.

Bell, Wendell, and Ernest M. Willis, "The Segregation of Negroes in American Cities," *Social and Economic Studies* 6:59–75 (March 1957).

Berry, L. H., "Black Men and Malignant Fevers," *Journal of the National Medical Association* 56:43–47 (January 1964).

Bird, Alan R., *Poverty in Rural Areas of the United States: Agricultural Economic Report No. 63,* Washington, D.C.: U.S. Department of Agriculture, June 1965.

Blalock, H. M., Jr., "Urbanization and Discrimination in the South," *Social Problems* 7:146–152 (Fall 1959).

Boskins, Joseph, "The Revolt of the Urban Ghettos 1964–1967," *Annals of the American Academy of Political and Social Science,* March 1969.

Bragen, George, and Francis Purcell, eds., *Community Action Against Poverty,* New Haven: College University Press, 1967.

Bremner, Robert H., *From the Depths: The Discovery of Poverty in the United States.* New York: New York University Press, 1964.

Brody, Eugene B., "Social Conflict and Schizophrenic Behavior in Young Adult Negro Males," *Psychiatry* 24:337–346 (November 1961).

Brown, Claude, "Harlem, My Harlem," *Dissent* 8:371–382 (Summer 1961).

Brown, Morgan C., "Selected Characteristics of Southern Rural Negroes Exchanged to a Southern Urban Center," *Rural Sociology* 27:64–70 (March 1962).

Burr, Charles W., *Housing-Health Relationships: An Annotated Bibliography.* Council of Planning Librarians, May 1969.

Carter, Wilmoth A., "Negro Main Street as a Symbol of Discrimination," *Phylon* 21:234–242 (Fall 1960).

Carter, Wilmoth A., *The Urban Negro in the South.* New York: Vantage, 1962.

Cervantes, Lucius F., *The Dropout: Causes and Cures.* Ann Arbor: University of Michigan Press, 1965.

Clark, Dennis, *The Ghetto Game,* New York: Sheed and Ward, 1962.

Clark, Kenneth B., *Dark Ghetto.* New York: Harper, 1965.

Clausen, J. A., "Drug Addiction," in R. K. Morton and R. A. Nisbet, eds., *Contemporary Social Problems*. New York: Harcourt Brace, 1961.

Cloward, R. A., and F. F. Piven, "Mississippi: Starving by the Rule Book: Hearings on Public Welfare Administration," *Nation,* April 3, 1967.

Coles, Robert, "What Migrant Farm Children Learn," *Saturday Review* 48:73–74+ (May 15, 1965).

Commission on Chronic Illness, *Chronic Illness in the United States. Vol. IV, Chronic Illness in a Large City: The Baltimore Study.* Cambridge: Harvard University Press, 1957.

Conant, James B., *Slums and Suburbs*. New York: McGraw-Hill, 1961.

Cooper, A. J., et al., "Biochemical Polymorphic Traits in a U.S. White and Negro Population," *American Journal of Human Genetics* 15:420–428 (December 1963).

Cornely, Paul B., "The Health Status of the Negro Today and in the Future," *American Journal of Public Health,* April 1968.

Cowhig, James D., and Calvin L. Beale, "Socioeconomic Differences Between White and Nonwhite Farm Populations of the South," *Social Forces* 42:354–362 (March 1964).

Cowles, Wylda, and Steven Polgar, with collaboration of Leonard Simmons and John Switzer, "Health and Communication in a Negro Census Tract," *Social Problems* 10:228–236 (Winter 1963).

Crawford, R. R., G. W. Hellins, and R. L. Sutherland, "Variations Between Negroes and Whites in Concepts of Mental Illness and its Treatment," *Annals of the New York Academy of Science* 84:918–937 (December 8, 1960).

Cultural Considerations in Changing Health Attitudes. Washington, D.C.: Department of Preventive Medicine and Public Health, Howard University, 1961.

David, Martin, "Incomes and Dependency in the Coming Decades," *American Journal of Economics and Sociology* 3:249–267 (July 1964).

DeMott, Benjamin, "An Unprofessional Eye: Project for Another Country," *American Scholar* 32:451–457 (Summer 1963).

Derbyshire, R. L., et al., "Family Structure of Young Adult Negro Male Mental Patients: Preliminary Observations from Urban Baltimore," *Journal of Nervous and Mental Disease* 136:245–251 (March 1963).

Deschin, Celia S., *Teen-agers and Venereal Disease.* Atlanta: U.S. Department of Health, Education and Welfare, 1961.

Deutsch, A., "The First U.S. Census of the Insane (1840) and Its Use as Pro-Slavery Propaganda," *Bulletin of the History of Medicine* 15:469–482 (December 1944).

"Dimensions of Poverty in New York City," Mayor's Council on Poverty, New York, March 23, 1964.

Drake, St. Clair, and Horace R. Cayton, *Black Metropolis: A Study of Negro Life in a Northern City.* New York: Harcourt, Brace, 1945; New York: Harper Torchbook, 2 vols., 1963.

Dulaney, William L., "The Negro and the City," *Journal of Negro Education* 31:198–201 (Spring 1962).

Dummett, C. O., "Dental Health Problems of the Negro Population," *Journal of the American Dental Association* 61:308–314 (September 1960).

Dunne, George H., ed., *Poverty in Plenty.* New York: Kenedy, for Georgetown University, 1964.

Egan, John J., "The Human Side of Neighborhoods," *Integrated Education* 1:20–25 (June 1963).

Engel, Leonard, "We Could Save 40,000 Babies a Year," *New York Times Magazine,* November 17, 1963.

English, W. H., "Minority Group Attitudes of Negroes and Implications for Guidance," *Journal of Negro Education* 26:99–107 (Spring 1957).

Fact Book on Youth in New York City. Community Council of Greater New York, 1956.

Faris, R. E. L., and H. W. Dunham, *Mental Disorder in Urban Areas.* Chicago: University of Chicago Press, 1939.

Frazier, E. Franklin, "The Urban Ordeal of Negroes," *Negro Digest* 12:26–32 (December 1962).

Fein, Rashi, *Economics of Mental Illness.* Joint Commission on Mental Illness and Health, Monograph Series, no. 2, New York: Basic Books, 1958.

Ferman, Louis A., Joyce L. Kornbluh, and Alan Haber, eds., *Poverty in America*. Ann Arbor: University of Michigan Press, 1965.

Fischer, R., "Thinking Style and Socioeconomic Status," *Perceptual and Motor Skills* 26:825–826 (June 1968).

Frumkin, Robert M., "Race and Major Mental Disorders: A Research Note," *Journal of Negro Education* 23:97–98 (Winter 1954).

Gist, Noel P., and L. A. Halbert, *Urban Society*. New York: Crowell, 1956.

Glazer, Nathan, and Daniel Patrick Moynihan, *Beyond the Melting Pot*. Cambridge: M.I.T. Press and Harvard University Press, 1963.

Goldstein, Marcus S., "Longevity and Health Status of Whites and Non-Whites in the United States," *Journal of the National Medical Association* 46:83–104 (March 1954).

Goldstein, Marcus S., "Longevity and Health Status of the Negro American," *Journal of Negro Education* 32:337–348 (Fall 1963).

Grabil, Wilson H., Clyde V. Kiser, and Pascal K. Whelpton, *The Fertility of American Women*. New York: Wiley, 1958.

Grant, F. W., and D. Groom, "A Dietary Study Among A Group of Southern Negroes," *Journal of the American Dietetic Association* 35:910–918 (September 1959).

Green, Constance McLaughlin, *The Rise of Urban America*. New York: Harper, 1965.

Green, Constance McLaughlin, *Washington: Capital City, 1879–1950*. Princeton: Princeton University Press, 1963.

Grey, Susan W., and R. A. Klaus, "An Experimental Pre-School Program for Culturally Deprived Children," *Child Development* 36:887–898 (1965).

Grier, Eunice, and George Grier, *Negroes in Five New York Cities: A Study of Problems, Achievements, and Trends*. New York State Commission Against Discrimination, 1958.

Grodzins, Morton, *The Metropolitan Area as a Racial Problem*. Pittsburgh: University of Pittsburgh Press, 1958.

Grodzins, Morton, "Metropolitan Segregation," *Scientific American* 198:33–41 (October 1957).

Groom, D., et al., "Coronary and Aortic Atherosclerosis in the Negroes of Haiti and the United States," *Annals of Internal Medicine* 51:270–289 (August 1959).

Grossack, Martin M., ed., *Mental Health and Segregation*. New York: Springer-Verlag, 1963.

Guralnick, Lillian, *Mortality by Occupation and Industry Among Men 20 to 64 Years of Age: United States, 1950*. Vital Statistics Special Reports, Vol. LII, No. 2, Washington, D.C.: G.P.O., 1962.

Hansen, Carl F., "Mental Health Aspects of Desegregation," *Journal of the National Medical Association* 51:450–456 (November 1959).

Hardy, Janet, *Tuberculosis in White and Negro Children*. 2 vols., Cambridge: Harvard University Press, 1958.

Harrington, Michael, "Harlem Today," *Dissent* 8:371–382 (Summer 1961).

Harrington, Michael, *The Other America: Poverty in the United States*. New York: Macmillan, 1962.

Henton, C. L., "The Effect of Socioeconomic and Emotional Factors on the Onset of Menarche Among Negro and White Girls," *Journal of Genetic Psychology* 98:255–264 (June 1961).

Herring, B. D., "Pernicious Anemia and the American Negro," *American Practitioner* 13:544–548 (August 1962).

Hill, Herbert, *No Harvest for the Reaper: The Story of the Migratory Agricultural Worker in the United States*. New York: NAACP, 1960.

Hilleboe, H. E., and B. W. Larimore, eds., *Preventive Medicine*. Philadelphia: Saunders, 1962.

Hilsheimer, G. von, "Child Care and the Migrant Farm Hand," *Journal of Nursing Education* 18:262–266 (September 1963).

Hingson, R. A., "Comparative Negro and White Mortality During Anesthesia, Obstetrics and Surgery," *Journal of the National Medical Association* 49:203–211 (July 1957).

Hollingshead, A. B., and F. C. Redlich, *Social Class and Mental Illness: A Community Study*. New York: Wiley, 1958.

Hunter, David R., *The Slums: Challenge and Response*. New York: Free Press, 1964.

Ivins, S. P., "Psychoses in the Negro: A Preliminary Study," *Delaware State Medical Journal* 22:212–213 (August 1950).

Ivy, A. C., "Physiological Differences Produced by Race and Diet," *Hawaii Medical Journal and Inter-Island Nurses' Bulletin* 16:21–25 (September–October 1956).

Jaco, E. G., *The Social Epidemiology of Mental Disorders.* New York: Russell Sage Foundation, 1960.

Jahoda, Marie, *Race Relations and Mental Health,* New York: Columbia University Press, 1960.

John, Vera P., "The Intellectual Development of Slum Children: Some Preliminary Findings," *American Journal of Orthopsychiatry* 33:813–822 (1963).

Johnson, Charles S., *Growing Up in the Black Belt.* Washington, D.C.: American Council on Education, 1941.

Jones, Lewis W., "The Negro Farmer," *Journal of Negro Education* 22:322–332 (Summer 1953).

Keeler, Martin H., and Mintauts M. Vitols, "Migration and Schizophrenia in North Carolina Negroes," *American Journal of Orthopsychiatry* 33:554–557 (April 1963).

Keller, Suzanne, "The Social World of the Urban Slum Child," *American Journal of Orthopsychiatry* 33:554–557 (April 1963).

Kelso, Louis Q. and Patricia Hetter, "Planning Economic Opportunity: Why Jobs are Not Enough," *Current* 94:52–57 (April 1968).

Killian, Lewis M., and Charles M. Grigg, "Urbanism, Race and Anomie," *American Journal of Sociology* 67:661–665 (May 1962).

Kitagawa, Evelyn M., and Philip M. Hauser, "Trends in Differential Fertility and Mortality in a Metropolis—Chicago," in E. W. Burgess and D. J. Bogue, eds., *Contributions to Urban Sociology.* Chicago: University of Chicago Press, 1964.

Kleiner, Robert J., and Seymour Parker, "Migration and Mental Illness: A New Look," *American Sociological Review* 24:687–690 (October 1959).

Kleiner, Robert J., and Seymour Parker, "Goalstriving, Social Status, and Mental Disorder: A Research Review," *American Sociological Review* 28:189–203 (April 1963).

Kleiner, Robert J., Jacob Tuckman, and Martha Lavell, "Mental Disorder and Status Based on Religious Affiliation," *Human Relations* 12:273–276 (August 1959).

Kleiner, Robert J., Jacob Tuckman, and Martha Lavell, "Mental Disorder and Status Based on Race," *Psychiatry* 23:271–274 (August 1960).

Lampman, Robert J., "Recent Thought on Egalitarianism," *Quarterly Journal of Economics* 71:234–266 (May 1957).

Lampman, Robert J., *The Low Income Population and Economic Growth,* Joint Economic Committee of the U.S. Congress, Study Paper No. 12, Washington, D.C.: G.P.O., 1959.

Langer, E., "Hospital Discrimination: HEW Criticized by Civil Rights Groups," *Science* 149:355–357 (September 17, 1965).

Lee, Everett S., and Anne S. Lee, "The Differential Fertility of the American Negro," *American Sociological Review* 17:437–447 (August 1952).

Lee, Everett S., and Anne S. Lee, "The Future Fertility of the American Negro," *Social Forces* 37:228–231 (March 1959).

Lepper, Mark H., et al, "An Approach to Reconciling the Poor and the System," *Inquiry* 1:37–42 (March 1968).

Lieberson, Stanley, *Ethnic Patterns in American Cities.* Glencoe, Ill.: Free Press, 1963.

Lyford, Joseph P., "The Talk of Vandalia," in *The Negro as an American.* Santa Barbara, Calif.: Center for the Study of Democratic Institutions, 1963.

McKay, Claude, *Harlem: Negro Metropolis.* New York: Dutton, 1940.

McLean, F. C., "Negroes and Medicine in Chicago," *Proceedings of the Institute of Medicine of Chicago* 23:2–6 (January 15, 1960).

Malzberg, Benjamin, "Mental Disease Among Native and Foreign-Born Negroes in New York State," *Journal of Negro Education* 25:175–181 (Spring 1956).

Malzberg, Benjamin, and Everett S. Lee, *Migration and Mental Disease.* New York: Social Science Research Council, 1956.

Martin, Roscoe C., *Metropolis in Transition: Local Government Adaptation to Changing Urban Needs.* Washington, D.C.: Housing and Home Finance Agency, September 1963.

Matsuda, R., "Relative Growth of Negro and White Children in Philadelphia," *Growth* 27:271–284 (December 1963).

Maxwell, Neil, "The Ailing Poor: Medical Team Combats Negroes' Dismal Health in Mississippi Delta," *Wall Street Journal,* January 19, 1969.

Mayo, Selz C., and C. Horace Hamilton, "The Rural Negro Population of the South in Transition," *Phylon* 24:160–171 (Summer 1963).

Mayo, Selz C., and C. Horace Hamilton, "Current Population Trends in the South," *Social Forces* 42:77–88 (October 1963).

Mirel, E., "Rural Negroes Need Help," *Science News Letter* 84:214 (October 5, 1963).

Moore, Truman E., *The Slaves We Rent*. New York: Random House, 1965.

Myrdal, Gunnar, *Challenge to Affluence*. New York: Pantheon, 1964.

National Commission Against Discrimination in Housing, *How The Federal Government Builds Ghettos*. 1967.

National Office of Vital Statistics, *Death Rates for Selected Causes by Age, Color, and Sex: United States and Each State, 1949–1951*. Washington, D.C.: G.P.O., 1959.

"Negro Families in Rural Wisconsin: A Study of Their Community Life," Madison, Wis.: Governor's Commission on Human Rights, 1959.

"Negro Farmers Get Unfair Deal," *Farm Journal* 89:78 (April 1965).

The Negro in Cleveland. Cleveland Urban League, June 1964.

"New Hope for Rural Dixie: Firms in Carolinas Create Jobs for Negroes," *Ebony* 19:50+ (June 1964).

New York City in Crisis: A Study in Depth of Urban Sickness. New York: McKay, 1965.

Nichaman, M. Z., E. Boyle, Jr., T. P. Lesesne, and H. I. Sauer, "Cardiovascular Disease Mortality by Race, Based on a Statistical Study in Charleston, South Carolina," *Geriatrics* 17:724–737 (November 1962).

Office of Economic Opportunity, *Congressional Presentation, April 1965*. 2 vols. Washington, D.C.: G.P.O., 1965. Vol. I, *The First Step on a Long Journey*, a description of all the programs provided for by legislation setting up the OEO; Vol. II, *Appendix*, statistical details of all programs.

Orshansky, M., "Aged Negro and his Income," *Social Security Bulletin* 27:3–13 (February 1964).

Orshansky, M., "Counting the Poor: Another Look at the Poverty Profile," *Social Security Bulletin* 28:3–29 (January 1965).

Osofsky, Gilbert, *The Making of a Ghetto*. New York: Harper, 1966.

Palley, Howard A., "The Migrant Labor Problem—Its State and Interstate Aspects," *Journal of Negro Education* 32:35–42 (Winter 1963).

Pasamanick, Benjamin, "Mental Subnormality," *New England Journal of Medicine* 266:1092–1097 (May 24, 1962).

Pasamanick, Benjamin, "Some Misconceptions Concerning Differences in the Racial Prevalence of Mental Disease," *American Journal of Orthopsychiatry* 33:72–86 (January 1963).

Pasamanick, Benjamin, "Myths Regarding Prevalence of Mental Disease in the American Negro: A Century of Misuse of Mental Hospital Data and Some New Findings," *Journal of the National Medical Association* 56:6–17 (January 1964).

Pasamanick, Benjamin, P. H. Knapp, eds., *Social Aspects of Psychiatry*. Washington, D.C.: American Psychiatric Association, 1958.

Pasamanick, Benjamin, and Hilda Knoblock, "Race, Complications of Pregnancy, and Neuropsychiatric Disorders," *Social Problems* 5:267–278 (Winter 1957–1958).

Passow, A. Harry, ed., *Education in Depressed Areas, New York.* Bureau of Publications, Teachers College, Columbia University, 1963.

Pavenstedt, Eleanor, "A Comparison of the Child-rearing Environment of Upper-lower and Very Low-lower Class Families," *American Journal of Orthopsychiatry* 35:89–98 (1965).

Payne, Raymond, "Organizational Activities of Rural Negroes in Mississippi," *Mississippi State College Agricultural Experiment Station Circular No. 192*, Starkville, Miss., 1953.

Payton, E., E. P. Crump, and C. P. Horton, "Growth and Development VII: Dietary Habits of 571 Pregnant Southern Negro Women," *Journal of the American Dietetic Association* 37:129–136 (August 1960).

Pederson, H. A., "Mechanized Agriculture and the Farm Laborer," *Rural Sociology* 19:143–151 (June 1954).

Pellegrin, Roland J., and Vernon J. Parenton, "The Impact of Socioeconomic Change on Racial Groups in a Rural Setting," *Phylon* 23:55–60 (Spring 1962).

Peter, Emmet, Jr., "On the Outside Looking Out," *New Republic* 152:18 (June 26, 1965).

Pettigrew, Ann Hallman, and Thomas F. Pettigrew, "Race, Disease, and Desegregation: A New Look," *Phylon* 24:315–333 (Winter 1963).

Phillips, J. H., and G. E. Burch, "Cardiovascular Diseases in the White and Negro Races," *American Journal of the Medical Sciences* 238:97–124 (July 1959).

Pomfret, John D., "Negro Farm Workers in Florida Fight Poverty Every Day," *New York Times,* April 20, 1964.

President's Committee on Urban Housing, *A Decent Home.* Washington, D.C., December 1968.

Rein, M., and S. M. Miller, "Poverty Programs and Policy Priorities," *Trans-Action* 4:60–71 (1967).

Riese, H., "Group Therapeutical Experience with Antisocial and Prepsychotic Negro Children," *Acta Psychotherapeutica et Psychosomatica* (Basel), Supplement to vol. 7:319–327 (1959).

Roberts, H. J., "The Syndrome of Narcolepsy and Diabetogenic Hyperinsulinism in the American Negro: Its Relationship to the Pathogenesis of Diabetes Mellitus, Obesity, Dysrhythmias, and Accelerated Cardiovascular Disease," *Journal of the National Medical Association* 56:18–42 (January 1964).

Robertson, Leon S., "Race, Status, and Medical Care," *Phylon,* Winter 1967.

Rose, Arnold M., "Psychoneurotic Breakdown Among Negro Soldiers in Combat," *Phylon* 17:61–69 (Spring 1956).

Rose, G., "Cardiovascular Mortality Among American Negroes," *Archives of Environmental Health* 5:412–414 (November 1962).

Ross, Arthur M., and Herbert Hill, eds., *Employment, Race and Poverty.* New York: Harcourt, 1967.

Russell, A. L., and P. Ayres, "Periodontal Disease and Socioeconomic Status in Birmingham, Ala.," *American Journal of Public Health* 50:206–214 (February 1960).

Rustin, B., "Lessons of the Long Hot Summer: Proposals to Widen War on Poverty," *Commentary,* Vol. 45 (January 1968).

Sabagh, Georges, F. Dingman, George Tarjan, and Stanley W. Wright, "Social Class and Ethnic Status of Patients Admitted to a State Hospital for the Retarded," *Pacific Sociological Review* 2:76–80 (Fall 1959).

Schermerhorn, R. A. "Psychiatric Disorders Among Negroes: A Sociological Note," *American Journal of Psychiatry* 112:878–882 (1956).

Schnore, Leo F., *The Urban Scene: Human Ecology and Demography.* New York: Free Press, 1965.

Scholz, B. W., "Medicine in the Slums," *New York State Journal of Medicine* 63:2132–2138 (July 15, 1963).

Sclare, A., "Cultural Determinants in the Neurotic Negro," *British Journal of Medical Psychology* 26:278–288 (Part 4 1953).

Scott, R. B., et al., "Growth and Development of Negro Infants: V. Neuromuscular Patterns of Behavior During the First Year of Life," *Pediatrics* 16:24–30 (July 1955).

Sexton, Patricia Cayo, *Spanish Harlem: Anatomy of Poverty*. New York: Harper, 1965.

Shane, M., "Some Subcultural Consideration in the Psychotherapy of a Negro Patient," *Psychiatric Quarterly* 34:9–27 (January 1960).

Smith, Earl B., "Medical Justice and Injustice," *Interracial Review* 35:254–255 (November 1962).

Smith, P. M., "Personal and Social Adjustment of Negro Children in Rural and Urban Areas of the South," *Rural Sociology* 26:73–77 (March 1961).

Smolensky, Eugene, "Public Housing or Income Supplements: The Economics of Housing for the Poor," *Journal of the American Institute of Planners,* March 1968.

Snyder, J. D., "Race Bias in Hospitals: What the Civil Rights Commission Found," *Hospital Management* 96:52–54 (November 1963).

Stevens, Rutherford B., "Interracial Practices in Mental Hospitals," *Mental Hygiene* 36:56–65 (January 1952).

Street, David, and John C. Leggett, "Economic Deprivation and Extremism: A Study of Unemployed Negroes," *American Journal of Sociology* 67:53–57 (July 1961).

Stringfellow, William, "Christianity, Poverty and the Practice of the Law," *Harvard Law School Bulletin* 10:4–7 + (June 1959).

Taeuber, Karl E., "Residential Segregation," *Scientific American* 213:12–19 (August 1965).

Taeuber, Karl E., and Alma F. Taeuber, *Negroes in Cities*. Chicago: Aldine, 1965.

U.S. Congress, Joint Committee on the Economic Report, *Characteristics of the Low-Income Population and Related Federal Programs*. Washington, D.C.: G.P.O., 1955.

U.S. Congress, Joint Committee on the Economic Report, *A Program for the Low-Income Population at Substandard Levels of Living.* Washington, D.C.: G.P.O., 1956.

U.S. Department of Labor, Bureau of Labor Statistics, *The Negroes in the United States: Their Economic and Social Situations,* Bulletin No. 1511. Washington, D.C.: G.P.O., June 1966.

U.S. Department of Labor, Bureau of Labor Statistics, *Social and Economic Conditions of Negroes in the U.S.,* BLS Report No. 332. Washington, D.C.: G.P.O., October 1967.

Vincent, M., and J. Hugon, "Relationships Between Various Criteria of Maturity at Birth," *Biologica Neonatorum* (Basel) 4:223–279 (1962).

Vitols, Mintauts M., "The Significance of the Higher Incidence of Schizophrenia in the Negro Race in North Carolina," *North Carolina Medical Journal* 22:147–158 (April 1961).

Weaver, Robert C., *The Negro Ghetto.* New York: Harcourt, Brace, 1948.

Weaver, Robert C., "Non-White Population Movements and Urban Ghettos," *Phylon* 20:235–241 (Fall 1959).

Weaver, Robert C., *The Urban Complex: Human Values in Urban Life.* Garden City, N.Y.: Doubleday.

Willie, Charles V., and William B. Rothney, "Racial, Ethnic, and Income Factors in the Epidemiology in Neonatal Mortality," *American Sociological Review* 27:522–526 (August 1962).

Wilson, D. C., and Edna M. Lantz, "The Effect of Culture Change on the Negro Race in Virginia as Indicated by a Study of State [Mental] Hospital Admissions," *American Journal of Psychiatry* 114:25–32 (July 1957).

Wright, Dale, *They Harvest Despair: The Migrant Farm Worker.* Boston: Beacon, 1965.

Zald, Mayer N., *Organizing for Community Welfare.* Chicago: Quadrangle Books, 1967.

The Black Family

Bell, R. R., "Lower Class Negro Mothers' Aspirations for their Children," *Social Forces* 43:493–500 (May 1965).

Bernard, Jessie, *Marriage and Family Among Negroes.* Englewood Cliffs, N.J.: Prentice-Hall, 1966.

Billingsley, Andrew, and Amy Tate Billingsley, *Black Families in White America.* Englewood Cliffs, N.J.: Prentice-Hall, 1968.

Billingsley, Andrew, and Amy Tate Billingsley, "Negro Family Life in America," *Social Service Review* 39:310–319 (September 1965).

Blau, Zena Smith, "Exposure to Child-Rearing Experts: A Structural Interpretation of Class-Color Differences," *American Journal of Sociology* 69:596–608 (May 1964).

Blood, Robert O., and Donald M. Wolfe, *Husbands and Wives: The Dynamics of Married Living.* New York: Free Press, 1963.

Brody, Eugene B., "Color and Identity Conflict in Young Boys: Observations of Negro Mothers and Sons in Urban Baltimore," *Psychiatry,* May 1963.

Burton, R. V., and J. W. M. Whiting, "The Absent Father and Cross-Sex Identity," *Merrill-Palmer Quarterly* 7:85–95 (April 1961).

Cavan, Ruth Shonle, "Negro Family Disorganization and Juvenile Delinquency," *Journal of Negro Education* 28:230–239 (Summer 1959).

D'Andrade, R. G., "Father Absence and Cross-Sex Identification," unpub. doc. diss., Harvard University, 1962.

Davis, Allison W., and Robert J. Havighurst, *The Father of the Man: How Your Child Gets His Personality.* Boston: Houghton Mifflin, 1947.

Deasy, Leila C., and Olive W. Quinn, "The Urban Negro and Adoption of Children," *Child Welfare,* November 1962.

Derbyshire, R. L., et al., "Family Structure of Young Adult Negro Male Mental Patients: Preliminary Observations from Urban Baltimore," *Journal of Nervous and Mental Disease* 136:245–251 (March 1963).

Duncan, Beverly, and Otis Dudley Duncan, "Family Stability and Occupational Success," *Social Problems* 16:273–285 (Winter 1969).

Edwards, G. Franklin, "Marriage and Family Life Among Negroes," *Journal of Negro Education* 32:451–465 (Fall 1963).

Erikson, Erik, "Memorandum on Identity and Negro Youth," *Journal of Social Issues* 20:29–42 (October 1964).

Frazier, E. Franklin, "Ethnic Family Patterns: The Negro Family in the United States," *American Journal of Sociology* 54:432–438 (May 1948).

Frazier, E. Franklin, *The Negro Family in the United States.* Chicago: University of Chicago Press, 1939; revised and abridged edition, with a new introduction by Nathan Glazer, 1966.

Frazier, E., Franklin, "Problems and Needs of Negro Children," *Journal of Negro Education* 19:269–277 (Summer 1950).

Frazier, E. Franklin, "The Negro Family in Chicago," in E. W. Burgess and D. J. Bogue., eds., *Contributions to Urban Sociology,* Chicago: University of Chicago Press, 1964.

Frumkin, Robert M., "Attitudes of Negro College Students Toward Intrafamily Leadership and Control," *Marriage and Family Living* 16:252–253 (August 1954).

Ginzberg, Eli, ed., *The Nation's Children;* Vol. I, *The Family and Social Change;* Vol. II, *Development and Education;* Vol. III, *Problems and Prospects.* New York: Columbia University Press, 1960.

Gipson, Theodore H., "Educational Status of the Negro Family in Louisiana," *Journal of Educational Sociology* 32:83–89 (October 1958).

Glazer, Nathan, and Daniel P. Moynihan, *Beyond the Melting Pot.* Cambridge, Mass.: Harvard University Press, 1963.

Gordon, Milton, *Assimilation in American Life.* New York: Oxford University Press, 1964.

Gould, Flo, and Richard K. Kerckhoff, "Family Life Education for the Biracial Community," *Journal of Negro Education* 29:187–190 (Spring 1960).

"Growing Up Negro," *American Child,* January 1963. Entire issue.

Herzog, Elizabeth, "Is There a Breakdown of the Negro Family?" *Social Work,* January 1966.

Hentoff, Nat, "The Other Side of the Blues," in *Anger and Beyond,* New York: Harper and Row, 1966.

Himes, Joseph S., "Interrelation of Occupational and Spousal Roles in a Middle Class Negro Neighborhood," *Marriage and Family Living* 22:362 (November 1960).

Himes, Joseph S., "Some Work-Related Cultural Deprivations of Lower-Class Negro Youths," *Journal of Marriage and the Family* 26:447–449 (November 1964).

Illegitimacy and its Impact on the Aid to Dependent Children Program. Washington, D.C.: Bureau of Public Assistance, U.S. Department of Health, Education and Welfare, 1960.

Jenkins, Wesley W., "An Experimental Study of the Relationship of Legitimate and Illegitimate Birth Status to School and Personal and Social Adjustment of Negro Children," *American Journal of Sociology* 64:169–173 (September 1958).

Kunstadter, Peter, "A Survey of the Consanguine or Matrifocal Family," *American Anthropologist* 65:56–66 (February 1963).

Lewis, Hylan, "The Changing Negro Family," in Eli Ginzberg, ed., *The Nation's Children*, vol. I. New York: Columbia University Press, 1960.

Lincoln, C. Eric, "The Absent Father Haunts the Negro Family," *New York Times Magazine*, November 28, 1965.

Middleton, Russell, and Snall Putney, "Dominance in Decisions in the Family: Race and Class Differences," *American Journal of Sociology* 65:605–609 (May 1960).

Moynihan, Daniel Patrick, "Employment, Income, and the Ordeal of the Negro Family," *Daedalus* 94:745–770 (Fall 1965).

Moynihan, Daniel Patrick, *The Negro Family: The Case for National Action*. Washington, D.C.: G.P.O., 1965.

Murray, Pauli, *Proud Shoes: The Story of an American Family*. New York: Harper and Row, 1956.

"Negro Families in Rural Wisconsin: A Study of their Community Life," Madison, Wis.: Governor's Commission on Human Rights, 1959.

Nordlie, Esther B., and Sheldon C. Rood, "Follow-up Adoption Counseling for Children of Possible Racial Admixture," *Child Welfare*, September 1962.

Opler, Marvin K., "The Influence of Ethnic and Class Structures on Child Care," *Social Problems* 3:12–21 (July 1955).

Orshansky, Mollie, "Children of the Poor," *Social Science Research Council Bulletin*, July 1963.

Radin, Norma, and Constance K. Kamii, "The Child-Rearing Attitudes of Disadvantaged Negro Mothers and Some Educational Implications," *Journal of Negro Education* 34:138–146 (Spring 1965).

Rainwater, Lee, "Crucible of Identity: The Negro Lower-Class Family," *Daedalus* 95:172–216 (Winter 1966).

Rainwater, Lee, and William L. Yancey, *The Moynihan Report and the Politics of Controversy*. Cambridge, Mass.: The M.I.T. Press, 1967.

Reiss, I. L., "Premarital Sexual Permissiveness Among Negroes and Whites," *American Sociological Review* 29:688–698 (October 1964).

Ross, Arthus M., and Herbert Hill, eds., *Employment, Race and Poverty*. New York: Harcourt, Brace, 1967.

Rovere, Richard, "Letter from Washington," *New Yorker,* September 11, 1965.

Ryan, William, "Savage Discovery: The Moynihan Report," *The Nation* 201:380–384 (November 22, 1965).

Schwartz, M., "Northern United States Negro Matriarchy: Status Versus Authority," *Phylon* 26:18–24 (Spring 1965).

Setleis, Lloyd, "Civil Rights and the Rehabilitation of the AFDC [Aid to Families with Dependent Children] Clients," *Social Work* 9:3–9 (April 1964).

Smith, Howard P., and Marcia Abramson, "Racial and Family Experience Correlates of Mobility Aspirations," Journal of *Negro Education* 31:117–124 (Spring 1962).

Strodtbeck, Fred L., "The Poverty-Dependency Syndrome of the ADC Female-Based Negro Family," *American Journal of Orthopsychiatry* 34:216–217 (March 1964).

Tietze, C., and S. Lewit, "Patterns of Family Limitation in a Rural Negro Community," *American Sociological Review* 18:563–564 (October 1953).

United States Department of Labor, Bureau of Labor Statistics, *The Negro in the West: Some Facts Relating to Social and Economic Conditions, #3 The Negro Family*. Regional Office, San Francisco, Calif.

Vincent, Clark, *Unmarried Mothers*. Glencoe, Ill.: Free Press, 1961.

Wakin, E., *Portrait of a Middle-Class Negro Family at the Edge of Harlem*. New York: Morrow, 1965.

Walker, Margaret, *Jubilee*. Boston: Houghton Mifflin, 1966.

Weinstein, E. A., and P. N. Geisel, "Family Decision Making over Desegregation," *Sociometry* 25:21–29 (March 1961).

Whitaker, Barbara, "Breakdown in the Negro Family: Myth or Reality?" *New South* 22:37–7 (Fall 1967).

Woods, Sister Frances Jerome, and Alice Cunningham Lancaster, "Cultural Factors in Negro Adoptive Parenthood," *Social Work,* October 1962.

History

Adler, Mortimer J., Charles Van Doren, and George Ducas, eds., *The Negro in American History*. 3 vols., Chicago: Encyclopaedia Britannica Educational Corp., 1969.

Aptheker, Herbert, *American Negro Slave Revolts*. New York: International, 1943.

Aptheker, Herbert, *Nat Turner's Slave Rebellion*. New York: Humanities Press, 1966.

Aptheker, Herbert, ed., *A Documentary History of the Negro People in the United States*. 2 vols., New York: Citadel, 1951; reissued 1962, 1964.

Ashmore, Harry S., *The Negro and the Schools*. Chapel Hill: University of North Carolina Press, 1964.

Barnes, Gilbert H., *The Anti-Slavery Impulse 1830–1844*. Gloucester, Mass.: Peter Smith Reprint, 1957.

Beals, Carleton, *War Within a War: The Confederacy Against Itself*. Philadelphia: Chilton, 1965.

Bennett, Lerone, Jr., *Before the Mayflower: A History of the Negro in America 1619–1962*. Chicago: Johnson, 1962.

Blaustein, Albert P., and Robert L. Zangrando, *Civil Rights and the American Negro: A Documentary History*. New York: Trident, 1968.

Bontemps, Arna, *100 Years of Negro Freedom*. New York: Dodd, Mead, 1961.

Bontemps, Arna, *Story of the Negro*. New York: Knopf, 1964.

Botkin, B. A., *Lay My Burden Down*. Chicago: University of Chicago Press, 1945.

Burchard, Peter, *One Gallant Rush*. New York: St. Martin's, 1965.

Burns, W. Hayward, *The Voices of Negro Protest in America*. New York: Oxford University Press, 1963.

Catterall, Helen T., *Judicial Cases Concerning American Slavery and the Negro*. 5 vols. 1927–1937, New York: Plenum.

"A Century of Struggle," *Progressive* 26:3–58 (December 1962).

Christman, Henry M., ed., *The South As It Is 1865–1866*. New York: Viking, 1965.

Coleman, J. Winston, Jr., *Slavery Times in Kentucky*. Chapel Hill, N.C.: University of North Carolina Press, 1940.

Cook, Samuel DuBois, "A Tragic Conception of Negro History," *Journal of Negro History* 45:219–240 (October 1960).

Cox, La Wanda, and John H. Cox, *Politics, Principle and Prejudice, 1865–1866: Dilemma of Reconstruction America*. New York: Free Press, 1963.

Cuban, Larry, *The Negro in America*. Chicago: Scott, Foresman, 1964.

Davidson, Basil, *Black Mother: The Years of the African Slave Trade*. Boston: Little Brown, 1961.

Davis, John P., ed., *The American Negro Reference Book*. New York: Prentice-Hall, 1966.

Donald, David, *The Politics of Reconstruction, 1863–1867*. Baton Rouge: Louisiana State University Press, 1965.

Drimmer, Melvin, ed., *Black History: A Reappraisal*. New York: Doubleday, 1968.

Duberman, Martin B., *In White America: A Documentary Play*. Boston: Houghton Mifflin, 1964.

Eaton, Clement, *The Growth of Southern Civilization*. New York: Harper, 1961.

Elkins, Stanley M., *Slavery: A Problem in American Institutional and Intellectual Life*. Chicago: University of Chicago Press, 1959; reissued, New York: Universal Library, 1963.

Fishel, Leslie H., and Benjamin Quarles, *The Negro Americans: A Documentary History*. Chicago: Scott, Foresman, 1967.

Forten, Charlotte L., *The Journal of Charlotte L. Forten: A Free Negro in the Slave Era*. New York: Collier, 1961.

Franklin, John Hope, *From Slavery to Freedom: A History of American Negroes*. New York: Knopf, 1947; 2nd ed., 1956.

Franklin, John Hope, "History of Racial Segregation in the United States," *Annals of the American Academy of Political and Social Science* 304:1–9 (March 1956).

Franklin, John Hope, *The Militant South*. Cambridge: Harvard University Press, 1956.

Franklin, John Hope, "The New Negro History," *Journal of Negro History*" 42:89–97 (April 1957).

Franklin, John Hope, *Reconstruction After the Civil War*. Chicago: University of Chicago Press, 1961.

Franklin, John Hope, *The Emancipation Proclamation*. Garden City, N.Y.: Doubleday, 1963.

Franklin, John Hope, "The Two Worlds of Race: A Historical View," *Daedalus* 94:899–920 (Fall 1965).

Frazier, E. Franklin, *The Negro in the United States*. Macmillan, 1965.

Gara, Larry, *The Liberty Line: The Legend of the Underground Railroad*. Lexington, Ky: University of Kentucky Press, 1961.

Garraty, John A., ed., *Quarrels That Have Shaped the Constitution*. New York: Harper, 1964.

Genovese, Eugene D., *The Political Economy of Slavery: Studies in the Economy and Society of the Slave South*. New York: Pantheon, 1965.

Ginzberg, Eli, and Hyman Berman, *The American Worker in the Twentieth Century: A History Through Biographies*. New York: Free Press, 1963.

Goldston, Robert, *Negro Revolution*. New York: Macmillan, 1968.

Hughes, Langston, and Milton Meltzer, eds., *A Pictorial History of the Negro in America*. New ed., rev., New York: Crown, 1963.

Huie, William B., *Three Lives for Mississippi*. New York: Trident, 1965.

Jordan, Winthrop D., *White Over Black: American Attitudes Toward the Negro 1550–1812*. Chapel Hill, N.C.: University of North Carolina Press, 1968.

Katz, William L., *Eyewitness: The Negro in American History*. New York: Pitman, 1967.

Kirwan, Albert D., *Revolt of the Rednecks: Mississippi Politics, 1876–1925*. Lexington, Ky.: University of Kentucky Press, 1951; New York: Harper Torchbook, 1965.

Lester, Julius, *To Be a Slave*. New York: Dial, 1968.

Lincoln, C. Eric, *The Negro Pilgrimage in America*. New York: Bantam, 1967.

Lincoln, C. Eric, and Milton Meltzer, *A Pictorial History of the Negro in America*. New York: Crown, 1968.

Litwack, Leon F., *North of Slavery: The Negro in the Free States, 1790–1860*. Chicago: University of Chicago Press, 1961.

Logan, Rayford W. and Irving S. Cohen, *The American Negro: Old World Background and New World Experience*. New York: Houghton Mifflin, 1967.

Logan, Rayford W., *The Negro in American Life and Thought: The Nadir, 1877–1901*. New York: Dial, 1954.

Logan, Rayford W., *The Negro in the United States: A Brief Review*. Princeton, N.J.: Van Nostrand, 1957.

McCarthy, Agnes, and Lawrence Reddick, *Worth Fighting For*. Garden City, N.Y.: Doubleday, 1965.

McPherson, James M., *Abolitionists and the Negro in the Civil War and Reconstruction*. Princeton University Press, 1964.

McPherson, James M., *The Negro's Civil War: How American Negroes Felt and Acted During the War for the Union*. New York: Pantheon, 1965.

Mannix, Daniel P., *Black Cargoes: The Story of the Atlantic Slave Trade, 1518–1865*. New York: Viking, 1962.

Mecklin, John N., *The Ku Klux Klan: A Study of the American Mind*. New York: Russell, 1963.

Meier, August, *Negro Thought in America, 1880–1915: Racial Ideologies in the Age of Booker T. Washington*. Ann Arbor: University of Michigan Press, 1964.

Meier, August, and Elliott M. Rudwick, eds., *Making of Black America*. 2 vols. New York: Athenaeum, 1968.

Meier, August, and Elliott M. Rudwick, eds., *From Plantation to Ghetto: An Interpretive History of the American Negro*. New York: Hill & Wang, 1966.

Meltzer, Milton, ed., *In Their Own Words: A History of the American Negro*. New York: Thomas Y. Crowell, 3 vols. 1964, 1965, 1967.

Meltzer, Milton, and August Meier, *Time of Trial, Time of Hope: The Negro in America 1919–1941*. New York: Doubleday, 1966.

Myrdal, Gunnar, *An American Dilemma*. New York: Harper & Row, 1962.

Osofsky, Gilbert, *The Burden of Race: A Documentary History of Negro-White Relations in America*. New York: Harper & Row, 1967.

Owens, William A., *Slave Mutiny: Revolt on the Schooner Armistad.* New York: John Day, 1963.

Patrick, John J., *The Progress of the Afro-Americans.* Westchester, Ill.: Benafic Press, 1968.

Ploski, Harry A., and Roscoe Brown, eds., *Negro Almanac.* New York: Bellwether, 1967.

Quarles, Benjamin, *Black Abolitionists.* New York: Oxford University Press, 1969.

Quarles, Benjamin, *The Negro in the American Revolution.* Chapel Hill: University of North Carolina Press, 1961.

Quarles, Benjamin, and Dorothy Sterling, *The Negro in the Making of America.* New York: Collier Books, 1964.

Record, Wilson, "The Development of the Communist Position on the Negro Question in the United States," *Phylon* 19:306–326 (Fall 1958).

Record, Wilson, *Race and Radicalism: The NAACP and the Communist Party in Conflict.* Ithaca: Cornell University Press, 1964.

Reimers, David M., *White Protestantism and the Negro.* New York: Oxford University Press, 1965.

Rose, Arnold M., "History with a Present Meaning," *Commentary* 24:542–546 (December 1957).

Salk, Erwin A., *A Layman's Guide to Negro History.* Chicago: Quadrangle, 1966.

Savage, Henry, Jr., *Seeds of Time, The Background of Southern Thinking.* New York: Holt, 1959.

Scheiner, Seth M., *Negro Mecca: A History of the Negro in New York City, 1865–1920.* New York: New York University Press, 1965.

Sellers, Charles Grier, ed., *The Southerner as American.* Chapel Hill: University of North Carolina Press, 1960.

Singletary, Otis A., *Negro Militia and Reconstruction.* Austin: Texas University Press, 1957.

Sloan, Irving J., *The American Negro: A Chronology and Fact Book.* Dobbs Ferry, N.Y.: Oceana Publications, 2nd ed. 1968.

Spangler, Earl, *The Negro in America.* Minneapolis: Lerner, 1967.

Stampp, Kenneth M., *The Peculiar Institution: Slavery in the Ante-Bellum South*. New York: Knopf, 1956.

Stampp, Kenneth M., *The Era of Reconstruction: 1865–1877*. New York: Knopf, 1965.

Tannenbaum, Frank, *Slave and Citizen: The Negro in the Americas*. New York: Knopf, 1947.

Thorpe, Earl E., *Negro Historians in the United States*. Baton Rouge, La.: Fraternal Press, 1958.

Thorpe, Earl E., *The Mind of the Negro: An Intellectual History of Afro-Americans*. Baton Rouge, La.: Ortlieb Press, 1961.

Wade, Richard C., *The Negro in American Life*. Boston: Houghton Mifflin, 1965.

Wade, Richard C., *Slavery in the Cities: The South, 1820–1860*. New York: Oxford University Press, 1965.

Weisberger, Bernard A., "The Dark and Bloody Ground of Reconstruction Historiography," *Journal of Southern History* 25:427–447 (November 1959).

Wiley, Bell Irvin, *Southern Negroes 1861–1865*. New Haven: Yale University Press, 1938.

Woodson, Carter G., and Charles H. Wesley, *The Negro in Our History*. Washington, D.C.: Associated Publishers, 1922; 10th ed. rev. and enlarged, 1962.

Woodward C. Vann, *Origins of the New South, 1877–1913*. Baton Rouge, La.: Louisiana State University Press, 1951.

Woodward, C. Vann, *The Strange Career of Jim Crow*. New York: Oxford University Press, 1955; 2nd rev. ed. and Galaxy paperback, 1966.

Woodward, C. Vann, *The Burden of Southern History*. Baton Rouge: Louisiana State University Press, 1960.

Woodward, C. Vann, "Flight From History: The Heritage of the Negro," *Nation* 201:142–146 (September 20, 1965).

Woofter, Thomas J., *Southern Race Progress: The Wavering Color Line*. Washington, D.C.: Public Affairs Press, 1957.

Wright, Richard, *Twelve Million Black Voices*. New York: Viking, 1941.

Black Psychology

Aichhorn, August, *Wayward Youth*. New York: Viking Press, 1935.

Allport, Gordon W., *Pattern and Growth in Personality*. New York: Holt, 1961.

Anastasi, Anne, "Psychological Research and Educational Desegregation," *Thought* 35:421–429 (Fall 1960).

Ausubel, D. P., "Ego Development Among Segregated Negro Children," *Mental Hygiene* 42:362–369 (July 1958).

Axline, Virginia M., "Play Therapy and Race Conflict in Young Children," *Journal of Abnormal and Social Psychology* 18:300–310 (July 1948).

Axline, Virginia M., "Play Therapy Procedures and Results," *American Journal of Orthopsychiatry* 25:618–626 (July 1955).

Ball, J. C., "Comparison of MMPI Profile Differences Among Negro-White Adolescents," *Journal of Clinical Psychology* 16:304–307 (July 1960).

Bandure, A., and R. H. Walters, *Adolescent Aggression*. New York: Ronald, 1959.

Baughman, Earl, and W. Grant Dahlstrom, *Negro and White Children: A Psychological Study in the Rural South*. New York: Academic Press, 1968.

Beck, Samuel J., et al., "Segregation-Integration: Some Psychological Realities," *American Journal of Ortho-psychiatry* 28:12–35 (January 1958).

Bender, Lauretta, "Behavior Problems in Negro Children," *Psychiatry* 2:213–228 (1939).

Berdie, R. F. B., "Playing the Dozens," *Journal of Abnormal and Social Psychology* 42:120–121 (January 1947).

Berger, E. M., "Relationships Among Acceptance of Self, Acceptance of Others, and MMPI Scores," *Journal of Counseling Psychology* 2:279–284 (Winter 1955).

Bernard, Viola W., "Psychoanalysis and Members of Minority Groups," *Journal of the American Psychoanalytic Association* 1:256–267 (April 1953).

Bovell, Gilbert Balfour, "Psychological Considerations of Color Conflicts Among Negroes," *Psychoanalytical Review* 30:447–459 (1943).

Brewster, Edward E., and Martelle D. Trigg, "Moral Values Among Negro College Students: A Study of Cultural and Racial Determinants," *Phylon* 23:286–293 (Fall 1962).

Brody, Eugene B., "Color and Identity Conflict in Young Boys, II," *Archives of General Psychiatry* 10:354–360 (April 1964).

Brown, B., "The Assessment of Self-Concept Among Four-Year Old Negro and White Children: A Comparative Study," New York: Institute for Developmental Studies (mimeo), 1967.

Burton, R. V., and J. W. M. Whiting, "The Absent Father and Cross-Sex Identity," *Merrill-Palmer Quarterly* 7:85–95 (April 1961).

Butcher, James, Brenda Ball, and Eva Ray, "Effects of Socio-Economic Level on MMPI Differences in Negro-White College Students," *Journal of Counseling Psychology* 11:83–87 (Spring 1964).

Butts, Hugh F., "Skin Color Perception and Self-Esteem," *Journal of Negro Education* 32:122–128 (Spring 1963).

Cannon, Walter B., *The Wisdom of the Body*. New York: Norton.

Charles, C. V., "Optimism and Frustration in the American Negro," *Psychoanalytical Review* 29:270–299 (1942).

Chein, Isidor, "What Are the Psychological Effects of Segregation Under Conditions of Equal Facilities?" *International Journal of Opinion and Attitude Research* 3:229 (1949).

Clark, Kenneth B., "Effect of Prejudice and Discrimination on Personality Development," Midcentury White House Conference on Children and Youth, 1950.

Clark, Kenneth B., *Prejudice and Your Child*. Boston: Beacon, 1955; 2nd ed. enlarged, Beacon paperback, 1963.

Clark, Kenneth B., "Color, Class, Personality and Juvenile Delinquency," *Journal of Negro Education* 28:240–251 (Summer 1959).

Clark, Kenneth B., and J. Barker, "The Zoot Effect in Personality: A Race Riot Participant," *Journal of Abnormal and Social Psychology* 40:143–148 (April 1945).

Clark, Kenneth B., and Mamie P. Clark, "Racial Identification and Preference in Negro Children," in Eleanor Macoby, et. al., eds., *Readings in Social Psychology*, New York: Holt, 1958.

Clinard, Marshall B., and Donald L. Noel, "Role Behavior of Students from Negro Colleges in a Non-Segregated University Situation," *Journal of Negro Education* 27:182–188 (Spring 1958).

Cobbs, Price M., "Journeys to Black Identity: Selma and Watts," *Negro Digest*, July, 1967.

Cobbs, Price M., "The Black Revolution and Education," *The Bulletin of the National Association of Secondary School Principals,* May, 1969.

Coles, Robert, *Children of Crisis.* Boston: Atlantic-Little Brown, 1967.

Coles, Robert, " 'It's the Same, but It's Different,' " *Daedalus* 94:1107–1132 (Fall 1965).

Coles, Robert, "Public Evil and Private Problems: Segregation and Psychiatry," *Yale Review* 54:513–531 (June 1965).

Coles, Robert, "Racial Conflict and a Child's Question," *American Journal of Orthopsychiatry* 34:218–219 (March 1964).

Coles, Robert, "Racial Identity in School Children," *Saturday Review* 46:56–57 + (October 19, 1963).

Coles, Robert, "Southern Children Under Desegregation," *American Journal of Psychiatry* 120:332–344 (October 1963).

Conyers, James E., and T. H. Kennedy, "Negro Passing: To Pass or Not To Pass," *Phylon* 24:215–223 (Fall 1963).

Cook, Studart W., "Desegregation: A Psychological Analysis," *American Psychologist* 12:1–13 (January 1957).

Dai, Bingham, "Problems of Personality Development Among Negro Children," in Clyde Kluckhohn and Harry A. Murray, eds., *Personality in Nature, Society and Culture.* New York: Knopf, 1953.

D'Amico, Louis A., "Problem Behavior in Negro Schools," *Journal of Negro Education* 26:72–74 (Winter 1957).

Davis, Arthur P., "Jesse B. Semple: Negro American," *Phylon* 15:21–28 (Spring 1954).

Derbyshire, Robert L., and Eugene B. Brody, "Social Distance and Identity Conflict in Negro College Students," *Sociology and Social Research* 48:301–314 (April 1964).

Deutscher, Isaac, and Isidor Chein, "The Psychological Effects of Enforced Segregation: A Survey of Social Science Opinion," *Journal of Psychology* 26:259–287 (October 1948).

Dreger, R. M., "Comparative Psychological Studies of Negroes and Whites in the United States: A Reclarification," *Psychological Bulletin* 60:35–39 (January 1963).

Dreger, R. M., and K. S. Miller, "Comparative Psychological Studies of Negroes and Whites in the United States," *Psychological Bulletin* 57:361–402 (September 1960).

Epps, Edgar G., Irwin Katz, and Leland Axelson, "Relation of Mother's Employment to Intellectual Performance of Negro College Students," *Social Problems* 11:414–418 (Spring 1964).

Erikson, Erik H., "The Concept of Identity in Race Relations: Notes and Queries," *Daedalus* 95:145–171 (Winter 1966).

Erikson, Erik H., "The Problem of Ego Identity," *Journal of American Psychoanalytic Association,* no. 4, 1956.

Fanon, Frantz, *Black Skins, White Masks* [reprint of *Peau Noire, Masques Blancs*]. New York: Grove Press, 1967.

Federn, Paul, "On the Distinction between Healthy and Pathological Narcissism," in *Ego Psychology and the Psychoses.* New York: Basic Books, 1952.

Fenichel, Otto, "Identification," in *The Collected Papers of Otto Fenichel.* New York: Norton, 1953.

Fishman, Jacob R., and Fredric Soloman, "Youth and Social Action, I: Perspectives on the Student Sit-in Movement," *American Journal of Orthopsychiatry* 33:872–882 (October 1963).

Fishman, Jacob R., and Fredric Soloman, "Youth and Social Action, II: Action and Identity Formation in the First Student Sit-in Demonstration," *Journal of Social Issues* 20:36–45 (April 1964).

Fishman, Joshua A., "Childhood Indoctrination for Minority Group Membership," *Daedalus* 90:329–349 (Spring 1961).

Fontinell, Eugene, "The Identity of James Baldwin," *Interracial Review* 35:194–199 (September 1962).

Frazier, E. Franklin, *Negro Youth at the Crossways.* Washington, D.C.: American Council on Education, 1940.

Freud, Anna, *The Ego and the Mechanisms of Defense.* New York: International Universities Press, 1946.

Freud, Sigmund, *A General Introduction to Psychoanalysis.* New York: Liveright, 1935.

Freud, Sigmund, "Instincts and Their Vicissitudes," *Standard Edition*, no. 14.

Freud, Sigmund, "On Psychotherapy," *Standard Edition*, no. 7.

Freud, Sigmund, "The Dynamics of Transference," *Standard Edition*, no. 12, London: Hogarth Press, 1958.

Freud, Sigmund, *The Ego and the Id*. London: Hogarth Press, 1927.

Gaier, Eugene L., and Helen S. Wambach, "Self-Evaluation of Personality Assets and Liabilities of Southern White and Negro Students," *Journal of Social Psychology* 51:135–143 (February 1960).

Gardner, George E., and Sadie Aaron, "The Childhood and Adolescent Adjustment of Negro Psychiatric Casualties," *American Journal of Orthopsychiatry* 16:481–495 (1946).

Gill, M. M., R. Newman, and F. C. Redlich, *The Initial Interview in Psychiatric Practice*. New York: International Universities Press, 1954.

Gist, Noel P., and William S. Bennett, Jr., "Aspirations of Negro and White Students," *Social Forces* 42:40–48 (October 1963).

Gordon, D. N., "Note on Negro Alienation," *American Journal of Sociology* 76:477–478 (January 1965).

Gore, Pearl M., and J. B. Rotter, "A Personality Correlate of Social Action," *Journal of Personality* 31:58–64 (March 1963).

Greenson, R. R., "The Mother Tongue and the Mother," *International Journal of Psychoanalysis* 31:18–23 (1953).

Greenson, R. R., "The Working Alliance and the Transference Neurosis," *Psychoanalysis Quarterly* 34:155–181 (1965).

Grier, William H., and Price M. Cobbs, *Black Rage*. New York: Basic Books, 1968.

Grier, William H., "Some Special Effects of Negroness on the Oedipal Conflict," *Journal of the National Medical Association*, November, 1966.

Grier, William H., "When the Therapist is Negro: Some Effects on the Treatment Process," *American Journal of Psychiatry*, June, 1967.

Grossack, Martin M., "Group Belongingness Among Negroes," *Journal of Social Psychology* 43:167–180 (February 1956).

Grossack, Martin M., "Group Belongingness and Authoritarianism in

Southern Negroes—A Research Note," *Phylon* 18:261–266 (Fall 1957).

Grossack, Martin M., "Psychological Effects of Segregation in Buses," *Journal of Negro Education* 25:71–74 (Winter 1956).

Grossack, Martin M., "Some Personality Characteristics of Southern Negro Students," *Journal of Social Psychology* 46:125–131 (August 1957).

Haggstrom, Warren C., "Segregation, Desegregation, and Negro Personality," *Integrated Education* 1:19–23 (October–November 1963).

Hammer, E. F., "Frustration-Aggression Hypothesis Extended to Socioracial Areas: Comparison of Negro and White Children's H-T-P's," *Psychiatric Quarterly* 27:597–607 (1953).

Hartmann, Heinz, "Comments on the Psychoanalytic Theory of Instinctual Drives," *Psychoanalysis Quarterly*, no. 17.

Hindman, Baker M., "The Emotional Problems of Negro High School Youth Which are Related to Segregation and Discrimination in a Southern Urban Community," *Journal of Educational Sociology* 27:115–127 (September 1953).

Hokanson, J. E., and G. Calden, "Negro-White Differences on the MMPI," *Journal of Clinical Psychology* 16:32–33 (January 1960).

Holloman, Laynard L., "On the Supremacy of the Negro Athlete in White Athletic Competition," *Psychoanalytical Review* 30:157–162 (1943).

Hughes, J. H., and G. C. Thompson, "A Comparison of the Value Systems of Southern Negro and Northern White Youth," *Journal of Educational Psychology* 45:300–309 (July 1954).

Iscoe, Ira, Martha Williams, and Jerry Harvey, "Age, Intelligence, and Sex as Variables in the Conformity Behavior of Negro and White Children," *Child Development* 35:451–460 (June 1964).

Jackson, Esther Merle, "The American Negro and the Image of the Absurd," *Phylon* 23:359–371 (Winter 1962).

Johnson, Edwina C., "The Child in the Prestige Vacuum," *Integrated Education* 1:13–26 (December 1963–January 1964).

Johnson, Robert B., "Negro Reactions to Minority Group Status," in Milton L. Barron, ed., *American Minorities*. New York: Knopf, 1957.

Kardiner, Abram, and Lionel Ovesey, *The Mark of Oppression: A Psychosocial Study of the American Negro.* New York: Norton, 1951.

Kardiner, Abram, and Lionel Ovesey, *The Mark of Oppression: Explorations in the Personality of the American Negro.* New York: Norton, 1951.

Karon, Bertram P., *The Negro Personality: A Rigorous Investigation of the Effects of Culture.* New York: Springer, 1958.

Katz, Irwin, and Charles Greenbaum, "Effects of Anxiety, Threat, and Racial Environment on Task Performance of Negro College Students," *Journal of Abnormal and Social Psychology* 66:562–567 (June 1963).

Kennedy, Janet A., "Problems Posed in the Analysis of Negro Patients," *Psychiatry* 15:313–327 (1952).

Kerckhoff, A. C., and T. C. McCormick, "Marginal Status and Marginal Personality," *Social Forces* 34:48–55 (October 1955).

Killens, John Oliver, "Explanation of the 'Black Psyche,' " *New York Times Magazine,* June 7, 1964.

Kris, Ernst, "The Development of Ego Psychology," *Samiksa,* no. 5.

Kvaraceus, William C., *Negro Self-Concept: Implications for School and Citizenship.* Medford, Mass.: Lincoln Filene Center for Citizenship and Public Affairs, Tufts University, 1964.

Lapouse, Rema, and Mary A. Monk, "Behavior Deviations in a Representative Sample of Children: Variation by Sex, Age, Race, Social Class and Family Size," *American Journal of Orthopsychiatry* 34:436–446 (April 1964).

Levin, David, "James Baldwin's Autobiographical Essays: The Problem of Negro Identity," *Massachusetts Review* 5:239–247 (Winter 1964).

Lewis, Nolan D. C., and L. D. Hubbard, "Epileptic Reactions in the Negro Race," *Psychiatry* 11:647–677 (1932).

Lewis, Nolan D. C., and L. D. Hubbard, "Manic-Depressive Reactions in Negroes," in *Manic-Depressive Psychosis.* Baltimore: Williams and Wilkins, 1931.

Liebow, Elliot, *Tally's Corner: A Study of Negro Streetcorner Men.* Boston: Little, Brown, 1967.

Lott, Albert E., and Bernice E., *Negro and White Youth.* New York: Holt, Rinehart and Winston, 1963.

Luchins, Abraham S., and Edith H., "Personality Impressions from Communications Reflecting Attitudes Toward Segregation," *Journal of Social Psychology* 58:315–330 (December 1962).

Marx, Gary T., *Protest and Prejudice: A Study of Belief in the Black Community.* New York: Harper and Row, 1967.

McLean, Helen V., "The Emotional Health of Negroes," *Journal of Negro Education* 18:283–290 (1949).

Menninger, Karl A., *Theory of Psychoanalytic Technique.* New York: Basic Books, 1958.

Middleton, Russell, "Alienation, Race, and Education," *American Sociological Review* 28:973–977 (December 1963).

Middleton, Russell, and John Moland, "Humor in Negro and White Sub-Cultures: A Study of Jokes Among University Students," *American Sociological Review* 24:61–69 (February 1959).

Miller, C., C. Wertz, and S. Counts, "Racial Differences on the MMPI," *Journal of Clinical Psychology* 17:159–161 (April 1961).

Millstein, G., "A Negro Says It with Jokes," *New York Times Magazine,* April 30, 1961.

Milner, Esther, "Some Hypotheses Concerning the Influence of Segretation on Negro Personality Development," *Psychiatry* 16:291–297 (August 1953).

Mischel, W., "Preference for Delayed Reinforcement and Social Responsibility," *Journal of Abnormal and Social Psychology* 62:1–7 (January 1961).

Mischel, W., "Delay of Gratification, Need for Achievement, and Acquiescence in Another Culture," *Journal of Abnormal and Social Psychology* 62:543–552 (May 1961).

Mischel, W., "Father-Absence and Delay of Gratification: Cross-Cultural Comparisons," *Journal of Abnormal and Social Psychology* 63:116–124 (July 1961).

Mitchell, Lonnie E., "Aspiration Levels of Negro Delinquent, Dependent, and Public School Boys," *Journal of Negro Education* 26:80–85 (Winter 1957).

Montagu, M. F. Ashley, "Origins of the American Negro," *Psychiatry* 7:163–174 (1947).

Montagu, M. F. Ashley, "The Physical Anthropology of the American Negro," *Psychiatry* 7:31–44 (1944).

Morland, J. Kenneth, "Racial Recognition by Nursery School Children in Lynchburg, Virginia," *Social Forces* 37:132–137 (December 1958).

Morland, J. Kenneth, "Racial Self-Identification: A Study of Nursery School Children," *American Catholic Sociological Review* 24:231–242 (Fall 1963).

Mussen, Paul, and Luther Distler, "Masculinity, Identification, and Father-Son Relationships," *Journal of Abnormal and Social Psychology* 59:350–356 (September 1959).

Myers, Henry J., and Leon Yochelson, "Color Denial in the Negro," *Psychiatry* 11:39–46 (February 1948).

"Negro American Personality," *Journal of Social Issues* 20:1–145 (April 1964).

Nunberg, Herman, "The Feeling of Guilt," in *Practice and Theory of Psychoanalysis.* New York: International Universities Press, 1955.

Oakes, Theresa, and Jerry M. Weiss, eds., *The Unfinished Journey.* New York: Webster Division, McGraw-Hill, 1967.

Palermo, D. S., "Racial Comparisons and Additional Normative Data on the Children's Manifest Anxiety Scale," *Child Development* 30:53–57 (March 1959).

Parker, Sam, and Paul Schilder, "A Specific Motility Psychosis in Negro Alcoholics," *Journal of Nervous and Mental Diseases* (90:1–18 (1939).

Parsons, T., and K. B. Clark, eds., *The Negro American.* Boston: Beacon Press, 1967.

Pennington, Stewart, and Lonnie E. Mitchell, "Sex Differences in Reactions to Minority Group Status," *Journal of Negro Education* 28:35–41 (Winter 1959).

Pettigrew, Thomas F., *A Profile of the Negro American.* Princeton, N.J.: Van Nostrand, 1964.

Powdermaker, Hortense, "The Channeling of Negro Aggression by the Cultural Process," *American Journal of Sociology* 48:750–758 (May 1943).

Price, Arthur Cooper, "A Rorschach Study of the Development of Personality Structure in White and Negro Children in a Southeastern Community," *Genetic Psychology Monographs* 65:3–52 (1962).

Proshansky, H. M., "The Development of Inter-Group Attitudes," L. W. Hoffman and M. L. Hoffman, eds., *Review of Child Development in Research*. New York: Russell Sage Foundation, 1966, pp. 311–371.

Prothro, James W., and Charles U. Smith, "Ethnic Differences in Authoritarian Personality," *Social Forces* 35:334–338 (May 1957).

Prothro, James W., and Charles U. Smith, "The Psychic Cost of Segregation," *Adult Education* 5:179–181 (1955).

Prudhomme, Charles, "The Problem of Suicide in the American Negro," *Psychoanalytical Review* 25:187–204 (1938).

Psychiatric Aspects of School Desegregation: Report No. 37. New York: Group for the Advancement of Psychiatry Publications Office, 1957.

Radzinski, J. M., "The American Melting Pot: Its Meaning to Us," *American Journal of Psychiatry* 115:873–886 (April 1959).

Redding, J. Saunders, *On Being Negro in America*. New York: Bantam Books, 1964.

Reik, T., *Listening with the Third Ear*. New York: Farrar, Straus, 1948.

Riessman, Frank, Jerome Cohen, and Arthur Pearl, *Mental Health of the Poor*. New York: Free Press, 1964.

Ripley, Herbert S., and Stewart Wolf, "Mental Illness Among Negro Troops Overseas," *Psychiatry* 103:499–512 (1947).

Roberts, J. K., ed., *School Children in the Urban Slum*. New York: Free Press, 1967.

Rohrer, J. H., and M. S. Edmonson, *The Eighth Generation*. New York: Harper, 1960.

Rosen, Bernard C., "Race, Ethnicity, and the Achievement Syndrome," *American Sociological Review* 24:47–60 (February 1959).

Rosenthal, Robert, and Lenore Jacobson, "Self-Fulfilling Prophecies in the Classroom: Teacher's Expectation as Unintended Determinants of Pupil's Intellectual Competence," in *Social Class, Race and Psychological Development*. Martin Deutsch, Irwin Katz, and Arthur Jensen, eds., New York: Holt, Rinehart, 1967.

Sachs, Wulf, *Black Anger*. Boston: Little, Brown, 1947.

Sachs, Wulf, *Black Hamlet*. London: Geoffrey Bles, 1937.

Schafer, R., "Generative Empathy in the Treatment Situation," *Psychoanalysis Quarterly* 28:342–373 (1959).

Schur, Max, "The Ego in Anxiety," in *Drives, Affects, Behavior.* R. M. Loewenstein, ed., New York: International Universities Press, 1953.

Secord, P. F., and E. S. Berscheid, "Stereotyping and the Generality of Implicit Personality Theory," *Journal of Personality* 31:65–78 (March 1963).

Seeman, Melvin, "Intellectual Perspective and Adjustment to Minority Status," *Social Problems* 4:142–153 (January 1956).

Seward, G., *Psychotherapy and Culture Conflict.* New York: Ronald Press, 1956.

Simpson, G. E., and J. M. Yinger, *Racial and Cultural Minorities.* 3rd ed., New York: Harper and Row, 1965.

Singer, S. L., and B. Stefflre, "A Note on Racial Differences in Job Values and Desires," *Journal of Social Psychology* 43:333–337 (May 1956).

Smith, Lillian, *Killers of the Dream.* New York: Norton, 1961.

Spock, Benjamin, "Children and Discrimination," *Redbook* 123:30+ (September 1964).

Stevenson, H. W., and E. C. Stewart, "A Developmental Study of Racial Awareness in Young Children," *Child Development* 29:399–409 (September 1958).

Sutherland, Robert L., *Color, Class and Personality.* Washington, D.C., 1942.

Taylor, Dalmas A., "The Relationship Between Authoritarianism and Ethnocentrism in Negro College Students," *Journal of Negro Education* 31:455–459 (Fall 1962).

Trent, Richard D., "The Relation Between Expressed Self-Acceptance and Expressed Attitudes Toward Negroes and Whites Among Negro Children," *Journal of Genetic Psychology* 91:25–31 (September 1957).

Vaughan, Graham M., "Concept Formation and the Development of Ethnic Awareness," *Journal of Genetic Psychology* 103:93–103 (September 1963).

Vaughan, Graham M., "Ethnic Awareness in Relation to Minority Group Membership," *Journal of Genetic Psychology* 105:119–130 (September 1964).

Veroff, J., J. W. Atkinson, Schiela C. Feld, and G. Gurin, "The Use of Thematic Apperception to Assess Motivation in a Nationwide Interview Study," *Psychological Monographs* 74:1–12 (1960).

Volkan, U., "Five Poems by Negro Youngsters Who Faced a Sudden Desegregation," *Psychiatric Quarterly* 37:607–617 (October 1963).

Vontress, Clemmont E., "The Negro Against Himself," *Journal of Negro Education* 32:237–242 (Summer 1963).

Waelder, Robert, *Basic Theory of Psychoanalysis*. New York: International Universities Press, 1964.

Waelder, Robert, "Notes on Prejudice," *Vassar Alumni Magazine*, May, 1949.

Weaver, E. K., "How Do Children Discover They are Negroes?" *Understanding the Child* 24:108–112 (1955).

Winnicott, D. W., "Hate in the Counter-Transference," *International Journal of Psychoanalysis* 30:69–74 (1949).

Witmer, Helen, and Ruth Kotinsky, eds., *Personality in the Making*. New York: Harper, 1952.

Woronoff, Israel, "Negro Male Identification Problems," *Journal of Educational Sociology* 36:30–32 (September 1962).

Yarrow, Marian R., and Bernard, Lande, "Personality Correlates of Differential Reactions to Minority Group-Belonging," *Journal of Social Psychology* 38:253–272 (November 1953).

Zetzel, E., "Current Concepts of Transference," *International Journal of Psychoanalysis* 37:369–376 (1956).

Black-Jewish Relations

Asher, Joseph. "To Speak Out Loud," *American Judaism* (Union of American Hebrew Congregations). Fall 1963. pp. 6, 48.

Band, Jordan C. *The Human Rights Revolution-Role and Relation of Federation*. Council of Jewish Federations and Welfare Funds, 1964. 8 pp., mimeo.

Berson, Lenora E. *Case Study of a Riot: The Philadelphia Story*. Institute of Human Relations Press, American Jewish Committee, 1966. 72 pp.

Brody, Eugene B. and Robert L. Derbyshire. "Prejudice in American Negro College Students: Mental Status, Antisemitism and Antiforeign Prejudice," Archives of General Psychiatry. December 1963. pp. 619–628.

Clark, Dennis. "Urban Negro and Urban Jew," *The Crisis*. May 1958. pp. 275–280.

Clark, Kenneth B. "Candor About Negro-Jewish Relations." *Commentary*. February 1946. pp. 8–14.

Cohen, Seymour J. *The Negro-Jewish Dialogue*. Synagogue Council of America, 1963. 7 pp.

Cohen, Seymour J. "Negroes and Jews," *Jewish Spectator*. November 1962. pp. 9–13.

Conservative Judaism, "Jews and the Racial Crisis," Summer 1965. pp. 1–27.

Council of Jewish Federations and Welfare Funds, *The Revolution of Our Time*, 1964. 28 pp.

Engel, Gerald. "Breathing Freedom in Mississippi." *Jewish Life*. Spring 1965. pp. 51–55.

Fiedler, Leslie A. "Negro and Jew-Encounter in America," *Midstream*. Summer 1956. pp. 5–17.

Fishman, Joshua A. "Southern City," *Midstream*. Summer 1961. pp. 39–56.

Fleischman, Harry. *Negro Anti-Semitism and the White Backlash*. American Jewish Committee, 1968.

Fleischman, Harry. *Negroes and Jews: Brotherhood or Bias*. American Jewish Committee, 1967. 4 pp.

Gibel, Ingle Lederer. "The Negro-Jewish Scene: A Personal View," *Judaism*. Winter 1965. pp. 12–21.

Glazer, Nathan. "Jews and Poverty," *Midstream*. January 1966. pp. 30–36.

Glazer, Nathan. "Negroes and Jews: The New Challenge to Pluralism," *Commentary* December 1964. pp. 29–34.

Gold, Bertram H. *Jews and the Urban Crisis*. American Jewish Committee, 1968.

Goodman, Arnold M. "The Equity of Redemption," *Reconstructionist* April 2, 1965. pp. 7–13.

Gordis, Robert. "Race and the Religious Tradition," *Jewish Frontier*. March 1962. pp. 68–77.

Gordis, Robert. *The Root and the Branch: Judaism and the Free Society.* University of Chicago Press. 1962. 254 pp.

Gordon, Albert I. "Negro-Jewish Marriages: Three Interviews," *Judaism.* Spring 1964. pp. 164–184.

Heller, Celia Stopnicka and Alphonso Pinkney. *Social Forces.* March 1965. pp. 364–369.

Hero, Alfred O. Jr. "Southern Jews, Race Relations and Foreign Policy," *Jewish Social Studies.* October 1965. pp. 213–235.

Hertz, Richard C. "Rising Tide of Negro-Jewish Tensions," *Ebony.* December 1964. pp. 117–125.

Hertsberg, Arthur, et al. "Changing Race Relations and Jewish Communal Service: A Symposium," *Journal of Jewish Communal Service.* Summer 1965. pp. 323–364.

Levine, Irving, *The Urban Crisis and the Jewish Community.* American Jewish Committee, 1968. 8 pp.

Maslow, Will. *Negro-Jewish Relations. (In Freedom Now! The Civil-Rights Struggle in America.* Alan F. Westin, editor). Basic Books. 1964. pp. 297–301.

Midstream. "The Civil Rights Front," September 1964. pp. 15–35.

Moon, Henry Lee. *Of Negro, Jews and Other Americans,* American Jewish Committee, 1968. 8 pp.

Morsell, John A. *Jewish Community Agencies and Negro-Jewish Relations.* (In *Proceedings of the Association of Jewish Community Relations Workers Conference.* Arden House, January 10–12, 1960. Jewish Community Relations Workers. 1960. 10 pp. mimeo.)

Moss, James A. "The American Jew and the Negro Civil-Rights Struggle," *Chicago Jewish Forum.* Fall 1965. pp. 15–18.

Muravchik, Emanuel. "Troubled Allies," *Jewish Life.* March–April 1963. pp. 9–16.

Negro-Jewish Relations in the United States. The Citadel Press. 1966 96 pp.

Palnick, Elijah E. "Southern Jewry and Civil Rights," *CCAR Journal* (Central Conference of American Rabbis). June 1965. pp. 62–65.

Podhoretz, Norman. "My Negro Problem—and Ours," *Commentary.* February 1963. pp. 93–101.

Polier, Shad. *The Jew and the Racial Crisis.* American Jewish Congress. 1964. 7 pp.

Raab, Earl. *The Black Revolution and the Jewish Question,* American Jewish Committee, 1969. pp. 12.

Religious Education. "Race Relations and Religious Education," January–February 1964. pp. 2–120.

Rose, Arnold M. *The Negro's Morale: Group Identification and Protest.* University of Minnesota Press. 1949. 153 pp.

Rothschilde, Jacob M. "One Man's Meat . . . A Personal Experience," *CCAR Journal,* June 1965. pp. 57–61.

Rubenstein, Richard. "Why 19 Conservative Rabbis Went to Birmingham," *National Jewish Monthly.* July–August 1963. pp. 6–7.

Schick, Marvin. "The Orthodox Jew and the Negro Revolution," *The Jewish Observor.* December 1964. pp. 15–17.

Schulweis, Harold M. "The Voice of Esau," *Reconstructionist* December 10, 1965. pp. 7–14.

Shapiro, Manheim S. "The Negro Revolution—and Jews," Reprinted from *Council Woman* (National Council of Jewish Women). April 1964. American Jewish Committee. 1964. 4 pp.

Sheppard, Harold L. "The Negro Merchant: A Study of Negro Anti-Semitism," *The American Journal of Sociology.* September 1947. pp. 96–99.

Sherman, C. Bezslel, "In the American Jewish Community: Negro and Jewish Relations," *Jewish Frontier.* July 1964. pp. 16–18.

Tanenbaum, Rabbi Marc H. *The American Negro: Myths and Realities.* American Jewish Committee, Institute of Human Relations, 1968. 4 pp.

Teller, Judd L. and Nahum Guttman, editors. *American Ethnic and the New Nations.* (In *The Free World and the New Nations.* A. S. Barnes. 1964. pp. 112–176.

Teller, Judd L. "Negro and Jew," *Jewish Frontier.* September 1963. pp. 9–13.

Union of American Hebrew Congregations. *Why We Went.* 3 pp. mimeo.

Vorspan, Albert. "The Negro Victory and the Jewish Failure," *American Judaism* (Union of American Hebrew Congregations). Fall 1963. pp. 7, 50–54.

Vorspan, Albert, "Ten Ways Out for Tired Liberals," *American Judaism,* Fall 1964. pp. 14–15, 57–58.

Weinstein, Jacob J. "How One Congregation Faced the Problem of Integration," *Jewish Frontier*. March 1959. pp. 13–17.

Wilkins, Roy. "Jewish-Negro Relations: An Evaluation," *American Judaism*. Spring 1963. pp. 4–5.

Wilson, James Q. *Negro Politics: The Search for Leadership*. Free Press, 1960. 342 pp.

Religion

Abbott, Walter M., "The Bible Abused," *Interracial Review* 36:26–27+ (February 1963).

Ahmann, Mathew, ed., *Race: Challenge to Religion*. Chicago: Regnery, 1963.

Alexander, W. W., *Racial Segregation in the American Protestant Church*. New York: Friendship, 1946.

American Friends Service Committee of the Society of American Friends, *Race and Conscience in America*. Norman: University of Oklahoma Press, 1959.

Bailey, Kenneth K., *Southern White Protestantism in the Twentieth Century*. New York: Harper, 1964.

Ball, William B., "New Frontiers of Catholic Community Action," *Interracial Review* 35:49–51 (February 1962).

Baltzell, E. Digby, *The Protestant Establishment: Aristocracy and Caste in America*. New York: Random House, 1964.

Barbour, Russell, *Black and White Together: Plain Talk for White Christians*. Philadelphia: United Church Press, 1968.

Bell, John L., "The Presbyterian Church and the Negro in North Carolina," *North Carolina Historical Review* 40:15–36 (January 1963).

Bennett, John C., "Faith and Responsibility," *Christian Century* 75:1394–1397 (December 3, 1958).

Bennett, John C., "The Demand for Freedom and Justice in the Contemporary World Revolutions," in Walter Leibrecht, ed., *Religion and Culture: Essays in Honor of Paul Tillich*. New York: Harper, 1959.

Bardolph, Richard, "Negro Religious and Educational Leaders in 'Who's Who in America,' 1939–1955." *Journal of Negro Education* 26:182–192 (Spring 1957).

Bernard, Raymond, "The Negro Prospect," *Social Order* 7:135–136 (March 1957).

Bernard, Raymond, "Some Anthropological Implications of the Racial Admission Policy of the U.S. Sisterhoods," *American Catholic Sociological Review* 19:124–135 (June 1958).

Berrigan, Phillip, S.S.J., *No More Strangers.* New York: Macmillan, 1965.

Beynon, Erdmann Doane, "The Voodoo Cult Among Negro Migrants in Detroit," *American Journal of Sociology* 43: 894–907 (May 1938).

Boggs, Marion, "The Crucial Test of Christian Citizenship," *New South* 12:7–8 (July–August 1957).

"Bonds of Union," *New York Times,* November 17, 1963.

Bontemps, Arna, "Rock, Church, Rock," in Sylvester C. Watkins, ed., *Anthology of American Negro Literature,* New York: Random House, 1944.

Bouton, Ellen Naylor, and Thomas F. Pettigrew, "When a Priest Made a Pilgrimage," *Christian Century* 80:863–865 (March 20, 1963).

Boyd, Malcolm, ed., *On the Battle Lines.* New York: Morehouse-Barlow, 1964.

Brewer, J. Mason, *The Word on the Brazos.* Austin: University of Texas Press, 1953.

Britts, Maurice W., "Interracial Justice: An Issue for Youth," *Interracial Review* 35:220–221 (October 1962).

Brown, Aubrey N., Jr., "Presbyterians, U.S.: En Route to Broader Concerns," *Christian Century* 80:1577–1580 (December 18, 1963).

Brown, Robert R., *Bigger Than Little Rock,* Greenwich, Conn.: Seabury, 1958.

Burr, Nelson R., *Critical Bibliography of Religion in America.* Princeton: Princeton University Press, 1961. See pp. 348–381.

Buswell, J. Oliver, *Slavery, Segregation and Scripture.* Grand Rapids: Erdman, 1964.

Campbell, Ernest Q., and Thomas F. Pettigrew, "Racial and Moral Crisis: The Role of Little Rock Ministers," *American Journal of Sociology* 64:509–516 (March 1959).

Campbell, Ernest Q., and Thomas F. Pettigrew, *Christians in Racial Crisis: A Study of Little Rock's Ministry, Including Statements on Desegregation and Race Relations by the Leading Religious Denominations of the United States.* Washington, D.C.: Public Affairs Press, 1959.

Campbell, Will D., "Perhaps or Maybe," *Christian Century* 79:1133 (September 19, 1962).

Cantril, Hadley, *The Psychology of Social Movements.* New York: Wiley, 1941.

"Cardinal McIntyre: A Ramparts Special Report," *Ramparts* 3:35–44 (November 1964).

Carnell, Edward John, "A Christian Social Ethics," *Christian Century* 80:979–980 (August 7, 1963).

Carr, Warren, "Notes from an Irrelevant Clergyman," *Christian Century* 80:879–881 (July 10, 1963).

Cartwright, Colbert S., "The Southern Minister and the Race Question," *New South* 13:3–6 (February 1958).

Cartwright, Colbert S., "Band Together for Genuine Unity," *New South* 16:6–10 (January 1961).

Catchings, L. Maynard, "Interracial Activities in Southern Churches," *Phylon* 13:54–56 (March 1952).

Cayton, Horace, "E. Franklin Frazier: A Tribute and a Review," *Review of Religious Research* 5:137–142 (Spring 1964).

"'Christian Guide' to Race Attitudes," *New South* 13:3–7 (May 1958).

"A Church Looks at Civil Rights in North Carolina," *New South* 18:13–15 (April 1963).

Clark, Elmer T., *The Small Sects in America.* Nashville, Tenn.: Abingdon, 1937; rev. ed. 1949.

Clark, Henry, "Churchmen and Residential Segregation," *Review of Religious Research* 5:157–164 (Spring 1964).

Cleague, Albert B., Jr., *The Black Messiah.* New York: Sheet & Ward, 1968.

Cogley, John, "The Clergy Heeds a New Call," *New York Times Magazine,* May 2, 1965.

Collie, Robert, "A 'Silent Minister' Speaks Up," *New York Times Magazine,* May 24, 1964.

Communism, Christianity and Race Relations. Valparaiso, Ind.: Lutheran Human Relations Association of America, 1960.

Conference on Jewish Social Studies, *Negro-Jewish Relations in the United States.* New York: Citadel, 1966.

Congar, Yves M. J., *The Catholic Church and the Race Question.* Paris: UNESCO, 1953.

Cox, Harvey, "Letter from Williamston," *Christian Century* 80:1516–1518 (December 4, 1963).

Creger, Ralph, with Erwin McDonald, *A Look Down the Lonesome Road.* Garden City, N.Y.: Doubleday. 1964.

Crook, Roger H., *No South or North.* St. Louis, Mo.: Bethany, 1959.

Culver, Dwight W., *Negro Segregation in the Methodist Church.* New Haven: Yale University Press, 1953.

Cuninggim, Merrimon, "The Southern Temper," *New South* 13:7–8 (July–August 1958).

Daniel, Vattel E., "Ritual and Stratification in Chicago Negro Churches," *American Sociological Review* 7:353–358 (June 1942).

Daniels, Jonathan, and Judith Upham, "Report from Selma," *Episcopal Theological School Journal* 10:2–8 (May 1965).

Davis, Lloyd, "The Religious Dimension of Interracial Justice," *Interracial Review* 35:46–48 (February 1962).

"Discrimination and the Christian Conscience," *Journal of Negro Education* 28:66–69 (Winter 1959).

Drake, St. Clair, and Horace Cayton, *Black Metropolis.* New York: Harcourt, Brace, 1945; Harper Torchbook, 1963.

DuBay, Father William H., *The Human Church.* New York: Doubleday, 1966.

Dunne, George H., " 'I Expect More of Christians,' " *Interracial Review* 35:39–41, 53 (February 1962).

Egan, John J., "Compassion and Community Life," *Interracial Review* 35:66–69 (March 1962).

Ehle, John, *Shepherd of the Streets: The Story of the Reverend James A. Gusweller and His Crusade on the New York West Side.* New York: Sloane, 1960.

Elston, Wilbur, "Social, but Little Action," *Christian Century* 79:106–108 (January 24, 1962).

Evans, John B., "Alabama," *Christian Century* 80:188–190 (February 6, 1963).

Fauset, Arthur H., *Black Gods of the Metropolis*. Philadelphia: University of Pennsylvania Press, 1944.

Fey, Harold E., "Reconciliation in Rochester," *Christian Century* 80:1125–1127 (September 18, 1963).

Fey, Harold E., "Disciples on Civil Rights," *Christian Century* 80:1326–1327 (October 30, 1963).

Fey, Harold E., "Churches Meet Racial Crisis," *Christian Century* 80:1572–1573 (December 18, 1963).

Fey, Harold E., "N.C.C. Acts on Racial Crisis," *Christian Century* 80:1602–1604 (June 19, 1963).

Fey, Harold E., "Uniting and Marching," *Christian Century* 80:926–927 (July 24, 1963).

Fichter, Joseph H., *Social Relations in the Urban Parish*. Chicago: University of Chicago Press, 1954.

Fichter, Joseph, "Negro Spirituals and Catholicism," *Interracial Review* 35:200–203 (September 1962).

Fichter, Joseph H., "The Catholic South and Race," *Religious Education* 59:30–33 (January–February 1964).

Fichter, Joseph H., "American Religion and the Negro," *Daedalus* 94:1085–1106 (Fall 1965).

Fichter, Joseph H., and George L. Maddox, "Religion in the South, Old and New," in John McKinney and Edgar Thompson, eds., *The South in Continuity and Change*. Durham, N.C.: Duke University Press, 1965.

Fitzpatrick, Joseph P., "The Dynamics of Change," *Interracial Review* 35:7–9 (January 1962).

Foley, Albert S., *God's Men of Color*. New York: Farrar, Straus, 1955.

Foshey, Gerald, "Divided Flocks in Jackson," *Christian Century* 80:1469–1471 (November 27, 1963).

Frazier, E. Franklin, *The Negro Church in America*. New York: Schocken, 1963.

Fry, John K., "United Presbyterians: Prophecy vs. Tradition," *Christian Century* 80:1235–1237 (October 9, 1963).

Gallagher, Buell, *Color and Conscience: The Irrepressible Conflict.* New York: Harper, 1946.

Gasnick, Roy M., "Franciscan Pledge to Interracial Justice," *Social Order* 12:173–177 (April 1962).

Geier, Woodrow A., "Tennessee," *Christian Century* 79:1302 (October 24, 1962).

Geier, Woodrow A., "Tennessee: Students and Race," *Christian Century* 80:56 (January 9, 1963).

Geier, Woodrow A., "Tennessee," *Christian Century* 80:1526–1527 (December 4, 1963).

"A Gandhi Society?" *Christian Century* 79:735–736 (June 13, 1962).

Gillard, John T., *The Catholic Church and the Negro.* Baltimore: St. Joseph's Society Press, 1929.

Gillard, John T., *Colored Catholics in the United States.* Baltimore, Md.: The Josephite Press, 1941.

Gillespie, G. T., "A Christian View of Segregation," Greenwood, Miss.: Publications of the Association of Citizens' Councils of Mississippi, no date.

Gleason, Robert W., "Immortality of Segregation," *Thought* 35:138 (Autumn 1960).

Glenn, Norval D., "Negro Religion and Negro Status in the United States," in Louis Schneider, ed., *Religion, Culture, and Society.* New York: Wiley, 1964.

Glock, Charles F., and Rodney Stack, *Christian Beliefs and Anti-Semitism.* New York: Harper and Row, 1966.

Greeley, Andrew M., "White Parish—Refuge or Resource," *Interracial Review* 35:168–169 (July 1962).

Grimes, Alan P., *Equality in America.* New York: Oxford University Press, 1964.

Gustafson, James M., "The Clergy in the United States," *Daedalus* 92:724–744 (Fall 1963).

Hacket, Allen, *For the Open Door.* Philadelphia, Penn.: United Church Press, 1964.

Hapgood, Hulchins, *The Spirit of the Ghetto: Studies of the Jewish Quarter.* New York: Schocken, 1966.

Harbutt, Charles, "The Church and Integration," *Jubilee* 6:6–15 (February 1959).

Harte, Thomas J., *Catholic Organizations Promoting Negro-White Race Relations in the United States.* Washington, D.C.: Catholic University Press, 1947.

Hartnett, Robert C., "The 'Divine Doctrine' of Brotherhood," *Interracial Review* 35:96–97 (April 1962).

Haselden, Kyle, *The Racial Problem in Christian Perspective.* New York: Harper, 1963. 1st ed., 1959.

Haselden, Kyle, "Too Busy to Hate," *Christian Century* 80:392–393 (March 27, 1963).

Haselden, Kyle, "The Birmingham Lull," *Christian Century* 80:1294–1295 (October 23, 1963).

Haselden, Kyle, "Religion and Race," *Christian Century* 80:133–135 (January 30, 1963).

Haselden, Kyle, "Eleven A.M. Sunday is Our Most Segregated Hour," *New York Times Magazine,* August 2, 1964.

Haselden, Kyle, *Mandate for White Christians.* New York: John Knox Press, 1967.

Haynes, Leonard L., *The Negro Community Within American Protestantism.* Boston: Christopher, 1953.

Herberg, Will, *Protestant, Catholic, Jew.* Garden City, N.Y.: Doubleday, 1955.

Herskovits, Melville J., "Social History of the Negro," in C. Murchison, ed., *Handbook of Social Psychology.* Worcester, Mass.: Clark University Press, 1935.

Herskovits, Melville J., *The Myth of the Negro Past.* New York: Harper, 1941; Boston: Beacon, 1958.

Hill, Samuel S., Jr., "The South's Culture Protestantism," *Christian Century* 79:1094–1096 (September 12, 1962).

Hill, Samuel S., Jr., "Southern Protestantism and Racial Integration," *Religion in Life* 33:421–429 (Summer 1964).

Holden, Anna, "A Call to Catholics," *Interracial Review* 35:140–143 (June 1962).

Horchler, Richard, "The Layman's Role in the Changing Community," *Interracial Review* 35:12–13 (January 1962).

Hough, Joseph C., Jr., *Black Power and White Protestants: A Christian Response to the New Negro Pluralism.* New York: Oxford University Press, 1968.

Hurley, Denis E., "Second Vatican and Racism," *Interracial Review* 36:11 (December 1963).

Hurley, Phillip S., "Role of the Churches in Integration," *Journal of Intergroup Relations* 1:41–46 (Summer 1960).

James, Willis Laurence, "The Romance of the Negro Folk Cry in America," *Phylon* 16:15–30 (Spring 1955).

Johnson, Benton, "Do Holiness Sects Socialize in Dominant Values?" *Social Forces* 39:309–316 (May 1961).

Johnson, Benton, "Ascetic Protestantism and Political Preference in the Deep South," *American Journal of Sociology* 69:359–366 (January 1964).

Johnson, Charles S., *Growing Up in the Black Belt.* Washington, D.C.: American Council on Education, 1941.

Johnson, James Weldon, *God's Trombones.* New York: Viking, 1927.

Johnston, Ruby F., *The Development of Negro Religion.* New York: Philosophical Library, 1954.

Johnston, Ruby F., *The Religion of Negro Protestants.* New York: Philosophical Library, 1956.

Jones, Madison, "On the Neighborhood Level," *Interracial Review* 35:22–23 (January 1962).

Jones, Raymond J., *A Comparative Study of Religious Cult Behavior Among Negroes with Special Reference to Emotional Conditioning Factors.* Howard University Studies in the Social Sciences, vol. 2 no., 2, Washington, D.C.: Howard University Graduate School, 1940.

Katz, Shlomo, ed., *Negro and Jew.* New York: Macmillan, 1967.

Kean, Charles D., "For Law and Integration," *Christian Century* 75:1262–1263 (November 5, 1958).

Kean, Charles D., "Pressures on Episcopalians," *Christian Century* 78:1102–1103 (September 20, 1961).

Kean, Charles D., "District of Columbia," *Christian Century* 80:725–726 (May 29, 1963).

Kearney, John, "Interracial Justice and the Indwelling of Christ

Among All Men of Earth," *Interracial Review* 35:263 (December 1962).

Kelsey, George D., *Racism and the Christian Understanding of Man.* New York: Scribner, 1965.

Kenealy, William J., "Racism Desecrates Liberty, Perverts Justice and Love," *Social Order* 13:5–20 (May 1963).

Kitagawa, Daisuke, *Race Relations and Christian Mission.* New York: Friendship, 1964.

Kitagawa, Daisuke, *The Pastor and the Race Issue.* New York: Seabury Press, 1965.

Klausler, Alfred P., "Chicago Area," *Christian Century,* July 17, 1963.

Kogan, Lawrence A., "The Jewish Conception of Negroes in the North: An Historical Approach," *Phylon* (Winter 1967).

Kramer, Alfred S., "Patterns of Racial Inclusion Among the Churches of Three Protestant Denominations," *Phylon* 16:283–294 (Summer 1955).

Kruuse, Elsa, "The Churches Act on Integration," *National Council Outlook* 7:6–8 (March 1957).

La Farge, John, *The Race Question and the Negro.* New York: Longmans, Green, 1943.

La Farge, John, *The Catholic Viewpoint on Race Relations.* Garden City, N.Y.: Doubleday 1956; 2nd ed., Garden City, N.Y.: Hanover House, 1960.

La Farge, John, "American Catholics and the Negro, 1962," *Social Order* 12:153–161 (April 1962).

La Farge, John, "Why Say 'Interracial'?" *Interracial Review* 35:44–45 (February 1962).

La Farge, John, "Translating into Action," *Interracial Review* 35:92–95 (April 1962).

La Farge, John, "Pope John on Racism," *Interracial Review* 36:110–111+ (June 1963).

La Farge, John, "Direct Action," *Interracial Review* 36:159+ (September 1963).

Lally, Francis J., "Needed—A People's Program," *Interracial Review* 35:2–3 (January 1962).

Lee, J. Oscar, "The Churches and Race Relations—A Survey," *Christianity and Crisis* 17:4–7 (February 4, 1957).

Lee, Robert, ed., *Cities and Churches: Readings on the Urban Church.* Philadelphia: Westminster, 1962.

Lee, J. Oscar, "Religion Among Ethnic and Racial Minorities," *Annals of the American Academy of Political and Social Science* 332:112–124 (November 1960).

Lenox, G. Merrill, "Michigan," *Christian Century,* September 11, 1963.

Lenski, Gerhard, *The Religious Factor: A Sociologist's Inquiry.* Garden City, N.Y.: Doubleday, 1961.

Leonard, Joseph T., *Theology and Race Relations.* Milwaukee: The Bruce Publishing Co., 1964.

Lincoln, C. Eric, *The Black Muslims in America.* Boston: Beacon Press, 1961.

Lipman, Eugene J., and Albert Vorspan, *A Tale of Ten Cities.* New York: Union of American Hebrew Congregations, 1962.

Liu, William T., "The Community Reference System, Religiosity and Race Attitudes," *Social Forces* 39:324–328 (May 1961).

Loescher, F. S., "Racism in the Northern City Churches," *Christian Century* 73:174–176 (February 8, 1956).

Long, Herman H., "Fellowship for Whom?" Nashville, Tenn.: Race Relations Department, Fisk University, no date.

McGill, Ralph, "The Agony of the Southern Minister," *New York Times Magazine,* September 27, 1959.

McLaughlin, Wayman B., "Symbolism and Mysticism in the Spirituals," *Phylon* 24:69–77 (Spring 1963).

McManus, Eugene P., *Studies in Race Relations.* Baltimore: Josephite, 1961.

McMillan, George, "Silent White Ministers of the South," *New York Times Magazine,* April 5, 1964.

McNeill, Robert, *God Wills Us Free: The Ordeal of a Southern Minister.* New York: Hill & Wang, 1965.

McPeak, William, "Social Problems are Human Problems," *Interracial Review* 35:253–254 (November 1962).

Malev, William S., "The Jew of the South in the Conflict on Segregation," *Conservative Judaism* 13:35–46 (Fall 1958).

Mantinband, Charles, "From the Diary of a Mississippi Rabbi," *American Judaism,* Winter 1962–1963.

Maston, T. B., *Segregation and Desegregation: A Christian Approach.* New York: Macmillan, 1959.

Mather, P. Boyd, "Religion and Race: Local Efforts," *Christian Century* 80:412–414 (March 27, 1963).

Mather, P. Boyd, "Search for Sufficiency," *Christian Century* 80:1139–1140 (September 18, 1963).

Mathews, Donald G., *Slavery and Methodism: A Chapter in American Morality 1780–1845.* Princeton, N.J.: Princeton University Press, 1965.

Mays, Benjamin E., *Seeking To Be Christian in Race Relations.* New York: Friendship, 1957.

Mays, Benjamin E., and Joseph W. Nicholson, *The Negro's Church.* New York: Institute of Social and Religious Research, 1933.

Mays, Benjamin E., *Negro's God as Reflected in His Literature.* New York: Atheneum, 1968.

Mehan, Joseph, "Catholic Perspectives on Interracialism," *Interracial Review* 35:222–223 (October 1962).

Meyer, Sylvan, "They Share a Mission," *Christian Century* 79:1103–1105 (August 22, 1962).

Miller, Robert M., *American Protestantism and Social Issues.* Chapel Hill: University of North Carolina Press, 1958.

Miller, William Robert, *Nonviolence: A Christian Interpretation.* New York: Association Press, 1965.

"Ministers' Statement of Conviction on Race," *New South* 12:3–6 (April 1957).

"A Missionary Presence in Mississippi 1964," *Social Action* 31:1–48 (November 1964).

Moellering, Ralph, *Christian Conscience and Negro Emancipation.* Philadelphia: Fortress Press, 1965.

Moss, James A., "The Negro Church and Black Power," An address, *Journal of Human Relations* 17:119–28 (First Quarter 1968).

Muelder, Walter, "Recruitment of Negroes for Theological Studies," *Review of Religious Research* 5:152–156 (Spring 1964).

Mulholland, Joseph A., "The Community and Crime," *Interracial Review* 35:18–19 (January 1962).

Murray, Andrew E., *Presbyterians and the Negro—A History*. Philadelphia: Presbyterian Historical Society, 1966.

Murray, Florence, ed., *The Negro Handbook*. New York: Macmillan, 1949.

National Catholic Conference for Interracial Justice, *The New Negro*. Matthew Ahmann, ed., Notre Dame, Ind.: Fides Publishing Co., 1961.

National Catholic Conference for Interracial Justice, "Statement and Resolutions Adopted by Council Delegates in Convention, November 17, 1963, at Washington, D.C.," *Interracial Review* 37:1+ (January 1964).

National Conference of Christians and Jews, 73 Tremont St., Boston, Mass., Grambs, Jean, "Education in a Transition Community," 1955.

National Conference on Religion and Race, "An Appeal to the Conscience of the American People," *Christian Century* 80:135 (January 30, 1963).

Nelson, J. Robert, "Race and Denomination—One Issue," *Christian Century* 78:1154–1555 (December 27, 1961).

New South 18:1+ (March, 1963). "The Other Mississippi."

New York Times, February 10, 1957. Survey by Protestant Council of the City of New York.

Nichols, Lee, and Louis Cassels, "The Churches Repent," *Harper's Magazine* 211:53–57 (October 1955).

Niebuhr, Reinhold, "The Crisis in American Protestantism," *Christian Century* 80:1498–1550 (December 4, 1963).

Niebuhr, H. Richard, *The Social Sources of Demoninationalism*. New York: Holt, 1929.

Northwood, Lawrence K., "Ecological and Attitudinal Factors in Church Desegregation," *Social Problems* 6:150–163 (Fall 1958).

O'Connor, John J., "Catholic Interracial Movement," *Social Order* 10:290–295 (September 1960).

O'Neill, Joseph E. ed., *A Catholic Case Against Segregation*. New York: Macmillan, 1961.

Officers of the United Church Board for Homeland Ministries, "Are 'Sanctions' Sub-Christian?" *Social Action* 30:12–16 (May 1964).

Olson, Bernhard E., *Faith and Prejudice: Intergroup Problems in Protestant Curricula*. New Haven: Yale University Press, 1963.

"Open or Closed Cities?" *Christian Century* 78:579–580 (May 10, 1961). "Woodlawn—Open or Closed," *ibid*. 78:685–688 (May 31, 1961), *ibid*. 78:711 (June 7, 1961).

Osborne, William, *The Segregated Covenant*. New York: Herder and Herder, no date.

Parker, Robert A., *The Incredible Messiah*. Boston: Little, Brown, 1937.

Peerman, Dean, "Death Down a Dark Street," *Christian Century* 80:166–167 (February 6, 1963).

Pettigrew, Thomas F., "The Myth of the Moderates," *Christian Century* 78:649–651 (May 24, 1961).

Pettigrew, Thomas F., "Our Caste-Ridden Protestant Campuses," *Christianity and Crisis* 21:88–91 (May 29, 1961).

Pettigrew, Thomas F., "Wherein the Church has Failed in Race," *Religious Education* 59:64–73 (January–February 1964).

Pohlhaus, J. Francis, "Catholic Involvement in Civil Rights Legislation," *Interracial Review* 36:192–195 (October 1963).

Pope, Liston, "Caste in the Church," *Survey Graphic* 36:59–60, 101–104 (January 1947).

Pope, Liston, *The Kingdom Beyond Caste*. New York: Friendship, 1957.

Pope, Liston, "The Negro and Religion in America," *Review of Religious Research* 5:142–152 (Spring 1964).

Posey, Walter B., "The Protestant Episcopal Church: An American Adaptation," *Journal of Southern History* 25:3–30 (February 1959).

Powdermaker, Hortense, *After Freedom: A Cultural Study in the Deep South*. New York: Viking, 1939.

"Race Tension is Costly," *Christian Century* 78:1068 (September 13, 1961).

Raines, Robert A., *The Secular Congregation*. New York: Harper and Row, 1968.

Ramsay, Paul, *Christian Ethics and the Sit-In*. New York: Association, 1961.

Rasky, Frank, "Harlem's Religious Zealots," *Tomorrow* 9:11–17 (November 1949).

Reid, Ira De Augustine, "Let Us Prey!" *Opportunity* 4:274–278 (September 1926).

Reimers, David M., "The Race Problem and Presbyterian Union," *Church History* 31:203–215 (June 1962).

Reimers, David M., *White Protestantism and the Negro.* New York: Oxford University Press, 1965.

Reissig, Herman F., *Man's New Home.* Philadelphia: United Church Press, 1964.

Religion in Racial Crisis: A Report on the National Conference on Religion and Race and Recommendations. New York: National Conference on Religion and Race, 1963.

Reuter, George S., Jr., August M. Hintz, and Helen H. Reuter, *One Blood.* New York: Exposition Press, 1964.

"Revolution—What Kind?" and "Politics—What Kind?" *Christian Century,* July 18, 1962; and replies: "Inner-City Realities," *ibid.,* August 22, 1962.

Root, Robert, *Progress Against Prejudice.* New York: Friendship Press, 1957.

Rose, Stephen C., "Student Interracial Ministry: A Break in the Wall," *Christian Century* 79:327–328 (March 14, 1962).

Rose, Stephen C., "N.C.C. Visits Clarksdale," *Christian Century* 80:1104–1106 (September 11, 1963).

Rosen, Alex, "The Negro and the Jew," *Journal of Jewish Communal Service,* Fall 1967.

Rubinstein, Richard L., "Jews, Negros and the New Politics," *Reconstructionist* vol. 33, pp. 7–16, Nov. 11, 1967.

Schomer, Howard, "Race and Religion in Albany [Georgia]," *Christian Century* 79:1155–1156 (September 26, 1962).

Schuyler, Joseph B., *Northern Parish: A Sociological and Pastoral Study.* Chicago: Loyola University Press, 1961.

Schuyler, Joseph B., "Apostolic Opportunity," *Interracial Review* 35:20–21 (January 1962).

Sellers, James, *The South and Christian Ethics.* New York: Association Press, 1962.

Senn, Milton, "Race, Religion and Suburbia," *Journal of Intergroup Relations* 3:159–170 (Spring 1962).

Senser, Robert, *Primer on Interracial Justice*. Baltimore: Helicon, 1962.

Seymour, Robert, "Interracial Ministry in North Carolina," *Christian Century* 80:109–111 (January 23, 1963).

Shriver, Donald W., Jr., ed., *The Unsilent South*. Richmond, Va.: John Knox Press, 1965.

Simms, David McD., "Ethnic Tensions in the 'Inner-City' Church," *Journal of Negro Education* 31:448–454 (Fall 1962).

Sklare, Marshall, *Jewish Identity on the Suburban Frontier: A Study of Group Survival in the Open Society*. New York: Basic Books, 1967.

Smith, Lauren A., "Saints in the Basement," *Christian Century* 75:1050–1052 (September 17, 1958).

Smythe, Lewis S. C., ed., *Southern Churches and Race Relations: Report of the Third Interracial Consultation*. Lexington, Ky.: College of the Bible, 1961.

Southard, Samuel, "Self-Criticism in the South," *Christian Century* 79:1488–1490 (December 5, 1962).

Southard, Samuel, "Are Southern Churches Silent?" *Christian Century* 80:1429–1432 (November 20, 1963).

Spike, Robert W., *The Freedom Revolution and the Churches*. New York: Association Press, 1965.

Stotts, Herbert E., and Paul Deats, *Methodism and Society: Guidelines for Strategy*. New York: Abingdon, 1962.

Stringfellow, William, "Race, Religion and Revenge," *Christian Century* 79:192–194 (February 14, 1962).

Stringfellow, William, *My People is the Enemy: An Autobiographical Polemic*. New York: Holt, 1964.

Sweet, William W., *The American Churches*. New York: Abingdon, 1948.

Tanenbaum, Marc H., "The American Negro: Myths and Realities," *Religious Education* 59:33–36 (January–February 1964).

Thomas, Mary S., "The Ordeal of Koinonia Farm," *Progressive* 21:23–25 (January 1957).

Thurman, Howard, *Deep River: Reflections on the Religious Insight of Certain of the Negro Spirituals*. New York: Harper, 1955.

Thurman, Howard, *Footprints of a Dream: The Story of the Church for the Fellowship of All People*. New York: Harper, 1959.

Thurman, Howard, *The Luminous Darkness*. New York: Harper and Row, 1965.

Tilson, Everett, *Segregation and the Bible*. Nashville, Tenn.: Abingdon, 1958.

Ungar, Andre, "To Birmingham and Back," *Conservative Judaism* 18:1–17 (Fall 1963).

"U.S. Bishops on Racial Harmony: Joint Pastoral," *Interracial Review* 36:182–183 (October 1963). Issued August, 1963.

Vissert, Hooft, W. A., *The Ecumenical Movement and the Racial Problem*. Paris: UNESCO, 1954.

Vorspan, Albert, "Segregation and Social Justice," *American Judaism* 7:10–11 (January 1958).

Vorspan, Albert, "The Negro Victory—And the Jewish Failure," *American Judaism* 13:7, 50–52, 54 (Fall 1963).

Walton, O. M., "Presbyterians Aware," *Christian Century* 77:718–719 (June 15, 1960).

Waltz, Alan K., and Robert L. Wilson, "Ministers' Attitudes Toward Integration," *Phylon* 19:195–198 (Summer 1958).

Washington, Joseph R., Jr., "Are American Negro Churches Christian?" *Theology Today* 20:76–86 (April 1963).

Washington, Joseph R., Jr., *Black Religion: The Negro and Christianity in the United States*. Boston: Beacon, 1964.

Washington, Joseph R., Jr., *Politics of God*. Boston: Beacon, 1967.

Weatherford, Willis Duke, *American Churches and the Negro: An Historical Study from Early Slave Days to the Present*. Boston: Christopher, 1957.

Whitman, Frederick L., "Subdimensions of Religiosity and Race Prejudice," *Review of Religious Research* 3:166–174 (Spring 1962).

Williams, Ethel L., *Biographical Directory of Negro Ministers*. New York: Scarecrow Press, 1965.

Williamson, E. M., "Brownsville Justice," *Christian Century*, January 3, 1962; Ernest Bromley, "Another View on Brownsville," *ibid.*, January 31, 1962.

Wilmore, Gayraud S., Jr., "The New Negro and the Church," *Christian Century* 80:168–171 (February 6, 1963).

Wilson, Robert L., and James H. Davis, Jr., *The Church and the Racially Changing Community*. Nashville: Abingdon Press Original, 1966.

Winter, Gibson, *The Suburban Captivity of the Churches*. Garden City, N.Y.: Doubleday, 1961.

Wogaman, Philip, "Focus on Central Jurisdiction," *Christian Century* 80:1296–1298 (October 23, 1963).

Woodson, Carter G., *The History of the Negro Church*. Washington, D.C.: Associated Publishers, 1921.

Young, Andrew J., "Demonstrations: A Twentieth Century Christian Witness," *Social Action* 30:5–12 (May 1964).

Young, Merrill Orne, "For Church's Sake," *Christian Century* 78:1300–1301 (November 1, 1961).